Malt Whisky

GRAHAM MOORE

Airlife

First published in 1998 by Swan Hill Press

Revised edition published in 2003 by
Airlife Publishing, an imprint of The Crowood Press Ltd,
Ramsbury, Marlborough, Wiltshire SN8 2HR

www.crowood.com

British Library Cataloguing-in-Publication Data
A catalogue record for this book
is available from the British Library.

ISBN 1 84037 290 7

The information in this book is true and complete to the
best of our knowledge. All recommendations are made
without any guarantee on the part of the Publisher, who
also disclaims any liability incurred in connection with
the use of this data or specific details.

The illustrations on pages 5, 6, 8 and 12 are reproduced with
the kind permission of Allied Distillers.

Typeset by Rowland Phototypesetting Ltd, Bury St Edmunds

Printed and bound in Hong Kong

ACKNOWLEDGEMENTS

Crossing the border from Scotland into England one invariably passes a road sign bearing the traditional farewell 'haste ye back', and after publishing my first book, *Malt Whisky – A Contemporary Guide*, I looked forward to doing so. I have enjoyed writing this book every bit as much as the first – it has, after all, taken me on a further tour of the distilleries – and once again I have enjoyed the hospitality and kindness of a great many people, both at the distilleries and 'behind the scenes' at head offices.

My thanks are due to all the distillers, to all the distillery managers and their staffs for their valuable help and

hospitality, and to the independent bottlers Gordon & MacPhail, Wm Cadenhead, The Whisky Castle, The Adelphi Distillery, Signatory, The Master of Malt, James MacArthur, The Vintage Malt Whisky Co. and Murray McDavid. Working on this book has introduced me to people I did not meet whilst writing *Malt Whisky*, and so I should also thank Ian MacMillan, Gavin Durnin, John Peterson, Richard Beattie, Steve Tulewicz, Yvonne Thackerey, Jacqui Seargeant, Malcolm Cannon, Terence Hillman, Tom Pearson, Rebecca Richardson, James Macpherson, Leslie Duroe and Aoife Martin.

I am also indebted to David Livingston-Lowe, lecturer in the Celtic Studies Programme at St Michael's College of the University of Toronto, for his invaluable research into the Gaelic derivations of the distillery names. Not all of these agree with the distillers' own ideas, which are sometimes over-romanticised, or the Gaelic has been inaccurately interpreted. Some may be speculation, based on David's studies, and the debate rages in some quarters. The Scottish Place Names Society has a website at www.gaelic.net/cli/links.htm for those readers wishing to join in.

All photographs and illustrations in this book are my work unless otherwise indicated.

Finally, thanks once again to Jill for her support.

This book represents a portrait of the whisky industry at the time of going to press. The industry has been in a state of flux for some time now and changes are ongoing. Similarly, distillers change their bottlings from time to time and it cannot be guaranteed that the same ones featured here will always be available. This goes doubly so for the independent bottlers who are often dealing with small bottling runs from single casks and so stocks of their products are necessarily finite. Readers are kindly asked to bear these points in mind.

For those readers who prefer metric units to Imperial ones the conversion of proof gallons to litres of pure alcohol is simply a matter of multiplying the former by a factor of 2.59.

FOREWORD

A distillery manager once commented that 'what happens inside a whisky cask is part of the magic and mystery, and long may it remain so, because the day we lose the mystery we've lost everything'.

Malt whisky is not only shrouded in mystique, it positively plays on it. It is the last of the great cottage industries, still persisting as we enter the twenty-first century. The beautiful old stone buildings with their characteristic pagoda-style roofs are home to a process which is as old as the surrounding hills and, like any other Scottish tradition, is wrapped in a blanket of history and romance which almost smothers it.

The object of this book is to loosen that blanket a little!

CONTENTS

INTRODUCTION

Whisky is not difficult to make; there are only three ingredients involved, four if you count the peat which flavours both the malt and the water. The process takes place in distinct stages and was certainly no problem to operate for the many smugglers who thrived on it in the eighteenth and nineteenth centuries. However, every ingredient and every stage of the process contributes to the mystique which surrounds malt whisky. There are literally hundreds of variables, each with some influence on the final product, and although distillers now have an intimate knowledge of the biochemistry involved the process still seems to be only one step removed from alchemy. The four alchemical elements of earth, air, fire and water all play a part in the making of whisky – the earth grows the barley and provides the peat; the air is the atmosphere in which the casks mature; fire drives the distillation process itself; and water is the vehicle of the final spirit.

There have been many attempts to duplicate Scotch whisky outside its homeland. All have failed. Some countries have resorted to importing tanker-loads of Speyside water, and one town in Japan was renamed Aberdeen so that its distillers could have an authentic 'Scots' name on their labels. What all these people have failed to realise is that Scotch whisky is what it is because Scotland is what it is. That particular combination of geology and climate shapes both raw materials and final product alike in an absolutely unique fashion. Scientific analysis has proved that whisky contains something like 800 chemical compounds, but exactly how these compounds relate to each other and interact has never been discovered. It has never been more true that ignorance is bliss, because until that discovery is made Scotch whisky will remain a magical substance, and if that discovery is made the magic will die.

Since the mid-eighteenth century over 700 legally licensed malt distilleries have been

Knockando

recorded as having operated in Scotland. There are now less than ninety, yet malt whisky is more freely available now than ever before ('freely' is perhaps the wrong word, considering the proportion of the price tag which is accounted for by profit and duty). The introduction of blended whisky, a result of the invention of the patent still and its prodigious rate of output, led to a vast increase in whisky consumption, on the back of which came the opportunity to stimulate the market for single malts. Although the Scots themselves have been privy to the delights of malt whisky for many years much of the credit for its success outside Scotland must go to Wm Grant and that company's efforts in the early 1960s in bringing Glenfiddich to a wider audience. Malt whisky is a gift to the marketing people now responsible for its sales – no other product comes with such a powerful marketing tool built in: two centuries of mystique fuelled by the illegality of the smugglers' occupation.

Its past history is now an important facet of the whisky industry, as though a dollop of it goes into every bottle. Some might say that it actually does. Although distilling is a fairly simple industrial process, now refined and controlled by the application of modern technology, it is surprising how late some parts of Scotland were in catching up with the twentieth century. Many Highland distilleries were not connected to the national grid until the 1950s. Aberlour was still using a steam-powered mill up to 1973, and some of the equipment at Glen Grant was powered by waterwheel as late as 1979. This is not merely olde-worlde traditionalism, taken for granted by those working in the industry; for a long time it was simply what they had. Today it is all part of the magic and to the distillers it is a heritage which is to be preserved. Whilst speaking to one manager about the article on his distillery which appears later in the book I mentioned that the

stillhouse looked modern. 'For God's sake don't call it modern,' he said, 'that's entirely the wrong image'! It is for reasons such as these that throughout this book I have used Imperial units of measurement. The Scots were forging their whisky industry at the same time as the Wild West was being won, and to describe the craft in terms of litres, kilograms and degrees Celsius hardly seems appropriate.

Today more and more people appreciate and enjoy malt whisky, a statement for which there are two particular pieces of evidence: the number of distilleries opening their doors to the public, some attracting tens of thousands of visitors each year; and the range of brands which can be found on the shelves of virtually any big supermarket, the malts outnumbering the blends in many places.

This market growth has taken place in relatively recent times – largely since 1980 – and some of today's top-selling single malts have only become available in their present form during that period. However, despite this increase in malt whisky's popularity certain questions still remain. Why is whisky made in Scotland? How did the Scots learn the art of distillation in the first place? What makes Scotch whisky unique, and how does it vary from one region of the country to another? We are not concerned here simply with what whisky tastes like – there are enough tasting guides on the market already which look at that aspect of the subject. This book looks at what makes whisky what it is. It actually examines all of Scotland's malt distilleries and places them in their historical and geographical context. It describes the background and heritage of each distillery and tells of the characters who populate the industry. It shows what a distillery is actually like and details the process it operates, from raw materials to bottled malt whisky – a process which can take upwards of ten years to complete. Malt whisky is unique amongst alcoholic beverages in having acquired such an aura of mystique and making that mystique such an integral part of its charm. This book takes a fascinating peek behind the façade of malt whisky and shows that there really is a little bit of history in every glass.

A History of Distilling

Distilling is an extremely ancient art. It has been suggested that like paper and gunpowder it was discovered by the Chinese, who were known to have been distilling liquor from rice in around 800 BC. Hippocrates used it as a method of making medicines around 400 BC and it was also known to Aristotle, who wrote of it in his *Meteorology* the following century. It was certainly known in Asia at around this time, where it was used to make perfumes; and from the Middle East, where medicines were made by distillation, the craft was brought to Europe by the Moors, who also introduced the guitar to Spain. In Europe it would have come to the attention of Irish missionary monks, and with them to Ireland itself, and in particular to the court of the clan O'Donnell, a prince of which would later become St Columba. Columba would not have been the only Christian missionary attempting to spread the Celtic Church to Scotland but he would certainly have been the most important; his political position was necessary in negotiating a truce with the Picts who were now threatening the Kingdom of Dalriada, an area of Argyll settled by Celtic people from northern Ireland in the early sixth century and comprising what is now Kintyre and the Inner Hebrides.

It is fairly certain that distilling at this time was a Celtic craft, unknown to other Britons, and was spreading through the offices of the Church. This is borne out by the first written record of whisky in Scotland, the oft-quoted 'eight bolls of malt to Friar John Cor wherewith to make aqua vitae', found in the Exchequer Rolls of 1494. Monasteries have always made their own alcoholic beverages; they still do, it being regarded as an extension of their agricultural activities. Friar Cor was certainly no novice; eight bolls is over half a ton of malt. The climate and geography of a particular area would dictate the type of drink they would make. Monasteries in the south would make wine, whereas those in the north would not have the climate for growing grapes, but would have good conditions for growing barley and hence distilling aqua vitae. After the dissolution of the monasteries monks travelled throughout the country to earn their living wherever possible, and so their knowledge and skills spread with them.

In 1505, the surgeons of Edinburgh were granted a monopoly for making aqua vitae within

Castle Stalker

the city for medicinal purposes, and magistrates forcibly prevented others from making and selling the spirit. In 1577 Holinshed, in his *Chronicles*, noted that whisky 'helps digestion and cures the dropsy', although the accuracy of his claims can be judged from a later observation that it also 'keeps the head from whirling'! Two years later the Scottish parliament passed an act to restrict the use of grain for distilling, to ensure that enough was being kept for use in making food. Shortages occurred again in 1597 when the barley crop failed, and distilling was limited to 'Lords of Barony and Gentlemen of such degree'. In 1609 the public order Statutes of Ilcomkill were introduced in the Western Isles in an effort to reduce consumption by restricting people to home-made drink, which naturally resulted in a major boost in home distilling!

The first Excise tax was imposed on whisky in 1644 by Charles I. The English at this time were mostly distilling a form of brandy from wine but the Scots were distilling from malt. Most of their stills were small but a few larger ones were beginning to appear, openly selling whisky in contravention of the 1579 Act. The most famous of these was called Ferintosh, which was owned by Duncan Forbes of Culloden. As compensation for damage done to his estate when it was sacked by the Jacobites in 1689 he was granted the right to make aqua vitae free of duty, save for a small annual fee of about £22. Although this still seems a lot of money for the late seventeenth century it was saving him an annual Excise duty of something like £20,000! He was restricted to using barley grown on his own farm, but by buying more land Forbes expanded his business to four distilleries and was making a profit of £18,000 a year. His privilege lasted for almost a century until the outcry from other distillers led to its retraction. Although they received further compensation from the government Forbes's descendants withdrew from

distilling, causing Robbie Burns to mourn 'Thee Ferintosh, o sadly lost!'

During this same period the nature of aqua vitae was to change considerably. Until the mid-eighteenth century it was common practice to add berries, herbs and spices to the spirit and it would be drunk quite young, usually within weeks of leaving the still. Fermentation was often accomplished by leaving the wort open to the air for several weeks to allow wild yeasts to reach it, and without the addition of these flavourings the result would no doubt have been undrinkable. By the 1750s methods had improved and the term

'aqua vitae' had come to mean 'malt spirit'.

After the Act of Union in 1707, parliament tried to align England and Scotland by imposing a malt tax. The attempt failed as it would have affected the price of ale as well as whisky throughout the country. A second attempt in 1725 led to riots in both Glasgow and Edinburgh, although this time the tax became law. Lowland distilleries began to mix their malt with increasing amounts of unmalted grain, and the quality of their whisky began to suffer. The Highland distilleries continued to use malted barley but they were distilling illicitly and the Act had little effect on them. Eventually the Wash Act was passed in 1784, in which the government seemed to take into account the economic advantage that the

Lowland distiller had over his Highland compatriot, Highland whisky being less severely taxed. A licence was introduced with a fee based on the still capacity, and an import tax of 2s (10p) a gallon imposed on Scotch whisky brought into England. The Act encouraged legal distilling in the Highlands but did nothing to discourage smuggling. It was generally recognised that the Highlanders' small stills produced a higher-quality spirit than did the big stills then in use in the Lowlands and so the smuggling trade was a profitable one, becoming more widespread as the government steadily increased both licence fee and duty. In fact, it was estimated that spirit consumption in Scotland at that time was at least four times the production capacity of the licensed stills then operating! Even when caught illicit distillers often escaped justice as the Justices of the Peace themselves were often local landowners who enjoyed a dram or two of the contraband spirit.

The industrial revolution began in Scotland in about 1779 and some of the largest manu-facturing concerns to emerge almost immediately were the distilleries built by the Haig and Stein families. The Wash Act, with its licence fee based on still capacity, encouraged distillers to work more efficiently, extracting more spirit from a given volume of wash. The Haigs and Steins adopted this approach with a vengeance and developed special shallow stills which could be worked and recharged extremely rapidly, running forty-seven charges in twelve hours! Between them, the two families held a vice-like grip on Lowland distilling which they protected by buying competitors' distilleries and decommissioning them. They even bought a mill which they used to deprive one distillery of its water supply.

Eventually the government was forced to adopt a new licensing system, and the regulations governing the English gin distillers were extended to encompass the Scots' whisky industry. In 1814 a standard fee was introduced of £10 for a still together with a duty on wash. Stills smaller than 500 gallons in capacity were declared illegal above the Highland Line (it being too easy to conceal a small still in Highland country), and at the Lowlanders' insistence the Highland distillers were barred from selling their whisky below the Highland Line. Lowland distillers were forced to register for trading on the English market and a minimum still capacity of 2,000 gallons was imposed.

The new Act failed because the Highlanders, like the monks before them, viewed distilling as an extension of their farming activities and considered it their right. Poorer farmers also needed the extra money that came from selling their whisky, even if only to their neighbours, and could ill afford to spend £10 on a licence. A year after the Act was passed there were estimated to be 200 stills in the Glenlivet area alone, and the Excise man's job was not made any easier by the public, who were more interested in partaking of the illicit produce. Even King George IV declared that he drank nothing but Glenlivet.

Legal distilling in the Highlands increased in 1816 with the introduction of the Small Stills Act and the number of licensed distilleries increased five-fold within the next two years. The Act permitted stills as small as 40 gallons (the smugglers' small stills traditionally made good whisky) but it also introduced the saccharimeter for checking the strength of the wash. Smugglers generally distilled from thin washes and in the Highlanders' opinion the Act demanded the use of washes which were too strong to produce a good spirit. In order to compete on quality, the licensed distillers were forced to use thinner washes than were permitted under the new law. This effectively made it pointless to take out a licence in the first place and led to a resurgence in illicit distilling.

In 1820 the Duke of Gordon spoke on the subject in the House of Lords. He was sure that if only the law were more reasonable he and his fellow landowners would be able to persuade their tenants to take out proper licences if they were to continue distilling. A commission was set up and, acting with typical alacrity, passed the Act to Eliminate Illicit Distilling (the Excise Act) some three years later. By this time, about 14,000 illicit stills had been discovered and distillers greeted the new Act with reticence, despite pressure from the landowners. The following year the first licence was granted to George Smith, owner of The Glenlivet Distillery, and despite a great deal of intimidation others followed his lead.

The new Act effectively broke the monopoly of the Haig and Stein families and within two years there were 263 licensed distilleries operating in Scotland. Only seventeen of the malt distilleries founded during that period still survive today, most of which are in the Highlands although two are on Islay. One of these, Port Ellen, was the distillery at which Robert Stein conducted his experiments in continuous distillation, which led to the introduction of the patent still in 1826. Haig's installed a patent still in their Cameronbridge Distillery in Fife, and in fact continued to use an original Stein still until 1929. The design was improved upon by Aeneas Coffey, the Inspector General of Excise in Ireland. Coffey resigned from the Excise in 1824 to take up distilling, and for a time ran the Dock Distillery in Dublin. He subsequently invented a twin-column version of the patent still in 1830. Coffey's idea was not well received in Ireland, the Irish being too inured in pot-still distilling (probably understandable, as the Irish had distilleries by the late twelfth century, but the attitude was to be their downfall) and he had no success with it until he took it to Scotland. The new design was patented in 1832, but due to an oversight whisky from patent stills did not come under Excise control for another six years! A Coffey still could distil 3,000 gallons of wash per hour and, as more were installed, grain whisky production trebled in the space of one year. The surge in production of this duty-free whisky was inevitably matched by an increase in illicit distilling in the Highlands, but as licensed production in general rose the illicit distillers found it impossible to compete and the smuggling trade began to wane. Ten years after the Excise

Act became law only 111 stills were seized in Scotland (compared to an incredible 8,233 in Ireland) and by 1865 the number had fallen to single figures.

The grain spirit from the patent stills was mostly sold locally or sent to England to be made into gin. New spirit from a patent still is colourless and characterless and can just as easily be made into whisky, gin or vodka, depending on its alcoholic strength. Gin, for instance, is made by redistilling the spirit after the addition of various herbal flavourings. Merchants and innkeepers were mindful that malt whisky was quite strong and had a characteristic flavour that was not to everyone's taste, and grain whisky could do with some character adding to it. The obvious conclusion was to blend the two types together to make a whisky that would appeal to a wider range of consumers. Malt distillers were already vatting together batches of whisky to achieve some continuity of flavour and colour, a practice approved by Customs and Excise and one which continues today. Andrew Usher is reckoned to have been the first to blend on a commercial scale with Usher's Old Vatted Glenlivet appearing in 1852. The Blending Act, covering the blending of malt and grain whiskies, was passed in 1865. The Scots' adoption of large-scale blending transformed the industry and effectively ended the dominance of Irish whiskey. The Irish distillers failed to join the revolution that was taking place, either because they failed to see it or because they simply misjudged the market response.

The introduction of the patent still led to the foundation of a number of new distilleries in the Lowlands. The resulting increase in competition led to cut-throat price wars which in turn led to bankruptcies. In 1857, six leading Lowland grain distillers formed a 'trade arrangement' to try to share out the available trade and avoid overproduction. A new agreement was concluded in 1865 in an attempt to influence whisky prices. A subsequent slump in output, together with the acknowledged advantages of regulating prices and production, led to an amalgamation of six of the leading Lowland grain distillers: Cambus, Cameronbridge, Carsebridge, Glenochil,

Kirkliston and Port Dundas. The arrangement proved successful and the consortium was christened the Distillers Company Ltd.

At about the same time, the French wine growers suffered a catastrophe. They had begun to augment their vineyards with imported American vines. The American species carried a vine louse known as *Phylloxera vastatrix*, to which it was immune. However the French vines were not and the pest rapidly spread. It started in about 1860, was firmly established by 1865, and by 1880 had reached the Cognac region. Within a few years brandy had all but disappeared from England and by the time the French industry recovered its place had been taken by whisky, and so the boom period began.

When the law allowed the Scots to send whisky to England in bottles, as opposed to kegs, the idea of branding emerged and merchants began to promote their own unique blends. Improvements in communications were highly significant at this time: the country's railway network linked Scotland with the south and steamships opened access to the islands. Large numbers of Scots moved to England or emigrated overseas, spreading the popularity of whisky as they went. Merchants began to travel to London in search of success. The 'big five' were to appear in this period, starting with James Buchanan and his Buchanan Blend, the first brand to become known. He was followed by the flamboyant self-publicist Tommy Dewar, Peter Mackie of White Horse, Johnnie Walker and John Haig.

The late 1880s saw the adoption of advertising on a wide scale. Better standards of printing, including colour pictures, led to the use of many kinds of promotional items such as showcards, mirrors and stone crocks. Romantic images of Scotland were strongly played upon (as indeed they still are), and labels and slogans became important in publicising the newly emerging brands. Much of the wording which appeared on the new labels survives to this day: 'Special', 'Finest', 'Oldest', etc. In addition to brands such as Haig's Pinch and Mackie's White Horse, single malts were also being promoted and adverts appeared for The Glenlivet, Caol Ila, Bowmore and Springbank. It became fashionable to invest

in whisky and banks were happy to lend money to finance stocks. New distilleries were built, existing ones enlarged, and more blenders and merchants appeared to sell their products. The industry was heading for a fall.

It came in 1898. Pattison's Ltd was a large-scale blender and wholesaler based in Leith, Edinburgh, which had started as a grocery business founded by two brothers. They became a limited company in order to raise capital and expand, but unfortunately the flotation was based on a fraudulent balance sheet. As the money rolled in they began to produce more and more whisky for which it was eventually realised there was no market. The brothers themselves were also leading extravagant lifestyles and put much of the money they raised into lavish offices and houses. Confidence waned and the share price began to fall. Eventually, doubts were expressed about the company's future and in December the shares collapsed. Both brothers ended up in prison on fraud charges. It was later found that Pattison's had been selling cheap unmatured grain whisky to which no more than a tiny amount of malt whisky had been added. The company had close links with certain distilleries, including Glenfarclas, Oban, Aultmore and Dallas Dhu, and the distillers were lucky to survive the crisis. In the recession which followed the Pattison debacle, the number of operating distilleries in Scotland fell from 161 to 132.

At the turn of the century the Highlanders were still not comfortable in their relationship with the grain distillers and blenders, and petitioned MPs for laws governing trade descriptions and minimum periods for maturing whisky before sale. An attempt to table a bill in parliament in 1904 met with no success, but the break came in 1906 when Islington Borough Council charged a publican and an off-licence trader for selling whisky which contravened the Merchandise Marks Act. James Davidge, the off-licensee, was charged with selling 'malt' whisky which was found to contain 90 per cent grain spirit. The court found in favour of the council, but the wording of the judge's conclusion implied that a blend of pot-still and patent-still spirits could not be sold as 'whisky' and the arguments

which followed led to the appointment in 1908 of yet another Royal Commission, whose job this time was to investigate the Highland malt distillers' proposals. It took them thirty-three sittings over eighteen months to come up with a legal definition of whisky, namely that it was 'a spirit obtained by distillation from a mash of cereal grains saccharified by the diastase of malt'. They also concluded, somewhat obviously, that whisky must be distilled in Scotland if it is to be called 'Scotch' whisky. It was not until 1915 that the Immature Spirits Act defined a compulsory bonding period and this Act was amended the following year to specify a minimum of three years in bond, a regulation which still applies.

It took the temperance movement to unite the malt and grain distillers. Lloyd George was a confirmed temperance man and Chancellor in the Liberal government. His decision in 1909 to increase duty on spirits by 34 per cent and change the licensing system, ostensibly to contribute to his pensions and unemployment benefit schemes, gave malt and grain distillers a common cause. Peter Mackie publicly called him 'a crank'. His Finance Bill was rejected by the Lords and precipitated a general election which resulted in the Liberals being re-elected with a majority of just two seats. An alliance with the Irish Nationalists enabled Lloyd George to get his punitive measures through parliament at the second attempt and the consequence was a fall in sales, together with an ominous build-up of stocks at the distilleries. Distillers began to turn their attention towards the export market.

At the outbreak of World War I Lloyd George took steps to cut down production and consumption of alcoholic beverages, setting up the Central Liquor Control Board. Licensing hours were shortened and the proof strength at which whisky could be sold was reduced. Before the war all whisky was bottled straight from the cask. Lloyd George wanted to limit its strength to 30 per cent volume. Objections from distillers brought about a compromise of 40 per cent volume, which is still the legal minimum strength for whisky today. The government took over pubs in all areas where there were military bases or munitions were being made – in other words

Strathisla

virtually every urban area. Pot-still distilling was regulated to 70 per cent of its previous level and banned completely in 1917. Grain distilling continued at about half its previous level, the patent stills being needed to produce industrial alcohol and baker's yeast, for which the Distillers Co. Ltd (DCL) became a major supplier. Even so, these measures were far less draconian than those Lloyd George had originally proposed, which had included nationalisation of brewery properties and the temporary prohibition of spirits. Further taxation was introduced in 1918 and 1919, which

more than trebled the amount of duty and forced demand down even further as the government attempted to claw back some of the enormous cost of the war effort. The Central Liquor Control Board was not dissolved until late in 1921, and the last of the pubs taken into state ownership under its powers was not sold by the government until 1975.

The Depression saw the closure of many distilleries and many companies either disappeared or merged with others in order to survive. American companies began to buy into

the Scottish industry, possibly to ensure that some kind of market would exist for them during Prohibition, and to build up stocks of whisky which would be available to them as soon as Prohibition was repealed. Prohibition was not an overnight occurrence. Thanks to the temperance movement, Maine became 'dry' in 1846 and by 1906 another seventeen states had followed suit. The Eighteenth Amendment was not passed until October 1919 and was initially vetoed by President Wilson. All drinks with an alcoholic content of more than 0.5 per cent were banned.

Prohibition put the distillers in a quandary: whether to break the American laws by sending in whisky directly or stand by and see the market for Scotch ruined by counterfeiters and their moonshine. The answer was to export to Canada or to the French islands off Newfoundland. It was then up to the bootleggers to deliver the goods to US territory. The expression 'the real McCoy' was coined in this period. Berry Bros blended a new 'light' whisky especially for the Americans' taste. It was called Cutty Sark and was delivered by a Nassau bootlegger who was known for supplying only genuine goods. His name was Bill McCoy, and thanks to his efforts Cutty Sark established a reputation in the States which it still has today. The distinctive yellow label was designed by Scots artist James McBey. The sketch of the ship, the hand lettering, and even the name, are all his work. The yellow colour was a printing error!

Many Scottish companies considered that they were doing the Americans a favour, saving them from the infernal products of their own illicit stills. As long as the genuine article was to be found there were plenty of buyers for it and the Scottish distillers used the period well, building up the reputation of their products. The exception was to be seen in Campbeltown which, in its attempts to keep up with demand, let its standards slip to the point where it fell from grace altogether. Of the twenty distilleries existing in the town at the onset of Prohibition, only two managed to keep their honour intact.

Prohibition was repealed in 1933 and the US government, knowing how much duty it could have charged on all the illicit liquor sold during that period, sued the Canadian distillers for some $60 million unpaid tax, a figure which was later settled at $3 million, half of which was paid by Seagram. America was inundated with literally thousands of brands of liquor, and the smarter of the American companies were falling over themselves to be appointed agents for the leading brands of Scotch. Joseph Kennedy, a Boston politician, had spent the Prohibition years building up a stock of whisky imported under special licence for 'medicinal' purposes, a loophole in the Prohibition Act. When the Act was repealed he was not only at an advantage over his competitors but also managed to secure the New England agency for both Dewar's and Haig's whiskies.

Macallan – Easter Elchies

If things were beginning to pick up again they turned sharply downwards six years later. World War II brought with it a complete ban on grain distilling, although malt distilling was allowed to continue until October 1942. A complete ban was then imposed until 1944, and a significant black market grew up which could have got out of hand if the Scotch Whisky Association had not stepped in and bought up all whisky stocks available at auction, regardless of cost. The first half of the war saw an increase in duty of almost 100 per cent, from 72s 6d (£3.62½) to 137s 6d (£6.87½) per proof gallon. After the war ended the distillers found they had an ally in none other than Churchill himself, who declared that whisky was a valuable dollar-earning export and its production should not be curtailed. The Labour government which deposed him in July 1945 had other ideas however, and decreed that all cereals were to be used primarily for food production. Between them, Dalton and Cripps hiked the rate of duty up to 210s 10d (£10.54) per proof gallon. Distillers found themselves working at less than half capacity, and it was not until 1953 that grain rationing was lifted.

A period of expansion followed at last. The Spirits Act, which made it illegal to mash and distil at the same time, and to work on Sundays, was reformed in 1952. Mothballed distilleries were refurbished and brought to life, and new distilleries were built. However the process was slow and hampered by the government, which regarded the industry in much the same way that they regarded the motorist: an easy target from which to elicit revenue. Taxation was increased ten times throughout the 1960s and 1970s, taking duty up to £27.09 per proof gallon. The exception was in 1973 when Britain entered the EEC, and duty was actually reduced for the first time since 1896. Not to be denied their pound of flesh however, the government introduced value added tax the same year which almost made up the difference.

The 1950s saw an increase in foreign investment in the Scottish industry, notably from North America and Canada, with the government granting subsidies to these foreign companies in order to encourage their investment. Seagram acquired Strathisla in 1950, beginning a chain of

acquisitions which was to give them control of nine distilleries by the end of the 1970s. Hiram Walker, which already owned three distilleries and had taken over Ballantine's in 1936, doubled the size of its portfolio in the fifties with the acquisition of Glencadam, Scapa and Pulteney. Long John, a name going back to the foundation of Ben Nevis Distillery in 1825, was taken over by the New York-based company Schenley Industries in 1956. More foreign influence would be brought to bear in the seventies and eighties, this time from Europe and the Far East.

The 1960s heralded a genuine advance for malt whisky drinkers. It was at this time that Glenfiddich began to export its single malt to markets outside Scotland. It is difficult for many people to think of England as an export market for Scottish products, yet south of Hadrian's Wall the public were blissfully unaware of the distilleries' contribution to the national heritage. Wm Grant & Sons Ltd saw a gap in the market and went about filling it with an admirable dedication to the cause. There are many distillers with products just as good and histories just as long, and who could well be in the same position today, but with Glenfiddich Grant's were the first to identify the 'export' market for bottled single malts and were in the position to capitalise on the success of their blended whisky Grant's Standfast. Their efforts were rewarded with a Queen's Award to Industry for Export Achievement in 1974, and thanks to their foresight awareness of the qualities of malt whisky has grown significantly ever since. Not so long ago you would have been lucky to find more than a couple of malts on a supermarket shelf alongside the blends. These days there are plenty of stores where the malts outnumber the blends, and enthusiasts are actively seeking out new ones to try. It is surprising to learn how many single malts which are today amongst the big names were never available in that form until the seventies or early eighties.

The eighties was not an auspicious decade for the industry. Recession forced the closure of a number of distilleries, some permanently, and created conditions which led to another wave of foreign take-overs. DCL closed twelve of its

distilleries, including all three in Inverness. Some were completely demolished, although Millburn was converted into a restaurant and St Magdalene into flats. Dallas Dhu gained a new lease of life as a museum. Glenugie, the most easterly distillery in Scotland, was closed by Long John in 1983 and the plant sold for scrap. The 1990s saw around a dozen further closures, some permanent. Rationalisation within the industry, and a general pulling-in of horns, was expected to account for the loss of at least 700 jobs during the decade. The recession came just as United Distillers' increasing market share had prompted them to introduce their Wildlife Series (now known as the Flora & Fauna Series), a collection of less well-known malts sold mainly within Scotland itself. The range includes a long-awaited malt from Pittyvaich, a distillery which then suffered the indignity of being mothballed shortly after its product went on sale. The closures follow a long-established DCL practice of regulating supply to match demand, a lesson originally learned in the mid-nineteenth century when overproduction led to bankruptcies, and eventually to the Pattison crash, but the ramifications range beyond the distilleries themselves. In remote rural areas a distillery can be a major employer and its staff may have little chance of finding other jobs locally. A closure will also affect farmers who rely on the distillers as a market for their barley and a supplier of draff for animal feed.

Japan has had a whisky industry since 1923 and the founder of Nikka Distillers, now the owner of Ben Nevis Distillery, actually studied at Campbeltown. It has become an important market not only for bottled whisky but also for bulk stocks, which are shipped to Japan to be blended with the domestic product in order to give it a more authentic 'Scotch' taste. About 15 per cent of the malt content of a Japanese blend is actually Scotch. Tomatin became the first Scottish distillery to come entirely under Japanese control. Vastly expanded between 1956 and 1975, it has an awesome production capacity of some 5 million proof gallons per annum, although it is perhaps a telling indication of the industry that it has never operated at anything like its full capability. It is now the second largest distillery in

Edradour

the world, after Suntory's Hakushu Distillery in Japan itself. Suntory is the world's biggest distilling company and has interests in Morrison Bowmore Distillers and Macallan.

The late eighties saw the beginning of much reshuffling within the industry, and take-overs galore. The main event concerned the acquisition by Guinness of DCL, a bitterly fought battle with

their main rival, Argyll. Guinness had already acquired Bell's in 1986 and fought for control of DCL amid allegations of fraudulently inflating its share price, thereby increasing the value of its offer. Guinness's offer was finally accepted and in 1987 it merged Bell's with DCL and renamed the company United Distillers plc. The following year, Allied Distillers was formed when Hiram Walker

was acquired by Allied-Lyons, and there were management buy-outs at Invergordon and Barton International. The Nikka Company of Japan acquired Ben Nevis Distillery, and Whyte & Mackay was sold by Lonrho to Brent Walker. By 1991, Whyte & Mackay had passed to the American tobacco company Gallagher, and had come within a whisker of taking over

Invergordon. A strongly contested fight gained them a 42 per cent stake in the company, and a full take-over was achieved in November 1993. Whyte & Mackay later become JBB (Greater Europe) plc – Jim Beam Brands – a subsidiary of the American company Fortune Brands. In July 1994 Suntory took full ownership of Morrison Bowmore, and in 1996 took over Macallan in partnership with Highland Distilleries. Guinness then announced its merger with Grand Metropolitan to create Diageo, a move which saw the renamed United Distillers & Vintners (UDV) divest itself of four of its distilleries, and Dewar's, to Bacardi for £1.15 billion. In return UDV acquired the J & B brand and its related distilleries. Bacardi has emerged from this as a new force in the whisky industry, having increased its portfolio from one to five malt distilleries. The decade ended with the acquisition of Highland Distilleries by The 1887 Company, a joint venture between Wm Grant and existing Highland shareholders The Edrington Group, for a reported $1.45 billion.

Such changes within the industry are on-going. The start of the new century has already seen Bladnoch unexpectedly reopen, and Bruichladdich Distillery was sold by JBB to the independent bottlers Murray McDavid. Whyte & Mackay was subject to a £200 million management buy-out in October 2001 which split it from JBB to create the Kyndal company. Shortly before Christmas that same year Diageo and Pernod-Ricard completed their acquisition of Seagram's wine and spirits business, which included Chivas and its associated distilleries. The deal cost Diageo $5 billion and Pernod $3.15 billion. Needless to say, few Scottish distilleries are still in the hands of the founders' descendants. Also disturbing is the amount of spirit being shipped out of Scotland, sometimes before it has matured, to be blended overseas by the distilleries' foreign parents.

The 1980s also saw a new force at work within the industry: the marketing department. As a result of all the various take-overs, the parent companies found themselves in possession of many well-known but considerably under-exploited brand names. They also found that the world market for Scotch had become static. The marketing men worked on the principle that as people's affluence increases they tend to buy not more goods, but better goods (a phenomenon evidenced by the quadrupling in sales in some of the developing Far Eastern countries). When Guinness took over DCL its share of the malt whisky market was 4 per cent. Within a year of introducing its Classic Malts range its market share was 10 per cent and climbing. The increase was achieved by moving the market away from the average-priced whiskies and towards the high-priced premium brands. The importance of the duty-free market was also realised at this time. Premium brands sell well to Japanese businessmen, since strict protocol demands that they purchase gifts for wives and colleagues whilst on business trips abroad. It is in the export market that United Distillers have found a satisfactory niche for even the highest-priced whiskies, such as their Old Parr Elizabethan.

Malt whisky has now been firmly placed in the luxury goods sector by the imposition of premium prices, a simple enough practice of making your product appear better than your competitor's by raising your price above his. The actual whisky in the bottle is worth no more, it just appears to be. More than one malt is marketed this way – indeed some premium malts have a profit margin on them of 50 per cent. It is just unfortunate that the points scored by the marketing departments are at the expense of the consumer. The government too has done little to ease the situation. The tax on an average-priced blend, for instance, accounts for about half of the price tag.

The 1990s turned out to be a rerun of the 1980s and the decade did not get off to a good start, with much of the world suffering the effects of recession. The UK market seems to be recovering from the after-effects of recent increases in duty, but competition is strong and the distillers have had to sustain price cuts, rather than achieve price increases. As a result, the number of malt distilleries working at present is at its lowest peacetime level since the introduction of the Excise Act. Depression in the Far Eastern and South American markets has brought a drastic reduction in sales there, which has led to overproduction and subsequent mothballings or distilleries put on sporadic production regimes. People investing privately in whisky stocks, lured by the promise of extravagant returns, have seen their 'investments' flop and have been panicked into selling out in order to cut their losses. Some have accepted offers from their banks to sell their stocks for the price paid. Although this has meant that investors have not been left out of pocket it has also left the banks in possession of significant stocks of mature whisky, and as it is released onto the market prices have been depressed to an all-time low. Despite this, the news is not all bleak. Whisky is still one of Britain's top foreign exchange earners, with annual export revenue exceeding £2 billion for the last ten years running, thanks to the development of new markets in India, Latin America and southern Europe. Inver House Distillers expanded its portfolio of distilleries steadily during the 1990s with the acquisitions of Balblair, Balmenach, Pulteney and Speyburn, saving at least the first two of those from closure. Ardbeg was similarly rescued by Glenmorangie after two periods of inactivity. Three new distilleries have opened – Speyside near Kingussie, Kininvie at Dufftown, and Arran at Lochranza, and plans have been announced for at least three more (one of which is in the Shetlands) – which at least indicates that these companies have some measure of confidence in the industry's immediate future. Speyside is the latest incarnation of a much older distillery which occupied the same site at Drumguish. Kininvie belongs to Wm Grant, which has been building on Glenfiddich's success now for over thirty years. Both these distilleries have been in production now for over ten years, building up their stocks of mature whisky. Speyside was unique in bottling its malt as soon as it reached three years old, but as time has passed an older version has appeared. Arran is, at the time of writing, Scotland's newest malt distillery, opening in 1995. The island's climate means that Arran spirit matures quite quickly and the company bottled a batch of sherry-aged spirit at five years old. Wm Grant is keeping whisky enthusiasts guessing!

In two centuries the Scottish whisky industry has grown from being an occupation of smugglers to a multi-billion pound business which stretches across the face of the world. The value of whisky stocks maturing in bonded warehouses throughout Scotland, around a billion gallons, exceeds the national debt of some small countries. The first person to blend single malt and Lowland grain whiskies on a commercial scale was arguably Andrew Usher in 1852, and once the technique had been pioneered it became possible to develop exclusive blend recipes and to produce them consistently. The incredible rise in consumption is due largely to the efforts of the merchants who followed in Usher's footsteps, establishing and developing the blending trade and introducing branded bottled whisky. Just as some brand names have become accepted as generic terms for certain products, the names of some of those merchants have become so synonymous with their brands that it never occurs to some people that there actually was a Mr Bell or a Mr Teacher. It is also interesting to consider that, despite the market position of their brands today, neither Bell's nor Teacher's were regarded as being amongst the original 'big five' blenders; those were Mackie, Haig, and in particular Buchanan, Dewar and Johnnie Walker.

This chapter looks at the men who set the industry on the road to what it has become today. They changed the way in which whisky was sold, taking it out of the casks in the merchants' cellars and putting it instead into labelled bottles, each creating a brand and an image that would identify their whisky the world over. The whiskies to which they gave their names are all blends, but their distilleries were built to supply their trade (and still do) and those same distilleries now supply the market which has been created for bottled single malts. In recent times others have gone on to tread the path defined by the men

Arthur Bell
James Buchanan
John Dewar
William Grant
John Haig
'Long' John Macdonald
Peter Mackie
William Henry Ross
William Teacher
John Walker

described here – George Christie has seen his Speyside Distillery open for business after possibly one of the longest gestation periods seen in the industry, some thirty-four years from acquiring the site to commencing distilling; Harold Currie, a former managing director of Chivas, has successfully realised his ambition to open his own distillery on Arran; and Gordon & MacPhail have progressed from blending and bottling to becoming distillers in their own right with the acquisition of Benromach Distillery at Forres, near their home town of Elgin.

Not all the companies described here owe all their success to their founders. Some were built from modest beginnings by the founders' descendants and so this chapter considers their contribution too.

Arthur Bell

To say that Arthur Bell was one of the founding fathers of the whisky trade is slightly confusing in that there were actually two Arthur Bells, both of whom contributed to making the company one of the most successful in the industry. Bell's has dominated the home market for many years despite not being regarded as one of the original 'big' blending companies.

Arthur Bell senior first entered the liquor trade

with the firm of Sandeman's before setting up on his own as a wholesale wine and spirit merchant in Perth. Spirits, especially blended whisky, accounted for 90 per cent of the company's profits yet Bell had what could only be described as a cautious management style and felt he had to be involved in every aspect of the business. He was reluctant to borrow money, distrusted agents, and refused to advertise, confident that the quality of his products alone would generate sales.

The advantages of this approach were that the company had a loyal clientele, plenty of scope for expansion, and good stocks of mature whisky. The family also had many relations abroad and Bell called on their help in finding overseas agents. He was concerned about the state of trade at home and intended to set his son the task of building export markets, having failed to predict the boom which was about to begin.

Arthur's son, Arthur Kinmond Bell, was born in 1870 and entered the family business in 1889, becoming a partner six years later. His younger brother, Robert Duff Bell, entered the partnership the following year but withdrew in 1914 to pursue other interests. Arthur Bell died in 1900, after which Arthur junior, or 'AK' as he was known, began to expand the company, appointing more agents and using advertising for the first time. The brand name Bell's first appeared in 1904. Profits were ploughed back into the company, with the partners making only modest drawings. By 1915 the company had some £105,000 invested in mature whisky stocks, which helped it to withstand the shortages which followed the introduction in that year of the Immature Spirits Act. These reserve stocks also helped Bell's to ride out later recessions in the industry.

Bell's first became Scotch whisky distillers in 1933 when it acquired P. Mackenzie & Co. and hence Blair Athol and Dufftown distilleries. Inchgower followed in 1936. The company also built Pittyvaich in 1974 and acquired the most

Kilchurn Castle, Loch Awe

James Buchanan

James Buchanan was born in Brockville, Ontario, in 1849 and moved to Scotland at the age of 14. He earned an annual salary of £20 working for a customs house before taking up a job with his elder brother William, who was a grain merchant in Glasgow. At the age of thirty he moved to London as agent for Mackinlay & Co., a job which was to act as catalyst in the decision to start a business marketing his own whisky, the Buchanan Blend.

Buchanan began his business with little more than self-confidence and a natural talent for salesmanship. He was quoted later as admitting that 'the possibility of failure never once occurred to me'. In 1898 he bought the Black Swan Distillery in Holborn, London, for £87,000. Shortly afterwards the Pattison company failed and Buchanan was asked by the trustees to value Pattison's stocks, as he was the only person for the job who was acceptable to all the parties involved. Buchanan replied that he was 'too busy'! His company was incorporated in 1903 with a share issue of £700,000, of which Buchanan himself owned 98 per cent.

When blended whisky began to be sold in bottles Buchanan realised that a market existed for a blend which would appeal specifically to the English palate. The blend was created with the help of W. P. Lowrie, a Glasgow whisky broker from whom Buchanan drew all his stocks, and whose company Buchanan bought out in 1906, a move which also gave him the licence of Convalmore Distillery. The whisky was sold in distinctive black bottles with white labels.

Over a period of twenty years Buchanan built from nothing one of the premier Scotch whisky-blending companies, holding royal warrants from both Queen Victoria and King Edward VII. He realised early on that success would come from selling his whisky in prominent outlets, and his use of advertising and publicity was ahead of his time. His association with the prima donna Adelina Patti was one of the earliest examples of endorsement advertising. He supplied his whisky to the Members' Bar at the House of Commons, winning the contract from his former employer, Mackinlay's, and also to the London music halls.

southerly distillery in Scotland, Bladnoch, from Inver House in 1983.

The Bell brothers died in 1942. AK's philanthropy had led to him being created a Freeman of the City of Perth. He had purchased the Gannochy and Muirhall estates and set about building a 'model village' to provide cheap housing for unemployed railwaymen, and had rescued from bankruptcy a local linen company, a major employer in the district, by re-equipping the factory to produce man-made fibres. At the time of his death he was a director not only of Bell's but also of the North British Distillery Co. Ltd and John Shields & Co. of Perth, and left an estate valued at almost £½ million.

Bell's retained its independence until 1986, when it was taken over by Guinness which subsequently merged it with DCL to create United Distillers, now United Distillers & Vintners.

His initial approaches to the company which controlled the music halls were rebuffed, but the company was led by a man who was also the head of a large firm of accountants and Buchanan placed his own business with them in a successful attempt to win the contract. His whisky had inevitably come to be known as Black & White, from the appearance of the bottles, and Buchanan finally registered the name as his brand. The trademark logo of the black and white terriers was his own idea and the wording 'As specially selected for the House of Commons' was later added to the label. Buchanan owned a Highland estate at Torridon and created a stud farm at Lavington in Sussex, horse racing being a particular passion. His horses won both the St Leger and the Derby. He became Lord Woolavington in 1922 and died in 1935, leaving an estate valued at over £7 million.

John Dewar

As was the case with Bell's, the Dewar company was founded by a wholesale wine and spirit merchant and guided to far greater success by his offspring. John Dewar himself was the son of a crofter, born in Aberfeldy in 1806, and trained as a joiner. In 1828 he accepted an offer of a job with his uncle, a wine merchant, and moved to Perth. Nine years later he was made a partner in the firm, and nine years after that began his own business. When he died in 1880 he left a successful company, albeit one whose operations were mainly confined to the local area.

After John's death control of the company was assumed by his second son, John Alexander, who had been taken into partnership with his father the year before. He was twenty-three years old. He was joined in 1885 by his 21-year-old brother Thomas Robert, known throughout the trade as Tommy. The brothers both served apprenticeships with merchants in Leith and were chalk and cheese in character, but complemented each other well. John was quiet and cautious, with an affinity for the management side of the business, whilst Tommy was an extrovert who was to build himself a reputation as a flamboyant and talented salesman, one of the industry's true characters. Between them, the brothers increased

Rannoch Moor

the company's annual profits from £1,321, at the time of their father's death, to £1,198,154 when the firm merged with DCL in 1925.

Tommy Dewar realised early on the importance of publicity and reputedly pulled his most famous stunt at the Brewers' Show at London's Agricultural Hall in 1886, attracting attention to his wares by having a piper marching up and down playing non-stop. In 1891 he embarked on a two-year world tour on which he visited twenty-six countries and appointed thirty-two agents. The tour wiped out Dewar's profits for the whole of the two-year period, but established the company across the globe. Meanwhile, Tommy's brother John had negotiated a credit deal with DCL for the supply of grain whisky. The agreement stood the company in good stead when discussions got under way for the merger with DCL, Dewar's first merging with Buchanan until the arrangement was accepted by Johnnie Walker. Both Dewar brothers were appointed to the board of DCL in 1925.

John Dewar entered politics at the age of twenty-seven, when he served on Perth Town Council, and in 1900 became MP for Inverness-shire, an office he held for sixteen years. He purchased Dupplin estate from the Earl of Kinnoull in 1910 for £249,000, built the village of Forteviot, and became the first of the so-called 'whisky barons' when he was made Lord Forteviot of Dupplin in 1916. He died in November 1929 leaving an estate worth nearly £4 million, 81 per cent of which was invested in the whisky trade. Tommy also served as an MP, for St George's, Tower Hamlets, and became Lord Dewar of Homestall in 1919, The Homestall being his home at East Grinstead. He published a book on after-dinner speaking, a talent for which he was famous. He died within months of his brother, in April 1930, and left an estate valued at over £5 million, a far cry from the days of his arrival in London to open Dewar's office in Pall Mall, when he was forced to find security for the rent!

William Grant

Some of William Grant's background is covered in the section on Glenfiddich but it will do no harm to take a closer look at the story here, as Grant founded a company which, through foresight, determination and a willingness to take chances, now produces the most successful single malt whisky in the world.

Grant's ancestors were no strangers to hard life or hard work. His great-grandfather was a survivor of Culloden and was said to have lived to the age of 103. His father, William senior, was originally a tailor but joined what was to become the Gordon Highlanders and took part in the battle of Waterloo in 1815. He was only 4ft 11in tall and boasted that he survived the battle because all the bullets went over his head! After his discharge in Newcastle in 1817 he walked the 275 miles back home to Dufftown.

William Grant junior was born in 1839. He must have inherited his father's wanderlust as, when he first thought of starting his own business, he walked the 120-mile round trip to Balmoral and back to speak to a landowner. At the age of twenty-seven he took a job as book-keeper at Mortlach Distillery, where he eventually became manager.

The story of how Grant and his family worked to establish Glenfiddich is well documented and will be happily explained by any of the distillery's tour guides. Glenfiddich was literally the product of the family's own toil, built within a year, and with only a single mason and carpenter being hired for skilled labour. The original plant was purchased second-hand from Cardhu. When the distillery went into production all Grant's children helped to run the place, some whilst still at school, his sons working the distillery and his daughters cutting the peat for the kiln. The first spirit ran from the stills on Christmas Day 1887, and the family still have the copper cup from which it was drunk.

Such was Glenfiddich's success that after only five years Grant was able to build a second distillery next door on the site of Balvenie Castle, which he bought for £200. A third, Kininvie, was added on the same site in 1990. The company has always been good at marketing, even when it was not thought of as 'marketing'. During Prohibition, when all but six distilleries in Scotland were closed, Glenfiddich and Balvenie stepped up production and had a supply of mature whisky ready and waiting when the American market reopened. They were the first company to sell whisky in gift packs, and the first to open their distillery to the public. In 1963 Grant's began to sell Glenfiddich as a single malt outside Scotland and the rest, as they say, is history.

John Haig

The Haig family claim to be the oldest Scotch whisky distillers, tracing their ancestry back to 1627 when Robert Haig established his farm at Throst. It was not uncommon, or illegal, at that time to distil spirits for personal consumption and farmers often operated a still as a sideline. Sure enough, Robert Haig is recorded as having appeared before a Kirk Session in 1655 accused of working his still on the Sabbath.

The Haigs' grip on Lowland distilling began when Robert Haig's great-great-grandson John married Margaret Stein in 1751. The Stein family had built the Kilbagie and Kennetpans distilleries and John Haig, seeing his family's destiny, sent his five sons to Kilbagie to train as distillers. Four of them went on to build their own distilleries. The youngest son, William, took over Kincaple Distillery from Robert Stein and later built Seggie, which passed to his son John in 1837. It is this John Haig who is credited with really putting the House of Haig on the whisky map.

In 1824, whilst still in his early twenties, John Haig built Cameronbridge Distillery. On 12 May 1830 he installed under licence the first of a pair of new Stein stills, recently invented by his cousin Robert Stein at Kilbagie for the continuous distillation of 'silent malt' spirit. One of them remained in use until 1929. The emphasis at Cameronbridge turned more and more towards grain whisky production and by 1887 two Coffey stills had also been introduced. As one of the most prominent Lowland distillers Haig's was one of the six companies which banded together to form the Distillers Co. Ltd, and John Haig was one of the original directors.

Glenfinnan viaduct

John Haig had eleven children. Hugh was also a DCL director and William became company secretary. His youngest son, Douglas, was Commander-in-Chief of the British Expeditionary Force to France in 1915 and was created Earl Haig for his war service. He later became chairman of John Haig & Co. DCL acquired full control of Haig in 1919 and, four years later, Haig & Haig Ltd, a company set up by Hugh Haig's brother to sell whisky in the USA. Thus Haig & Haig became a subsidiary of Haig!

Haig is now owned by United Distillers & Vintners and holds the licences for three malt distilleries: Glenkinchie in the Lowlands, and Glenlossie and Mannochmore on Speyside. They also market a single grain whisky, Cameron Brig.

'Long' John Macdonald

The history of Long John is both long and complex and has seen ownership of both the brand name and the distillery with which it is associated, Ben Nevis, pass from one continent to another.

The origin of John Macdonald's nickname is not difficult to guess: he was 6ft 4in tall, an unusual height in the early nineteenth century. He is believed to have been born in 1796 at Torgolbin, the son of a farming family. The particular branch of the clan Macdonald from which he was descended can be traced back to Alexander Macdonald, a son of the Lord of the Isles, and himself a descendant of Somerled, King of Argyll. Long John's great-grandfather fought in both the 1715 and 1745 rebellions and was killed at Culloden.

In 1825 John Macdonald turned from farming to distilling, building a new distillery at Fort William. Taking the name of the most prominent local landmark, he called his whisky Long John's Dew of Ben Nevis. His reputation grew quickly and included royal patronage, Queen Victoria visiting the distillery in 1848 and being presented with a cask of whisky to be opened fifteen years later when the Prince of Wales came of age.

Some time after his death Long John's successors sold the brand name to W. H. Chaplin & Co., a London wine and spirit merchant. It in turn was acquired by Seager Evans, a company originally formed as a gin distiller, but which had diversified into the whisky trade. Seager Evans subsequently passed to the American company Schenley Industries then in 1969 to Rapid American Inc., which changed its name to Long John International.

Here, things start to become complicated. Long John International owned the Strathclyde grain distillery and four malt distilleries, including Tormore and Laphroaig. The company returned to British ownership when it was taken over in 1975 by Whitbread, which reunited Ben Nevis Distillery with the Long John brand name after many decades' separation. However, the industry suffered much upheaval during the 1980s and Long John did not escape its share of the action. Whilst Guinness was bidding for control of DCL, Long John International was renamed James Burrough Distillers and sold off Ben Nevis, which had been in mothballs for much of the decade, to the Japanese Nikka company. Whitbread relinquished its interests in malt distilling with the sale of Tormore and Laphroaig to Allied Distillers in 1990, the good news being that, in the hands of the Japanese, Ben Nevis is once more in business.

Peter Mackie

Peter Mackie was, by all accounts, one of the most outspoken and energetic members of the whisky trade and deserved his nickname 'Restless Peter'. He was born in Stirling in 1855 and started his career with a Glasgow firm owned by his uncle, James L. Mackie. James Mackie had by this time merged his business interests with those of the Graham family, the owners of Lagavulin, and he dispatched his nephew to Islay to learn the art of distilling.

Mackie applied his customary enthusiasm to the job and his uncle rewarded him with a partnership in a new firm, Mackie & Co. Offices were opened in London and the firm began to sell its bulk blends in the south. Mackie also promoted Lagavulin as a single malt, and it was one of those which most impressed Alfred Barnard when he toured all the Scottish distilleries in the 1880s, researching his definitive book *The Whisky Distilleries of the United Kingdom*. Within the next few years Mackie was to found Craigellachie Distillery and, prompted by the success of firms such as Johnnie Walker, whose sales were beginning to eat into the market for bulk blends, decided to introduce a branded blend of his own. He named the blend after an old Edinburgh inn, the White Horse, on the site of which was built the family's home in Canongate. The blend owes its distinctive flavour to Lagavulin and it was immediately successful, selling 24,000 cases in its first year on the market.

Mackie took a prominent role in the industry and was afraid neither of speaking his mind nor of the consequences of doing so. He publicly called Lloyd George 'a crank', his withering comment on the Budget of 1909 being 'What can we expect of a Welsh country solicitor?' His answer to the tax increases was to improve production at Craigellachie and Lagavulin by introducing more labour-saving equipment and better biochemical control measures. He fiercely lobbied the government for legislation on the blending and maturation of spirits, and created much antagonism with the owners of Laphroaig. In fact, Mackie had strong views on pretty much everything and enjoyed expressing them. He awarded prizes to his distillery workers for best-kept gardens, and compelled all his employees to use his own 'bran, bone and muscle' flour in their cooking, a product which was made to his own secret recipe by machinery underneath the boardroom floor at the company's office.

The company expanded after World War I when Mackie purchased Hazelburn Distillery at Campbeltown and also built a grain distillery in London. A laboratory was established at Hazelburn to carry out research into the process and materials of whisky-making, and it was there where Masataka Taketsuru, the founder of Nikka Distillers, came to study the craft.

Many of Mackie's ideas were quietly forgotten after his death in 1924. His public rhetoric was virtually silenced by the news of his son's death in Palestine in 1917, after which he became a peace campaigner. With no heir the chairmanship of the company, which had changed its name to White Horse Distillers only months earlier, was taken by his son-in-law.

Glenfinnan monument, Loch Shiel

William Henry Ross

The name William Henry Ross is unfamiliar to most whisky drinkers and does not appear on the labels of their favourite brands, yet Ross was an influential character in the whisky trade thanks to his meteoric rise through the ranks to the chairmanship of DCL.

Ross was born in 1863 and, like John Walker, was the son of a farmer. His father came from Carluke and moved to Westfield Farm on the Dundas estate near South Queensferry. Ross was educated at the local school and at George Watson's College in Edinburgh. At the age of fifteen he left school to become a clerk at the City of Glasgow Bank. However, the bank failed a year later and Ross took a job as a clerk at DCL. He was promoted to accountant at the age of twenty-two, to secretary at twenty-seven, to general manager at thirty-five and to the board as managing director at thirty-eight.

Ross's values were instilled into him by his experiences in his first job, when the bank collapsed, and by the Pattison crash which occurred around the time of his promotion to DCL general manager. He was a fervent believer in the advantages of amalgamation and rationalisation, and the regulation of supply and demand. He played an important role in the 'what is whisky' case, and led DCL to develop export markets and diversify into other fields of operation, notably the production of industrial alcohol, solvents and plastics.

Ross became chairman of DCL in May 1925, at the time of the company's merger with Buchanan-Dewar and Johnnie Walker. He retired in 1935 after a tragic accident aboard ship left him blinded in both eyes. He died in August 1944.

William Teacher

Like Bell's, Teacher's is a company which was not originally regarded as being one of the front-runners in the blending trade and was eclipsed by the so-called 'big five'. Also like Bell's, Teacher's stayed independent for many years after those companies had been swallowed up by DCL and now makes one of the top-selling blended Scotch whiskies.

William Teacher was a wine and spirit merchant and became the single biggest licence holder in Glasgow with a chain of eighteen shops. As he moved into wholesaling he developed a speciality of blending whiskies in bulk to his customers' specifications, and consequently built up a repertoire of blend recipes. His story parallels that of William Sanderson, who was working at around the same time, both men developing their own house blends from those recipes. Sanderson called his product Vat 69, Teacher's was to be called Highland Cream, and the name was first registered in 1884.

Highland Cream was not Teacher's only blend, although it is the one which has stood the test of time. At least three other brands were marketed including Australian Bonded Grand Liqueur, casks of which were dispatched by sea to Australia and back in order that the marrying process should be helped along by the rolling of the ship during the long voyage. Teacher's continued this practice until the 1920s and it was adopted shortly after by William Whiteley, the proprietor of Edradour Distillery, as an important step in the blending of King's Ransom.

Teacher's began exporting in 1875, first to New Zealand. This was followed by sales to Scandinavia, Canada, India, South America and the USA by 1903. As the company expanded so the need became apparent for ready supplies of whisky, and with this in mind Teacher's built its first malt distillery, Ardmore, at Kennethmont in 1898. In 1960 the company also acquired Glendronach from Captain Charles Grant, the fifth son of William Grant of Glenfiddich. One particular selling point of Teacher's Highland Cream is its malt whisky content; the company claims a minimum of 45 per cent.

Teacher's is now one of the biggest blending companies outside the United Distillers & Vintners conglomerate, and until its acquisition by Allied Brewers was the largest independent Scotch whisky producer still controlled by descendants of the founder. An approach was made by DCL in the early 1920s in an attempt to acquire its stocks, but the bid was unsuccessful and Teacher's remained independent until 1976. The company is now a subsidiary of Allied Distillers.

John Walker

John Walker first established a grocery, wines and spirits business in Kilmarnock in 1820, but it was another thirty years before he became involved in the whisky trade and it was his son, Alexander, who persuaded him to move from retailing into wholesaling. The firm built up a successful trade in Scotch whisky, selling both in England and overseas, and by the 1880s John Walker & Sons was one of Scotland's biggest blending companies. Alexander died in 1889 and control of the company passed to his three sons, in particular the youngest, Alexander junior, who had joined the company only the previous year yet was to become the driving force in its success.

Alexander was educated at Ayr Academy and received legal training before joining the company after serving an apprenticeship with Robertson & Baxter, learning his way around the processes of distilling, blending and bottling. He became a director in 1890 and organised the purchase of Cardhu Distillery from the Cumming family in 1893, the first of many take-overs. He was also responsible for the Johnnie Walker logo, which is still in use today. In 1908 he commissioned the artist Tom Brown to make a sketch of his grandfather, the original Johnnie Walker, the result being a rapidly executed drawing of a striding, top-hatted man which has been instantly identifiable with the brand ever since. Lord Stevenson, a close associate of Alexander's, created the accompanying slogan: Born 1820 – Still Going Strong.

Alexander had argued unsuccessfully to the Royal Commission for a minimum malt content in blends of 50 per cent, and his strong views on trade matters probably held up an amalgamation with other blenders, a move strongly advocated by James Buchanan in order to contain the effects of cut-throat competition. Unwilling to wait for Walker's decision, Buchanan and Dewar merged in 1915 and it was not for another ten years that Buchanan-Dewar and John Walker merged with the Distillers Company.

At fifty-six, Alexander Walker was one of the youngest directors on the board of DCL. He became a member of a committee which eventually brought about a change in the management structure of the company. He was put in charge of a division which controlled DCL's diversification into industrial chemicals, a move in which Walker had been influential against opposition from the blenders who sat on the DCL board, who believed that any such diversification should be no more than a temporary measure whilst the company rode out a depression in the whisky market.

Alexander Walker was knighted in 1920 for his service in the Ministry of Munitions. In 1946 he was given the Freedom of Troon, the first person to be granted the honour, in recognition of his charitable work on behalf of the town. He died at his home there in 1950 after an active and influential career, not only with DCL but also as a director of numerous other companies, including British Home Stores. His holding in DCL accounted for nearly a quarter of his estate, yet at £½ million its overall value was surprisingly low for a man who controlled Scotland's largest whisky blending company.

Kiln furnace, Springbank

HOW MALT WHISKY IS MADE

It is important to remember two significant features of malt whisky: it is made entirely from malted barley, and it is made in batches. This batch production applies not only to the distillation stage but also to all the other stages of the process as well, and one only has to look at samples of whisky taken from various casks filled over a period of weeks to see just how different the results can be after maturation. The process of making whisky has been greatly refined over the last two centuries as it has become more clearly understood, but despite its few simple ingredients and the fact that modern distillers take great pains to maintain consistency at each stage, every twist and turn of the process is fraught with variables, any of which are potentially capable of ruining the entire production run.

It will take a distillery two to three weeks to convert nature's raw materials into a fiery clear spirit, but by law it will be at least another three years before it will emerge as Scotch whisky, and in the case of most single malts more like eight to twelve years or even longer. The process can be thought of in seven distinct stages: malting, mashing, fermenting (or brewing), distilling, filling into casks, maturing, and finally bottling. Not all distilleries operate every stage of the process themselves. It is common practice these days for malt to be bought in from a centralised maltings, and for the mature whisky to be sent out for bottling, usually to a plant owned by the parent company or a sub-contractor somewhere in the Lowlands industrial belt. The introduction of computerised control systems has seen distilleries

move away from having specialist staff for each stage of production. It is now common for each member of staff to be trained in all aspects of the process, and quite often a distillery will be run by a single operator per shift. Distilleries vary, so it is impossible to look at any one in particular as being definitive in the exact details of the process. This chapter looks at a theoretical distillery which operates every stage of the process itself, but first let us take a look at the raw materials and the many factors which influence them.

Raw materials

There is nothing artificial about whisky; all the ingredients from which it is made are nature's gifts and are used in virgin condition. It is interesting to compare whisky in this respect with brandy, its

great rival. Brandy is distilled from fermented grape juice (it is not at a sufficiently refined stage to call it wine), and the grapes are pressed again and again, probably six or seven times in all, together with the pips and stems, in order to extract the very last drops of juice. It is this juice which is fermented and distilled, and which to me makes brandy appear to have been made from second-hand ingredients.

Whisky is made from only three basic materials: barley, water and yeast. In addition, peat plays an important part in the process in two ways. It is used to fire the kiln in which the malt is dried and it also flavours the water as it flows over or seeps through it. Each of these elements has a crucial part to play.

Barley

Distilling grew up in Scotland's religious establishments because of the abundance of barley grown on local farms. It was a major crop throughout Scotland, England and Ireland at that time but Scottish barley now accounts for only half the distillers' requirements. The rest is imported from other parts of the EU, yet strangely Scotland exports malt to distillers in Japan!

Barley is a cereal of the genus Hordeum, a grass-type crop which yields starchy seeds rich in carbohydrates and suitable for food. It is the easiest of all cereals to grow, hence its popularity from the earliest times. Developments in farming over the years have led to new varieties and better strains of barley such as Chariot, Optic, Derkado and Prisma which give higher yields in the field, tougher and shorter straw for better harvesting, improved malting capabilities and subsequently higher yields in the distillery. Some strains accept higher peating levels more readily, and this will be taken into consideration if a distiller is making a peaty whisky. However, a high phenol level in the malt will restrict the efficiency of the fermentation process and reduce the yield of alcohol from the wash. The maltster's chemists will test the barley for low nitrogen content and its useful carbohydrate content (nitrogen inhibits fermentation, and the higher the nitrogen the lower the amount of carbohydrate available which will turn into sugars during malting) and will check that it has the correct proportion of starch and protein. Only if it satisfies these conditions will it make it to the first stage of the process: malting.

Water

Water is taken for granted these days; turn a tap and out it comes. Of all the familiar substances which are single chemical compounds (salt, for instance, is another), water is by far the most complex. The *Encyclopaedia Britannica* devotes five pages to it.

Distilleries usually have their own water supplies, often a burn or spring to which they own exclusive rights. The available water usually dictates the siting of a distillery at the outset, and it is common for all distillers to claim that their water is the best in the whole of Scotland. Highland water is very pure, as there is no heavy industry or intensive farming to contaminate it, and it is usually used at the distillery untreated save for a basic filtering to remove foreign matter. The same source is used to steep the barley prior to malting and for mashing the grist in the mash tun. Cooling water for the condensers is often drawn from a dam and recycled, the dam sometimes fed from a nearby river.

Water is classified as being hard or soft, hard water being that which contains a high proportion of calcium and magnesium salts which causes limescale to build up in pipes and kettles. Hard water is often used by breweries but by very few distilleries. Glenmorangie, Glenkinchie, Highland Park and Scapa all use hard water, which rises in limestone. Highland water is generally soft, rising instead in red granite. The peat and heather over which it often flows impart their own flavour to it and determine whether it will be clear, or have a brown tinge and some fibrous content. If the water has enough peat flavour then it may be that no peat is needed at the kilning stage, and certainly not all distilleries use peated malt. The peat also makes the water very slightly acidic, and this is an advantage at the malting stage as the enzymes present in the barley function best in slightly acid conditions. Hard water tends to be acidic anyway.

The water temperature also affects the quality of the final spirit. Distilleries in sheltered locations where the water is colder tend to produce particularly clean whiskies. This may be due to the rapidity with which the alcohol vapour is condensed back into liquid, colder water making the condensers more efficient and causing extra reflux in the still, leading to a lighter spirit. The chemical make-up of the water will also change with the ambient temperature, the quality falling as the temperature rises, and this is one reason why distilleries usually close down during the warmest summer months. Distilleries need a reliable supply of water in large quantities and it would be unusual (although not unknown) to find the springs which supply them drying up in hot weather. Two-thirds of Scotland has over 40in of rain per year, and in the mountainous areas of the Highland region the average rainfall is more than double that.

Yeast

Yeast is a fungus which belongs to the same general family as truffles, mildew and the fungi which cause Dutch elm disease! It is a mould, a living single-cell organism which contains what are known as enzymes. Enzymes are biochemical catalysts which cause certain chemical reactions to take place. The reaction which particularly interests brewers and distillers is that which converts sugars into alcohol. Enzymes are also present in the barley grains and cause a change in the nature of their starch reserves during the malting process.

Yeast is usually inactive in its stored state. In baking, for instance, it is activated by the water and the warmth generated when dough is made, and then killed by the heat of the oven. In distilling, it is activated by the wort in the washback. The yeast multiplies at a phenomenal rate during the fermentation, feeding on the sugars in the wort, and eventually it is killed by the alcohol it produces.

Distillers commonly use two types of yeast, cultured yeast and brewer's yeast. Brewer's yeast is produced as a by-product in the brewing industry and is usually packaged as a paste in 25kg bags. It suffers with age and poor storage, so it is important that it is used promptly. Cultured yeast, as its name suggests, is grown under laboratory conditions on suitable nutrients such as molasses and has a far higher viability, usually above 90 per cent. The exact mixture of the two types does affect the final spirit and the new strains of yeast currently in use are capable of fermenting higher-gravity worts. Modern worts have an original gravity (OG) of 1058–1060, as opposed to the average OG of 1050 of twenty years ago, meaning they have a higher content of fermentable sugars, leading to more alcohol in the wash.

Peat

Peat is an organic fuel formed by the decomposition of plant remains in waterlogged areas such as bogs and swamps. It is a relic of the Carboniferous period some 300 million years ago when much of what is now Britain was swampland. As giant trees and ferns died they fell into the stagnant water and partially decomposed, but did not rot away entirely. Depending on their degree of decomposition they became brown and spongy, or black and compact, and as the sea advanced and withdrew it laid down new sediments over the deposits. Had the process advanced further, these would have become coal.

Scotland has vast deposits of peat, covering some 2,600 square miles of the country. A quarter of the island of Islay is peat, the Laggan Bog said to be 100ft deep in places. In the north of Scotland, the Altnabreac Bog in Caithness covers some 21,000 acres and is estimated to contain 13 million tons of peat. It is this ready availability that made it a natural domestic fuel, and early distillers found that when used for drying the grain the peat infused it with a characteristic flavour.

Today, many distillers own or rent areas of land from which to cut peat. Traditionally it is hand cut, a long knife-like spade cutting thin blocks from the top 18in of the bog. The top layer of heather is removed first and replaced after the peat has been dug out. Some distillers and private contractors have equipment for cutting and spreading it mechanically. Apart from efficiency, the main advantage of this method is that it does

Peat cutting on Islay

not require removal of the top layer, hence there is less disturbance of flora and fauna. Peat contains 90–95 per cent water so after cutting it must be dried. From the distillers' point of view it must also be 'matured', as when it is freshly cut it contains a high proportion of sulphur and other undesirable minerals and these will gradually disappear when the peat is left to dry naturally in the open air. Some distillers are now taking steps to preserve the supply of peat. Bowmore, for instance, have developed a method of kilning with chopped and moistened peat which cuts the amount they use to 20 per cent of the amount they used to burn in brick form. Peat is actually a renewable resource, but unfortunately the time it takes to renew is measured in thousands of years.

Let us now follow one single batch of raw materials through the process from beginning to end, from the barley in the field to the whisky in the bottle, and bear in mind that this process can take on average ten years. The first stage will be to malt the barley.

Malting

Barley contains starch which acts as a source of food for the new shoots when the grain germinates. The purpose of malting is to prepare the starch for conversion into sugars which can in turn be converted into alcohol by the yeast during the fermentation stage.

Few distilleries now operate their own maltings and this part of the process is more likely to take place at a centralised maltings, which often belongs to the distillery's parent company, and which will supply malt to a number of distilleries in the area. Dedicated maltings of this type do not just churn out malt continuously, but make it to order for each distillery they supply and to each distillery's individual specification. The economics of the operation mean that maltings of this type usually work on the drum or Saladin box system. There are now very few independent maltings which still use the traditional floor-malting method.

A drum malting may seem a fairly modern invention, yet Speyburn had one in 1897. Like a number of other contemporary inventions it failed to catch on at the time, and widespread acceptance took a further fifty to sixty years to achieve. It consists of a number of large revolving drums, each of which may contain anything from 20 to 50 tons of barley. Air is drawn into the centre of the drum as it revolves, turning and airing the grain as it germinates. The drum method is favoured by commercial maltings such as those at Port Ellen and Montrose, the drums at the Montrose plant being able to handle over 740 tons of barley at any one time. The Saladin box system, named after the French engineer who invented it, is a long, open-topped metal box in which a bed of grain about 3ft deep is turned by a series of revolving forks which move back and forth along the box. Saladin boxes first appeared in the Scotch whisky industry in

ABOVE AND BELOW: *Malt barns, Highland Park*

1948, at the North British grain distillery at Edinburgh. Tamdhu and Glen Ord were the first Highland distilleries to install them. These two methods notwithstanding, the time-honoured practice used by most distilleries is (or was) floor malting.

The malting process was originally largely determined by trial and error. Today it is a controlled scientific process and its biochemistry is well understood. Maltsters must be able to make consistent malts in bulk from grain from many different sources grown under a wide variety of conditions. They will take samples of barley grain and test its characteristics before buying it from the merchant or farmer, and these tests will establish the correct malting cycle to be used for that batch of grain. If, when it is delivered, the bulk quantity does not match the preliminary samples, it will be rejected.

The barley is delivered to the maltings, usually in bulk transporters, and is pre-cleaned and dried before being sent to the storage silos. At harvest time a vast quantity of grain suddenly becomes available, and it must be carefully stored to maintain its quality. The amount of grain in storage is a natural attraction for pests and in the nineteenth century it was common for distillers and maltsters to have a cat to control the number of rats and mice. These days, this is more likely to be achieved with approved poisons and the biggest menace is insect infestation. The best method of control is storing the grain at the correct temperature and humidity.

The first step in the malting process is to soak the grain in water, but before this happens it is passed through the dresser which removes dust and dirt and any foreign contaminants. Magnets remove any metallic objects such as nuts and bolts which may have found their way in amongst the grain from the farm machinery, and a vibrating sieve removes stones. About half a bucketful of small stones will be extracted from a 30-ton batch of barley, and the type of stone will give a good clue as to where the barley came from. A lot of chalky stones, for instance, would prove that the barley was not grown in Scotland.

The barley is then filled into the steep tanks where it will spend up to seventy-two hours,

although some floor maltings are able to complete steeping within as little as forty-eight hours. The steep cycle varies and will be determined for each new batch of barley by the maltster's chemists, but a typical cycle for a floor maltings would be to steep for up to twelve hours, then drain and stand for a similar period. This is repeated three times. Air may be blown through the water in the steep to aerate the grain and give it fresh oxygen, and carbon dioxide can be sucked from the bottom of the steep after the water has drained. The soaking is to trigger the germination of the barley, but if the seed grains are left submerged too long they will drown! Living barley respires just like humans, and the water must be drained from time to time to allow the seeds to breathe. Steeping increases the moisture content of the grain to 43–45 per cent and simulates the pre-germination phase which happens when the seed is sown in the ground. The next stage is to simulate the conditions which occur in spring, when the temperature and oxygen levels are at the optimum for the seed to germinate, and in order to do this the grain is spread out, or cast, on the malt floor.

Floor malting is back-breaking work, and the grain needs constant attention for the eight to twelve days that it spends in the malt barn. If left to its own devices for too long it will overheat and germination will stop. One manager at Glenmorangie even went so far as to tell apprentices that the maltings was haunted, to keep them from dozing off during their shifts.

The grain is delivered from the steeps at one end of the floor. In winter it will be warmed first by piling it into a heap, or ruck. It is then deposited in a series of piles across the stone floor, the maltmen using large, triangular pram-like barrows to shift the grain around. The piles of grain are raked out with 2ft-wide metal rakes so that the barley covers the floor to an even depth of about 6in. The bed of grain on a malt floor is known as a piece.

For a typical malt floor, around 15 tons of barley will be steeped (its weight increases by some 50 per cent during steeping as the grain absorbs moisture). The barley must be turned to maintain an even temperature throughout the piece, to keep the grains supplied with oxygen and to prevent the rootlets from becoming entangled. Either the rakes will be used for this task, or wooden shovels called shiels. The maltmen wear rope-soled shoes or plimsolls when walking on the grain so as not to bruise it. The piece will usually be turned by a team of two men, one turning to his right, the other to his left. The men are expected to be capable of turning to either side with equal skill but in practice each has his own preference and will work to that side most of the time. The evidence can be seen on the shiels, whose blades

Maltmen's soft shoes, Springbank.

Malt floor, Laphroaig

Barley

Green malt

Kilned malt

become slanted to one side as they wear down. A malt floor will take about three hours to turn by hand, and given that a distillery will have at least two, if not three floors, it can be imagined what an arduous job this is. Some maltings now use electric 'rotovators' to turn the grain.

Germination is a biochemical reaction and generates heat, and it is essential that the temperature is kept down to around 60°F. This is done by thickening or thinning the piece, and opening or closing the windows which line the walls of each malt floor. Thermometers are inserted into the barley so that a constant check can be kept on the temperature, and traditional maltsters still proudly use Fahrenheit thermometers.

As the barley germinates, a complex of starch-splitting enzymes is secreted which will break down its reserves of starch into fermentable sugars. The enzyme complex is called diastase, and makes some of the starch soluble. The final conversion to soluble starch is completed later in the mash tun. When the starch enters solution in the tun, it is ultimately converted to sugars by further action of the diastase complex. These dissolved sugars will make a suitable nutrient for the yeast at the brewing stage. The malt also contains soluble proteins which contribute something towards the flavour of the distillate and also act as nutrients for the yeast.

After germination the barley becomes what is known as green (undried) malt. Depending on the season this will take eight to twelve days on a malt floor, or about five days in a drum or Saladin box.

Linkwood

Each barley grain will have grown a root, which could be up to an inch long, and a sprout which grows up the inside of the kernel. The maltman will assess the colour, hardness, texture and smell of the grains, and when the sprout has grown to about three-quarters of the length of the kernel the green malt will be sent to the kiln. It is a popular misconception that kilning stops the germination process. It doesn't. A seed only spends so long germinating, then it actively begins to grow. At this stage, the barley has germinated and has become green malt. The malt, however, is still growing, and if its growth is not checked the seed will start to use up its stored food reserves, the now partly soluble starch. Kilning stops any further growth by removing the moisture which sustains it, and preserves both the stored starch within the seeds, and the potential for further enzyme activity.

The kiln

The kiln is the one part of a distillery which makes it instantly recognisable. Its roof is surmounted by a slatted square chimney, topped with a pyramid-shaped cover which is usually the home of the distillery's weather vane and from which the structure gets its common name, the pagoda. Sometimes the cover is sheathed in copper, which after many years' exposure has tarnished to a bright green. The pagoda roof was first developed in the 1890s by the distillery architect Charles Doig at Dailuaine. Before then, distillery kilns were based on the design of Kent oasthouses which generated less draught and tended to retain the peat smoke, giving the malt a more pronounced flavour. Not all distilleries have kilns. The last generation of distilleries built since the 1950s, for instance, generally buy in all their malt, although some have a pagoda just for show. Similarly, not all distilleries which have kilns still use them as such – Balblair uses its as a reception centre.

The kiln is a two-storey building with the roof space open to the upper floor. The chamber is about 25ft square and has a perforated metal floor on which 15–20 tons of green malt are spread out to a depth of between 1 and 3ft. Beneath the kiln floor is the furnace. It is surprisingly small considering the size of the kiln space, not much larger than a domestic fireplace. Bricks of peat burned in the furnace generate clouds of sweet-smelling smoke which swirl up through the perforations in the kiln floor and infuse the grain with a characteristic 'peat-reek'. Some distilleries also burn small quantities of heather along with

Glen Garioch

Kiln furnace, Highland Park

Laphroaig kiln

Malt bins

the peat. Fans in the pagoda roof help to draw the smoke upwards through the malt, which must be turned during kilning to ensure even drying and flavouring from the peat smoke, a punishing task in 120ºF heat. The kiln temperature will be kept below 158ºF to avoid damaging the enzymes in the malt, and affecting their subsequent viability.

It is unusual nowadays for distilleries to kiln entirely with peat. The necessary peat-reek is obtained after the first few hours' kilning and the rest of the drying cycle is accomplished by using a coal fire or blown hot air. Even so, it is not uncommon for a distillery to burn 10 tons of peat every week, and some distillers have developed ways of cutting this down in order to preserve their peat resources. The kilning cycle takes up to forty-five hours and dries the malt to a moisture content of 4–4.5 per cent. It then has to be cooled to arrest the decline in enzyme levels and reduce the chances of insect attack. The culm, or rootlets, will be separated from the malt before it is sent for storage, as they absorb moisture from the air. They will be sold for cattle food or burnt as fuel. The malt is stored in the malt bins, where it will be kept for four to six weeks before being sent for mashing. There is some evidence that this period of resting improves the subsequent wort quality.

Mashing

When the malt is required for mashing it is taken from the malt bins and passed through another dresser which removes any dust, loose husks and foreign matter. There is a danger of stones or pieces of metal getting into the mill and causing sparks, as malt dust is highly explosive! After screening, the malt is weighed and sent to the mill to be ground into grist.

This is akin to flour milling, but the grist is not uniform. In order to achieve the maximum extraction of soluble starch from the malt, it is ground into a mixture of approximately 10 per cent husk (to help drainage), 80 per cent middles, a medium grind which produces the extract, and 10 per cent flour. The aim is to produce a clear mash, as free as possible from dust and impurities. The husks are removed from the grain intact and these will form a filter bed in the mash tun. The

The malt mill

type of mill is important. A roller mill grinds the grain relatively gently. Other types which grind very finely can burn the grain, causing bitter flavours in the final spirit. It takes about fifteen minutes to mill a single ton of malt. From the mill, the grist is passed into a hopper from where it will be fed to the tun.

The mashing of grist in a distillery works on exactly the same principle as the mashing of tea in a teapot, although obviously on a vastly different scale. It takes place in the mash tun, a huge circular vessel originally made of iron but now more likely to be stainless steel. Some distilleries have preserved their original mash tuns with their highly-polished, domed copper tops, although the mechanics inside will probably now be modern. The latest design of mash tun, developed in the brewing industry, is the lauter tun (*lauter* is German for 'clarifying'), a stainless steel tun with filter plates in the base through which the wort is drained. Lauter tuns also have improved rake gear which can be adjusted for clearing the draff, thus avoiding the need for the mashman to climb into the tun and physically shovel it out himself. They

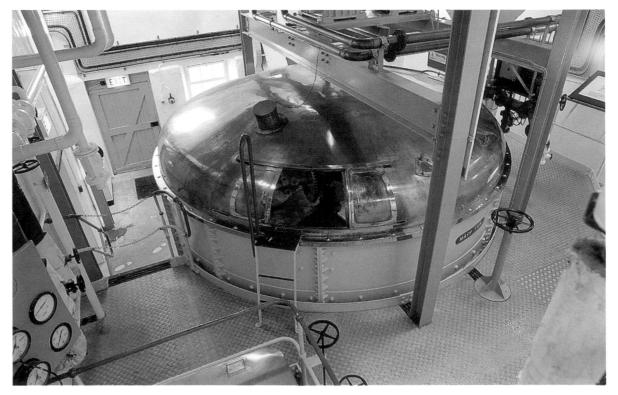
Traditional mash tun, Dallas Dhu

Rake gear in a traditional mash tun

Above: *Lauter mash tun and underback*
Below: *Sparging in a lauter tun*

tend to be larger than the old type of tuns as they mash a shallower bed of grist, and a lauter tun 23ft in diameter, and with a capacity of 11 tons of grist, is nothing out of the ordinary.

The purpose of the mashing process is to create a sugar solution from the carbohydrates in the malt. The conversion of unmodified starch to soluble starch and finally to sugars is completed by the diastase complex, at this point dormant in the malt but reactivated by the hot water in the mash tun. From the grist hopper the grist is fed into the mash tun through a large pipe, 1ft or more in diameter, called a Steel's masher. It is mixed as it enters this pipe with hot water at a temperature of about 155°F, a process known as sparging. The porridge-like mixture which results fills the mash tun and is agitated by the rake gear so that all the starch and sugars will be dissolved. The rake gear in a lauter tun consists of a revolving cross-bar from which a number of thin blades project downwards to stir the mash. The rake can be adjusted to avoid cutting into the filter bed of husks which lines the bottom of the tun. Rake gear in older mash tuns tends to look like some instrument of torture, a spinning shaft bearing curved, toothed arms and driven by a system of heavy cogs.

During a typical eight-hour mashing period, the water in the mash tun will be changed three or four times. Each refill will be progressively hotter than the last to ensure that all the malt extracts are dissolved, and each batch of the so-called extraction waters will be a weaker solution. The third and fourth extractions will be recycled and used for sparging the next batch of grist. The first and second extractions will be sent for fermenting and the bulk liquid is called wort.

Lauter tuns treat the mash more gently than the older tuns with their spinning rakes thrashing the grist. After the first sparging, the mash is stirred for about twenty minutes, during which time the starch in the malt grist is converted into sugars by enzyme action. After the extract has been drained, water is sprayed onto the grist as it is stirred by the rake. This is known as elution, and washes all the remaining sugars away from the grist solids. The original mash water has to be cool enough to preserve the diastase as it effects the conversion. The first and second elutions will be hotter, about 187°F and 210°F, to ensure that all sugars are dissolved, and correspond to the second and subsequent spargings in a conventional tun. Lauter tuns not only work faster but are capable of draining wort from finer grinds of grist, improving the yield of extract in the wort by up to 1 per cent, a significant quantity from an average 11-ton mash.

The first waste product is generated at this stage. The mass of spent grains left in the mash tun after the wort has been drawn off is called draff, and although it has given up its starch and sugars it is still rich in protein and makes an ideal cattle food. Some distilleries process it on site but the current trend is to send it to a centralised plant which processes the by-products from a number of distilleries. Getting the draff out of the mash tun used to be a job for a man with a shovel, but as we have seen modern lauter tuns are self-emptying. Some distilleries clear the pipes by sending footballs down them under pressure, the balls being collected at the draff hopper outside in a device resembling an over-sized snooker table pocket.

The wort is drawn off and passes through the underback on its way to the wort cooler. The underback is a semicircular tank, usually of stainless steel, that serves both to indicate the level of the wort draining from the mash tun and to balance the flow, enabling the tun to be drained slowly. The wort is still quite warm and must be cooled to a temperature at which the yeast can work. Most distilleries have no way of cooling the wort during the fermentation and heat is created during the reaction. If the wort temperature reaches 95°F there is a danger of killing the yeast, so the initial temperature must be set low enough to prevent it from rising that far. From the wort cooler, the wort is pumped to the washbacks for fermentation.

Fermentation

This step is sometimes called brewing, and up to this point the process bears a close resemblance to that operated in a brewery (indeed some distilleries started their lives as breweries), yet despite the antiquity of the brewing process the chemistry of fermentation was not understood until the late nineteenth century. The wort is fermented by yeast in large vats known as washbacks.

An average distillery will usually have six to eight washbacks, each with a capacity of up to 10,000 gallons or so. One notable exception to

Cragganmore's wort cooler

Tun room, Cragganmore

this is Glen Grant which has ten, each holding 20,000 gallons of wort. Traditionally, washbacks are made of larch or Oregon pine (or Douglas fir, as pine is sometimes called) although again this is another area where stainless steel is becoming more widely used. Steel is much easier to keep clean and steel vessels will either have a sprayhead inside for this purpose, which looks rather like a golf ball on a pipe, or will be pressure-washed after use. Wooden washbacks need to be scrubbed out with a caustic solution to kill bacteria. Any infection will turn a batch of fermented wort into nothing more than malt vinegar, yet many distillers prefer to stick with the wooden vats, believing that they exert their own influence on the end product in a way that stainless steel cannot. Wood is also a better insulator than steel and will retain more of the heat in the fermenting liquor. The temperature can rise by as much as 18°F during fermentation and wooden washbacks will retain more of this heat, which can be a problem in warm weather as the yeast will be killed above 95°F. Conversely, in cold weather steel vessels are prone to heat loss which will slow down the reaction.

The tun room, or fermenting hall, is a two-storey building in which the washbacks stand on the ground floor and project up through the floor above (this is why some people think that they are only 4ft deep). During the fermentation process carbon dioxide gas is given off. Being heavier than air it sinks to the ground, and for this reason the lower tun room is kept locked when the washbacks are in use.

Wort is pumped into the washback and yeast is pitched in to start the reaction as soon as the liquid covers the bottom of the vessel. A carbon dioxide blanket is quickly formed which prevents airborne wild yeasts and bacteria from reaching the wort and spoiling the flavour of the resulting wash and its yield of alcohol. Constant checks are made on the wort as it ferments as a sudden increase in acidity will be a sign of contamination. Only one batch of yeast is used in each washback but it will usually be a mixture of two types, about 40 per cent cultured yeast and 60 per cent brewer's yeast. About 8cwt will be added to 10,000 gallons of wort. Fermentation is actually a

Checking the fermentation's progress

Switcher

41

chain of biochemical reactions and is caused by a complex of enzymes collectively known as zymase, the maltose and other sugars in the wort being broken down to ethyl alcohol and carbon dioxide. The process is quite energetic and the wort froths up to the top of the washback. Inside the cover of the vessel a stirring paddle called a switcher slowly revolves, breaking up the bubbles and preventing the froth from overflowing. Before the introduction of switchers the froth would be beaten down by a man using a heather broom.

When touring a distillery, beware if you are invited to take a sniff inside a working washback. It is a source of constant amusement to distillery tour guides to see grown men reduced to tears because they have blithely stuck their head into the vessel and taken a deep breath, as though inhaling some sort of cold cure. The carbon dioxide inside the vat is sharp enough to buckle the strongest knees!

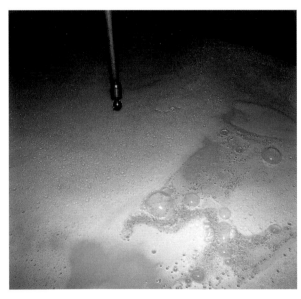

Wort ferments in the washback

A brewery will stop fermentation part-way through to allow for a little extra fermentation to take place in the cask, the so-called 'cask-conditioning'. Distilleries allow it to proceed to finality, at which point the yeast has been killed by the alcohol it has produced. Other secondary fermentations also take place during the reaction, each contributing to the end product. The process

Bowmore

takes in all up to forty-eight hours. With a mash tun producing three eight-hour mashes per day six washbacks will be filled in two days, at which point the first will have finished fermenting and will be ready for cleaning and refilling. Fermentation times are dropping now as new and better strains of barley and yeast become available, and it is not unknown these days for the process to take as little as twenty-seven hours.

The liquid which results from the fermentation is known as wash, and is the first occurrence of alcohol in the process. This is therefore the stage at which the Customs and Excise will first take an interest, as they are able to calculate the amount of spirit that should be obtained from a given volume of wash. Wash itself is like a strong beer, with an alcohol content of 7–8 per cent. It also contains some by-products of the fermentation process and some unfermentable matter. To eliminate these and concentrate the alcohol in the solution, the wash now passes to the most mystical part of the process: the distillation.

Distillation

The sight of the gleaming copper pot stills is the memory that remains longest to most distillery visitors. This is the part of the distillery where the illusion of alchemy is strongest, and the one part of the process where a mistake by the operator will have the gravest consequences. As an art-form, distillation has come a long way since the days when it used to be performed by smugglers in coastal caves and remote moorland hideaways.

The principle of distillation was first discovered almost 3,000 years ago. It is quite simply a method of separating two or more substances, usually liquids, which boil and vaporise at different temperatures. In the case of whisky distilling the two liquids are ethyl alcohol and water, the alcohol boiling and evaporating at 173.3°F (78.5°C), the water remaining liquid until

OPPOSITE: *Stillhouse, Laphroaig*

it reaches 212°F (100°C). In theory the process would also work in reverse, by cooling, as water and alcohol have different freezing points. However, apart from the expense and impracticality of doing it this way, it would mean that distilleries would not be such cosy places in which to work!

In the stillhouse of a malt distillery, the biggest difference between malt and grain distilling becomes instantly apparent. Whereas grain whisky is made in tall column stills which operate continuously, malt whisky is distilled in (relatively) small batches in the distinctive, onion-shaped pot stills. Just how large or small these batches are will vary from one distillery to another, but a couple of visits to Edradour and Glenfarclas will show how the scale of operation can differ.

A pot still is simply a large copper kettle, its general pear-shape defined as long ago as the sixteenth century. No two distilleries will use identical designs, even though they may appear similar at first sight, and every distiller will claim that his stills have some unique feature which makes them produce the finest whisky in Scotland! Talisker's bent lyne arms and Glen Grant's 'German helmet' mid-sections are cases in point, but no one knows exactly what effect such features have, and no distiller is prepared to risk changing the design of his stills in case it affects the character of the whisky. To take this argument to its absurd lengths, if a still is damaged in some way, dented say, then when that still needs to be replaced the dent will be reproduced in the new one. I have heard variations on this story many times, yet if the design of the still is that crucial, and a dent causes no detrimental change in the spirit when it first appears, why bother reproducing that dent when the still is replaced? Such is the mystique which has whisky in its grip.

It is true, however, that the general shape of the still has a bearing on the type of spirit it produces. Small squat stills, such as those at Macallan, will produce a heavy, oily spirit, as the heavier alcohols have less trouble climbing to the top of a small still. In contrast, a tall still such as those at Glenmorangie and Jura will produce a light spirit, as only the very lightest alcohols are volatile enough to climb the full height of the still

Edradour's tiny stills

neck. The shape of the still also determines the degree of reflux, the amount of spirit vapour condensing on the sides of the still neck and running back down into the boiling charge to be redistilled. Well-flavoured but not-too-heavy whiskies can be produced by using stills with a lantern neck (such as Auchroisk's), or a bulge in the neck such as the 'Balvenie ball'. A purifier, a sort of pre-condenser inserted in the still neck or lyne arm (as used at Glen Grant) will also influence the degree of reflux. Popular at one time in Hiram Walker distilleries was the Lomond still. Invented by one of the company's employees, it was a peculiar cylindrical still with a water jacket mounted vertically above it. Within the still neck were three rectifying plates which could be adjusted and water-cooled to vary the degree of reflux, and the still produced a rich,

heavy spirit. It seems to have rather fallen out of favour these days, as problems arose when the plates became 'gummed up' with residue, but some whiskies made with this system, such as Mosstowie and Glencraig, can still be found occasionally in independent bottlings.

All stills are custom-made from copper, the name of the coppersmith proudly emblazoned on a plaque or on the inspection hatch. This is one area in a distillery where stainless steel has not taken over, nor is likely to. Copper not only is one of the best conductors of heat but also acts as a catalyst, removing unwanted sulphurous compounds from the spirit which originate from the malt. A new still with an average capacity of 2,000–4,000 gallons will cost in the region of £35,000, with another £20,000 for the condenser, and can be expected to last on average about ten

Inspection hatch

to fifteen years. It would be unusual for a still to be replaced completely. The problems of access to the stillhouse mean that it is more likely that small sections will be replaced as and when necessary. The copper in a new still is about ¼ inch thick, and over a period of years' use will wear down to about half that thickness. Wash stills and spirit stills exhibit different patterns of wear but generally the bottom is the most vulnerable as it bears most of the heat, followed by the bend at the top of the neck where the boiling vapour is concentrated into a very small area. It is easy to see where patches of newer metal have been inserted. When the still begins to wear, the metal can be seen 'pumping' in and out when it is being filled and this is caused by the sudden change in pressure inside as the charge is drawn in. The mushroom-shaped device sprouting from all stills is an anti-collapse valve, designed to prevent damage to the still by sucking air in to counteract the rapid change in internal pressure when the heat is suddenly taken off.

The vast majority of malt distilleries use two stages of distillation and this usually means that the stills operate in pairs. There are exceptions to this rule though, for instance at Macallan, where the spirit stills are so small that two are used with each wash still. In some distilleries, the design of the spirit stills means having to have an extra one to handle the volume of low wines generated in the first distillation. Talisker and Laphroaig are examples of this, Talisker having a total of five stills and Laphroaig seven. The biggest distilleries

Glenfarclas has the biggest stills on Speyside

in Scotland are undoubtedly Tomatin and Glenfiddich. Steady expansion has given Tomatin a total of twenty-three stills, all in the same stillhouse. Glenfiddich has two separate stillhouses, with twenty-eight stills split between them.

Let's now see what happens to the wash, which has been pumped from the washback and stored in a holding tank called the wash charger.

The wash distillation

After fermentation the wash has an alcoholic content of 7–8 per cent and the first distillation will concentrate this to around 21–28 per cent, yielding a liquor known as low wines from which the yeast residue and any unfermented matter will have been eliminated. Some further cooking of secondary constituents also takes place which will influence the flavour of the final spirit. From the wash charger, the wash is filled into the first, or wash still.

There are four methods of heating the stills, all of which have their adherents. In the earliest times stills would have been coal-fired, although now the furnaces are just as likely to be fired by oil or gas. Some distilleries do not like to keep oil stored on the premises as there is some belief that the heavy vapours it gives off can taint the spirit. The latest heating method is by steam coil. Originally demonstrated in the latter part of the nineteenth century (Glenmorangie was using steam coils in the 1880s) it failed to catch on at the time, and it was not until the 1960s that it found widespread acceptance. The coil itself looks rather like a kettle element sitting in the bottom of the still, and steam from a boiler is passed through it to heat the wash. Being a milky liquid, wash takes a lot of effort to heat and many steam coils now have cylindrical attachments on them, known as cans, which distribute the heat more evenly through the liquid. Steam coils have the advantage of not scorching the liquid as an open flame can, but many distilleries still swear by their coal furnaces. Open flames are hotter and give a 'toasting' effect which colours the flavour of the distillate.

The main disadvantage of open flame is that if any yeast particles sink to the bottom of the still

Charging the still

they will be burned, and this will give rise to an unpleasant treacly taint which can be carried through to the final spirit. To prevent this, wash stills fired from below are fitted with rummagers. A rummager is a set of copper chains attached to a shaft which rotates inside the still, scraping loose any particles which sink to the bottom. Before the advent of mains electricity the rummagers, like all mechanical equipment in the distillery, would have been driven by water power and in some distilleries the old water wheels can still be seen. Today rummagers are driven by electric motor and you are unlikely to see any fitted with a bell, as they used to be years ago. This was to tell the stillman that they were working properly, as if the noise of the chains rattling inside the big copper pots was likely to leave him in any doubt! Where the system is still in use, the racket in the stillhouse is loud enough to preclude any attempt at conversation.

As the wash is heated, the alcohol vaporises and climbs the neck of the still. It passes along the lyne arm and to the condenser, where it will be cooled back into a liquid. Modern condensers consist of a vertical, cylindrical copper jacket

Steam cans in a wash still

Slit window in a wash still

containing a network of pipes through which cooling water runs, the distillate passing through the shell. The condenser may stand alongside the still or it may be outside, the lyne arms passing through the stillhouse wall. Whisky smugglers in the eighteenth and nineteenth centuries would have used for this purpose a coiled copper pipe called a worm, immersed in a barrel of cold water. Some distilleries still use a scaled-up version of this arrangement. Worm tubs look like washbacks, standing behind the stillhouse. An alternative is to immerse the worms in concrete tanks sunk into the ground.

The condensers act as heat exchangers, the boiling vapour heating the cooling water as it passes through. The water leaves the condensers at a temperature in excess of 158°F (70°C) and many distillers use this otherwise waste heat to heat water for mashing, although Glen Garioch has used it to heat a greenhouse, and Bowmore uses it to heat the public swimming pool built in one of its old bonded warehouses!

The first distillation takes five or six hours to run. As the wash is heated further and further it begins to boil up. If it boils too far there is a danger that it will boil right over the neck of the still, as a milk pan will suddenly boil over, and the wash will pass over the lyne arm undistilled. If this happens the whole batch will be ruined and the distillation will have to be started all over again. To prevent this the wash stills have slit-shaped windows fitted into their necks, and the stillman can see when the liquid starts to boil up this far and reduce the heat to a simmer. This is called 'breaking the still' and marks the point

when the alcohol starts to vaporise. Once the froth subsides the heat is increased again until all the alcohol has been driven off.

The end of the first distillation leaves a residue in the wash still known as pot ale, which is usually made into cattle feed. It can be evaporated to a syrup or mixed with draff and pelletised. The distillate is stored in the low wines charger until the spirit or low wines stills are ready to receive it.

The low wines distillation

It seems impossible to believe that a product which sells entirely on the merits of its flavour can only be judged during its manufacture by looking at it, yet for whisky this is precisely the case. From the low wines charger, all the apparatus is sealed with Crown locks to prevent any alcohol going 'astray'. This makes the stillman's job extremely skilled, as he alone is responsible for the quality and consistency of the final spirit.

The purpose of the second distillation is to concentrate the alcoholic content of the low wines. As the liquid is heated to 173.3°F the alcohol vaporises and rises up the still, passes over the lyne arm and through the condenser, where it liquefies. From the condenser, it runs into the spirit safe. The spirit safe was developed by Customs and Excise at Port Ellen Distillery in the 1820s and consists of a brass-bound glass tank through which the spirit flows, and contains hydrometers and thermometers for testing the spirit and a swivelling spout for directing it to one of two destinations. It is closed with a padlock which has an internal seal that will reveal to the Excise officers any sign of tampering.

The spirit safe

The low wines are heated until the alcohol starts to come off, then the heat is reduced to control the spirit flow. Distilling gently, rather than driving the still hard, encourages consistency of the final spirit, and the harder the still is run the less beneficial contact the spirit will have with the copper. First to come off are the lightest alcohols, known as foreshots, which are very volatile and do not make potable spirit. The stillman will test the specific gravity and quality of the spirit as it runs through the safe. By turning taps at the front of the safe, he is able to divert some of the flow into a glass jar containing a hydrometer. He is also able to mix the spirit with distilled water, a test in which impure spirit will

Labelling – an Excise requirement

turn milky. It is quite surprising to see for the first time just how fast the spirit gushes through the safe. Because of all the different liquids flowing this way and that around the place all the pipes in a distillery, and the stills themselves, are colour-coded. Red is for wash; blue for low wines, foreshots and feints; black for clear spirit and white for water. A further Excise requirement is that all the distillery's various vessels and utensils are labelled with their name and contents, and the visitor could well be excused for thinking that this thoughtfulness is for his benefit!

Foreshots will account for about 5 per cent of the distillation and are diverted to a tank called the feints receiver for redistillation along with the next batch of low wines. Small distilleries with only a single pair of stills will not generate enough foreshots and feints to need a separate receiver, and will simply direct them to the low wines charger. When the spirit coming through reaches a strength of about 75 per cent volume, the

stillman will divert the flow to the spirit receiver. This is called 'cutting on spirit' and this part of the run is called the middle cut, or heart of the run, and is the spirit which will be matured to become whisky. The middle cut can be up to 40 per cent of the spirit distillation, but most distilleries are very fussy and use a far smaller proportion than this, maybe as little as 15 per cent. The moments at which the stillman cuts on and off spirit are critical, as different flavour characteristics come through at different points during the distillation and undesirable congeners are carried in the foreshots and feints. The sweeter and fruitier flavours come through early in the middle cut, the oilier, drier and peaty elements towards the end. Cutting on spirit too soon will include more higher-strength alcohol in the middle cut, resulting in a spirit with a high ester content and giving rise to 'pear drop' flavours. Taking a short middle cut, cutting on spirit late and off spirit early, will lose flavour components. Running on spirit too long will take in an excess of feints with the middle cut which causes stale, fishy aromas and decreases the strength of the spirit. A certain amount of 'esteryness' in the spirit can be matured out, but 'feintiness' cannot.

By this time the still has been getting hotter and hotter, to the point where the heavier alcohols in the low wines – the feints – are beginning to vaporise. A certain amount of amylic alcohol, or fusel oil, is desirable to add character to the whisky, but when the strength of the distillate drops to about 63 per cent volume the stillman will direct the flow back to the feints receiver and the most critical part of the distillation process is over. The stillman cuts off spirit when the feints become too pungent, and the cut-off point is fixed and consistent for any particular distillery, although it will vary from one distillery to another.

Feints account for about 35 per cent of the total run, although only a tiny fraction of this will be kept along with the middle cut. After the stillman cuts off spirit the heat is increased to distil the last of the alcohol quickly, but the distillation will be stopped before the still becomes so hot that the water itself begins to vaporise – there is little point in adding water to

the contents of the feints receiver. Both the foreshots and the feints will be redistilled with the next batch of low wines. The liquid that remains in the spirit still is known as spent lees, and is little more than deoxygenated water. It is usually run to waste. A conscientious distiller will not return it to a river or stream without first treating it to put the oxygen back.

The second distillation takes six to eight hours and results in a fiery, clear spirit with a strength of about 68 per cent volume. This new spirit is held in the spirit receiver awaiting filling into casks. At this point the Excise officer will check his earlier calculations to ensure that the quantity of spirit obtained is as expected from the volume and strength of wash that was used. It is usually expected that 1 ton of malt will yield about 142 gallons (646 litres) of new spirit at the strength at which it will be filled into the casks (88 gallons of pure alcohol). If it does not then production managers and Excise officers alike will probably start asking awkward questions. If all is as it should be, the new spirit is piped to the filling store.

Triple distillation

Traditional Lowland (and Irish) distilleries use a method of triple distillation where the spirit is produced in three stages using an extra still called the intermediate still. In this method, low wines are produced as normal in the wash still and are sent forward to the intermediate still. From the intermediate distillation, strong alcohol and strong feints (from about 70 per cent volume to 20 per cent volume) are sent forward to the spirit still, with weak alcohol below 20 per cent volume recycled back to the intermediate still with the next batch of low wines (Irish distillers recycle this back to the wash still). From the spirit still, alcohol is collected starting at 81–82 per cent volume down to a strength of 78 per cent volume. Weaker alcohol is recycled back to the spirit still with the next batch from the intermediate still.

The result is a stronger spirit than that which comes from conventional double distillation, averaging 80 per cent volume, although this is not to say that the quantity produced is much less. Even though the parameters are finer the yield

Stillhouse, Springbank

from triple distillation is just over 80 per cent of that of the conventional process. It is also a lighter spirit and matures to become a characteristically clean-flavoured and fragrant whisky.

This method used to be much more widespread and was even popular on the west coast up to the 1920s, although today it is becoming exceedingly rare. The closure of Rosebank means that Auchentoshan is now the only distillery in Scotland still operating the process, although a variation on it is used at Springbank, where the manager and the stillman argue whether their whisky is distilled three times, or only two and a half!

Filling

In the filling store the spirit is held in a large tank where it is diluted, or cut, to the strength at which it will be filled into the casks. Some distilleries may use the same spring water that they use for steeping and mashing, although most now seem to use de-mineralised water for this purpose. The new spirit will be reduced to about 63.5 per cent volume as whisky seems to mature best at around this strength, and allowance must be made for the change in strength during maturation, bearing in mind the strength at which the whisky will finally be bottled. Before computerisation, the spirit would be held in a tank up in the roof of the filling store and simply piped into the casks by

gravity. Today it is not so simple. Automatic dispensers, rather like miniature petrol pumps, fill exactly the correct volume of spirit into each cask and record that amount on a digital display.

Every distillery used to have a resident Excise officer and it would have been his responsibility to oversee the filling process. A record is kept of every cask: the date it was warehoused, its location in the warehouse, the quantity and strength of its contents, and the name of its owner. This job is now entrusted to the distillers themselves, Customs and Excise checking from time to time that everything is being done to the letter of the law. The name of the distillery, together with the date and cask number, are stencilled onto the end of each cask, traditionally using a copper stencil. It is a sign of the times that casks can now be seen bearing bar-code labels, from which the computer can recall all the necessary information at the swipe of a light-pen.

Cask filling at ABOVE: *Glen Moray* BELOW: *Bowmore*

The casks

From this point on, the casks will shape the quality of what is to become fine malt whisky. They will be chosen and looked after with meticulous care.

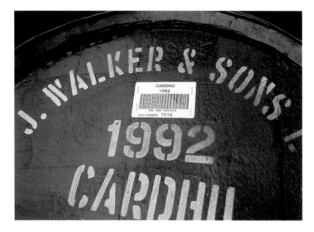

Bar-code labelling – a sign of the times

In the nineteenth century the cooper would probably have been the highest-paid man in the distillery, and coopers are probably the last traditional craftsmen still widely employed in Scotland. Few distilleries now have their own cooperages, and the casks are more likely to come from a central supplier, but the tools, techniques and materials they use are still largely the same as they were in the days of the guilds.

Casks are always oak, either American white oak or European oak, and the spirit develops both flavour and colour from its contact with the wood. Some distillers believe that over 50 per cent of a whisky's flavour is derived from the cask wood. American oak will give a lighter, cleaner spirit than European oak, which is used for sherry casks. The particular way in which the cooper cuts the staves from the log makes the cask water-tight, and a good cask can last up to sixty years. There are two sizes of cask in common use, the butt and the hogshead. Butts are traditionally sherry casks and have a capacity of 108 gallons. Hogsheads hold 55 gallons. There is also the puncheon, a shorter and fatter variation of the butt, and with the same capacity.

Scottish distillers enjoy a symbiotic relationship with both their compatriots in the USA, and the sherry bodegas in Spain. By law American bourbon casks can only be used once, so after the four-to-eight-year maturation period they are emptied and shipped to Scotland. The American barrels are slightly smaller than an Imperial hogshead, so when they are received at the cooperage they may be rebuilt with extra staves to increase their capacity from 42 US gallons to the hogshead's 55 Imperial gallons. Five American barrels will be remade into four hogsheads. Any staves which cannot be reused will be reduced to chippings, which are then used for smoking salmon. The convenience of container shipping now means that a load of barrels can be transported from an American to a Scottish distillery with minimal handling, and some distillers choose to forgo the rebuilding routine and use the American barrels unmodified. They will be rejuvenated by charring their insides, which cracks the surface and exposes new wood to the spirit.

Sherry casks add a very characteristic flavour to whisky matured in them, and many distilleries use them. Only Macallan uses them exclusively. Some distillery managers make annual visits to Jerez to personally select the butts that will be shipped back to Scotland. Because of the vagaries of the supply, some distillers commission Spanish cooperages to make butts for them. These are then used by a bodega for two or three years to mature sherry, a privilege for which the distiller has to pay, after which they are shipped intact to Scotland. A sherry butt will cost a distillery about £200, as opposed to the £40 or so for a bourbon hogshead.

Once the casks have been filled, identified and recorded, they are taken to the warehouse to begin their long period of hibernation.

Aberfeldy

Maturation

The beneficial changes which occur in malt whisky stored for a long period in oak barrels were discovered quite by accident and are still not fully understood even now. One thing is certain, and that is that the spirit is shaped into Scotch whisky by the Scottish climate and the outcome would be very different if it were matured elsewhere. Before the spirit can legally be called whisky it must be matured in (oak) wood for at least three years, and much of the whisky destined for the blenders is shipped from the bonds at this age. Spirit which is to be bottled as single malt whisky will normally be aged for much longer. Eight to twelve years is more usual, and there is no shortage of distillers who bottle versions much older than this.

The maturation period will be influenced by the character of the spirit, the size of the cask and the atmosphere in which it is kept. Distillery warehouses are traditionally long, low buildings in which the casks are stacked three or four high on racks or on top of each other, separated by wooden rails or dunnage. The floor is often bare earth, which allows the damp to penetrate the building, and a typical sight in a dunnage warehouse is that of the whitewash peeling off the walls inside. The alcohol fumes which permeate the stone encourage the growth of the black mould seen on the outside. Some newer warehouses use a system of palletised storage, where casks are stacked nine to a pallet on concrete floors, up to half a dozen or so pallets high. The system was pioneered at Tormore in the 1970s and has been adopted at numerous distilleries since. The pallets are handled by fork-lift trucks, whose LPG fuel must be filtered to avoid contaminating the atmosphere in the warehouse. Although this method of storage maximises a warehouse's capacity it is not always the most convenient for retrieving particular casks, or sequences of casks, as required by the blender, when compared to the old dunnage-type warehousing. From time to time the casks are inspected for leaks, and samples will be taken to check on the maturation's progress. As the temperature changes the whisky expands and contracts inside the cask, either pushing air out or

Warehouse, Balblair

at least forty come from the cask wood. Perfumiers have identified around two dozen different aromas in whisky, over half of which arise from the maturation process. Scientists in Scotland have isolated most of the chemicals which give rise to these scents and have been able to determine at which stage of production each is introduced. The malting, fermentation and distillation stages all make a critical contribution to the end result.

Every whisky is characterised by the level and ratio of isobutyl and isoamyl alcohols in it. The harsher alcohols evaporate first, with the effect of mellowing the spirit. Extracts from the wood colour the flavour, more so if the wood is new. If the casks have been used previously most of the wood extracts will have been given up to the first fillings, generally a desirable case for whisky. New oak, for instance, contains vanillic acid which is responsible for the pronounced vanilla flavour in bourbon. The first filling itself will also imbue the spirit with its own characteristics, particularly if the cask was first used for sherry. The type of sherry – whether it is oloroso, fino or amontillado – will also be significant. Some distillers and independent bottlers have experimented beyond the tried and trusted methods using other types of cask. Glenmorangie experimented with versions of its malt finished in port and Madeira wood, and have obviously been encouraged by the results as the company now bottles a range of wood finishes. Port wood finishing has caught on with a number of distillers, including Balvenie, Bowmore and Cragganmore. Glen Moray now finishes its malt in Chardonnay and Chenin Blanc barrels, and each of the six members of UDV's Classic Malts range has a partner finished in port or sherry wood.

A distillery's warehousing is what is known as bonded, or duty-free. This means that the whisky stored there is not assessed for the payment of tax, or duty, until it leaves the warehouse when it is sold. The reason for this unexpected leniency on behalf of the government is that during the maturation period a certain amount of spirit is lost from the casks due to evaporation, and both the volume of the contents and its alcoholic strength change. Whisky matured in a damp, misty

drawing it in through the porous oak. As the cask breathes, the atmosphere impresses its own personality on the spirit. This is particularly noticeable at coastal distilleries, where the whisky assumes the same salty, seaweed tang as the air itself. Some warehouses even have wire mesh in the windows instead of glass so that the air can more easily reach the casks.

Maturation is basically a long and complex series of chemical reactions which change the character of the distillate. Some changes are due

to compounds in the spirit reacting with each other, alcohols reacting with acids and oxygen to produce esters and aldehydes; some result from reactions with the oak itself, such as the extraction of tannins which give the whisky its colour. If the whisky remains in the wood for too long it will pick up too much tannin, giving it a sharp, woody taste, but it can quite happily spend twenty-five years or more in the cask if the cask is chosen carefully enough. Of the 800 or so chemical constituents present in whisky, it is reckoned that

The vaulted weaving shed warehouse at Deanston

his father was chairman of the Fettercairn Distillery Co.!

The angel's share, or ullage as it is otherwise known, also explains the high price of the older malt whiskies. It is expensive enough for a distillery to have warehouse space occupied by stocks of whisky in which their investment cannot be realised for some ten years. In addition to the extra expense of keeping it for eighteen to twenty-five years or longer, the angel's share of a cask over a 20-year period accounts for nearly half the contents! This illustrates perfectly why distillers do not pay duty on newly filled casks.

When the whisky leaves the distillery it is signed off the warehouse records. During the maturation period a record will have been kept detailing the life of each cask. Any samples taken will be recorded, as will any loss of spirit due to leakage from the cask, as this will all be accounted for in the eventual assessment of duty. Whisky usually goes from the distillery warehouse to the blender or bottler, and then to the wholesaler, under bond. Duty is only charged once it is shipped to the retailer.

Until recently it was a fairly practical proposition for a private individual to buy a cask of whisky at a distillery and lay it down for a private bottling, say to celebrate a child's coming of age. Distillers now seem to be discouraging this practice, although there are a couple of distilleries which operate schemes that enable people to buy a quantity of new spirit for bottling some years hence. The costs may look quite attractive but always remember that as soon as the whisky is taken out of bond the taxman will want his duty. With a cask yielding up to perhaps 300 bottles this will be a not inconsiderable sum!

There have also been cases of broking companies offering whisky as an investment, with promises of high returns. Investors should remember the old adage that 'if something looks too good to be true then it probably is'. Many people are currently out of pocket on these schemes as depression in some whisky markets means that their casks are worth less after three years than when first filled, and some brokers are taking advantage of investors who decide to sell and cut their losses instead of holding on to their

climate such as that in the Hebrides will lose its strength more quickly than its volume, the reverse being true of whisky matured in a relatively dry atmosphere such as that of Speyside. Each year, approximately 1½–2 per cent of a cask's contents will be lost to evaporation, the amount being greater from a hogshead than from a butt (whisky also matures more quickly in a hogshead, the compounds reacting more readily in the smaller volume of liquid). As it is forbidden by law to 'top up' casks during the maturation this loss is romantically called the angel's share and regulations were introduced by Gladstone to account for it, possibly prompted by the fact that stocks until the market revives. Some have decided to bottle their whisky themselves, only to find the results disappointing due to overused casks having being pressed into service again, probably with the thought that a private investor with no knowledge of the whisky trade will not know any better. There will always be reputable companies amongst the shady ones, but caution is the watchword with such schemes and the distillers themselves are often dismayed at the thought of their national drink being treated as a commodity to be traded on the open market.

The blending trade

It is not within the scope of this book to discuss blended whiskies, but a few words on the blender's art will not go amiss as blending plays a far greater part in the industry than does the bottling of single malts. Most malt distilleries send the vast proportion of their production for blending, even those whose single malts are well known and successful. Laphroaig, for instance, sends 90 per cent of its output for blending. Only the remaining 10 per cent is bottled as a single malt, yet it still manages to come in the top ten in the world sales rankings. Some distilleries exist primarily to supply whisky for blending and it would be very rare to see their products bottled as single malts, even by the independent merchants.

The blending trade sprang up in the nineteenth century as a result of the introduction of the patent still and its use in the production of grain spirit. The expression 'blending' is taken to mean the mixing of grain whisky from patent stills with varying proportions of pot-still malt whisky (when malt whiskies alone are mixed together, this is called 'vatting'). Blended whisky was an attempt by the whisky merchants to make a product which would appeal to a wider market, as malt whisky was then regarded by many people as being too much of an acquired taste. Grain whisky, which forms the major component of an average blended whisky, is mainly derived from cereals other than barley. Wheat is most commonly used, as it tends to be the cheapest available source of starch, and it is not malted, but simply cooked, before being mashed. A small proportion of malt will be added to the mash to introduce the necessary diastase which converts the starch to fermentable sugar. Patent-still spirit must be distilled at a strength below 94.7 per cent volume and matured for three years in oak wood before it is legally recognised as grain whisky.

The formula of every blend is the closely guarded secret of the manufacturer and is usually known only to a handful of people in the company on a need-to-know basis. Anything from fifteen to forty or more malts may be mixed with the grain spirit, and the malt content of blends varies enormously according to their price range. A cheap supermarket own-brand may contain less than 10 per cent malt whisky, whereas an average standard blend will usually contain 30–40 per cent. Teacher's Highland Cream is a notable exception to this with a minimum malt content of 45 per cent, and it makes a point of advertising this fact on its label. A deluxe blend, such as Johnnie Walker Black Label or Chivas Regal, will not only have a fairly high malt content, maybe 60 per cent, but it will also carry an age statement. The age will apply to the youngest whisky in the bottle, be that malt or grain. There will always be exceptions of course, but most whisky used in standard blends is used at the legal minimum age of three years.

Blending is a high art needing years of training and experience, and a blender's job will often last his working life. The task relies entirely on the physical senses of the blender himself, and is yet another variable in the process. Some whiskies

Vatting hall, Auchroisk

Sample room

will not successfully blend with others, and it is up to the blender to ensure that all the component whiskies are compatible. He will select whiskies according to their flavour and age, accounting for the type of cask used and the location in which it was matured. Islay malts, for instance, are especially important for the 'top notes' they impart to the overall flavour of a blend. Lighter blends may rely more on softer malts such as those from the Lowlands. The whiskies are assessed by 'nosing' them in a tulip-shaped glass, and a little distilled water will be added to release the spirit's aroma. The blender may use coloured (usually dark blue) glasses, so as not to be influenced by the colour of the whisky. Blenders rarely taste the whiskies, preferring to make their judgement simply by sense of smell. It is now becoming quite popular for the blender to supplement his own opinions with those of a trained tasting panel, rather than make all the decisions alone.

When the blender has sampled the various casks at his disposal and made his selection, the whiskies are mixed together in a large vat. At this point a small amount of colouring agent may be added, as the consistency of colour from one

bottle to the next seems to be a more important attribute in a blend than it is in a single malt. The colouring agent may be caramel, or even a little sherry may be added. The blended whisky will then be filled into casks to 'marry' for six to eight months before it is bottled. Another way of adding colour to a blend is to smear the insides of these casks with pajarete, a syrupy substance made from grape juice and used in Jerez for colouring certain sherries.

Malt whiskies also go through a similar process at the bottling stage. Each cask has its own individual characteristics, and the blender will achieve consistency of flavour and colour by selecting which of those casks will be married for each bottling. Malt whisky is usually reckoned to be ready for bottling when it displays a perfect 'ring of pearls' in the blender's glass, a ring of bubbles which form around the inside of the glass when the spirit is poured. Colouring agents are not usually added to single malts, all the colour coming from the cask wood. Up to 200 casks may be vatted for a single bottling run.

Bottling

Glenfiddich Springbank and Bruichladdich are the only malt distilleries to have their own bottling facilities on site. Most whisky is bottled at dedicated bottling plants in the Lowland industrial areas around Glasgow, Edinburgh and Perth. Bottlers are often sub-contractors who bottle whisky for a number of distillers. They are understandably cagey about naming their customers as it is not unknown for them to bottle blends for retailers to sell under their own brand, blends which may well be sold alongside the original distiller's own, higher-priced, product.

The casks of whisky are emptied into large, glass-lined tanks, and de-mineralised water is added to dilute the spirit to the required proof strength. It is then chill-filtered. At low temperatures impurities in the whisky cause a clouding effect which, although harmless, is deemed to be undesirable. The spirit is cooled and filtered to remove the impurities which cause this effect. Not all distillers allow their whisky to be chill-filtered, some arguing that it also filters out some of the character.

The most common packaging material is glass, as it is non-reactive. Plastic containers are usually eschewed for reasons of both economics and aesthetics, although they do have a use in certain areas of the duty-free market. Mechanised bottling lines clean the bottles, fill them and apply the cap, seal and label at a rate of up to 240 per minute. The standardisation of bottle sizes and shapes, and the use of high-strength glass, allows fully automated production. Of course, not all bottles are what would be regarded as 'standard', the main idea behind those that are not being to make them stand out on a retailer's shelf. Some very well-known designs have appeared over the years such as Glenfiddich's triangular green bottle, the square Johnnie Walker bottle, and the aptly named Haig Dimple.

Bottling line

The new EU standard bottle size is 70cl, as opposed to the old 75cl, and it was noticeable that the price of a bottle of whisky was not reduced along with its size! Duty-free allowances have popularised the 1-litre bottle, not only in duty-free shops but also in supermarkets, and some of the more popular blends are now sold in 1½-litre bottles. The idea is not new: Whyte & Mackay introduced a 40oz bottle (just over 1 litre) for pub optics in 1963, and Long John introduced the tregnum which was roughly twice this size. Occasionally, a distiller will make available special packages, either for a limited edition or for a special market. Good examples are Glenfiddich's Wedgwood crocks and Bell's china bell. For their super-deluxe blend Old Parr Elizabethan, United Distillers commissioned a special bottle with a pewter stopper and cotton thread embedded in the glass. The bottle accounts for almost 20 per cent of the £700 price tag.

One very important feature of whisky is that, unlike wine, it stops maturing when it is bottled. The age statement on the label refers to the length of time that it has spent in the cask. Some malts, mostly limited editions and independent bottlings, carry the year of distillation instead of an age quoted in years, but this will be qualified somewhere on the label with the year of bottling. You are then left to work out the age for yourself. One exception to this is Knockando, which has always used this method on its standard bottlings. In terms of the ageing process, keeping an unopened bottle of a ten-year-old malt for a further ten years does not really make that whisky any older as far as its maturity is concerned. When you open it, it will still only be a ten-year-old.

Drinking malt whisky

Although a noble drink, malt whisky is thankfully relatively free of the snobbery which infects the wine world. It is true that there are people who would have us believe that a malt should be drunk neat from a crystal tumbler with, at most, the water of Loch Katrine for company, but the best way of drinking malt is simply to take it in whichever way pleases you most. That way, you will get the greatest enjoyment from it. The Scots themselves will drink whisky at any time, and blended whisky is often taken as a long drink with lemonade.

The tumbler is the traditional vessel from which to drink whisky as it supposedly shows the colour to best advantage, but bear in mind that blenders will assess whisky in a plain, tulip-shaped glass similar to a sherry copita. Bowmore once ran a competition to find an ideal design for a whisky glass and came up with a pleasing result, appropriately bearing a resemblance to the Scottish thistle, but unfortunately the glasses are not widely available. The addition of a little pure water (not tap water, and certainly not ice cubes), will release the bouquet of a malt whisky, but malts do not appreciate, or need, to be warmed for this purpose. For this reason brandy balloons are best kept for brandy, and a good single malt will be wasted in a hip flask. Anyone who baulks at adding water to malt whisky would do well to consider the amount which has been added to it since it left the stills. A few drops more will not do any harm!

Malts are generally classified as being pre-dinner or after-dinner drinks, and there are certainly malts which have a beneficial effect after a heavy meal, but I tend to think that this is pigeon-holing them somewhat and my own instincts are that if a particular malt seems appropriate to the occasion, then drink it. The many tasting guides which are available these days act not only to point you in the direction of a malt which may suit your particular taste, but also give a qualitative indication of characteristics and flavours which you can recognise and identify. Always remember though that whisky is an incredibly subjective thing and like anything else which needs to be experienced and appreciated, be it art or music or anything else, it cannot simply be defined in terms of marks out of ten. Although some tasters use a scoring system, all such a system says is that a certain whisky made a particular impression on one particular palate on one particular day. It also causes unnecessary friction between the distillers. Distillery managers are unlikely to be pleased if they see their whisky scored below that of a close rival. Therefore, use tasting guides as just that: a guide. Do not be afraid to have your own opinion.

The rising popularity of single malts, coupled with the kudos of certain distilleries, has led to the emergence of the whisky collector. It is true that the rarity of certain whiskies, whether it is real or artificially created, has made them desirable but the problem with a whisky collection is that its value is entirely in the eye of the beholder. Other than the price paid for it, it has no value except to the collector. Once opened, it loses any value it might have had, and if it is not opened it may as well not exist. I have seen many esoteric whiskies, and if you are lucky enough to be able to afford one never forget that it has been made for drinking. If you are just going to hide it away then all the effort that went into making it was for nothing! Whisky is for drinking!

Legal implications

To understand the information given on a whisky label fully we need to know the legal definition of whisky itself, and as we have seen this was defined by the 1908 Royal Commission as 'a spirit obtained by distillation from a mash of cereal grains saccharified by the diastase of malt'. Obviously a pure malt whisky will only come from a mash of malted barley. The law also stipulates that whisky must be distilled in Scotland if it is to be called 'Scotch' whisky (you can not have Japanese 'Scotch'), and that the spirit must be matured in oak wood for a minimum of three years before it becomes whisky at all.

Malt whisky labels are generally informative and succinct, giving the name of the distillery, the whisky's age and alcoholic strength, and confirming that it was made in Scotland entirely

from malt. Given the constraints of the Trade Descriptions Act, the labels of blends are more often prone to flights of fancy and the blenders are fond of shoehorning superlatives into every available space. Words such as 'special', 'extra special', 'finest', 'old' and 'reserve' are common and usually denote nothing more exclusive than a standard blend. An exception would be a blend described as deluxe, where one can assume a higher malt whisky content than in a standard blend, and an age statement will confirm a higher degree of maturity as it must by law refer to the youngest whisky in the blend, whether that is a malt or grain whisky.

Sometimes, what the label does not say can be more telling than what it does. For instance, if it is a blend does it say 'distilled, blended and bottled

in Scotland', or does it omit 'blended' or 'bottled'? If so, then where was it blended or bottled? If it is a malt whisky does it say 'single malt Scotch whisky'? Each of these four words is significant. If there is no distillery name, or the word 'single' is missing, it will be a vatted malt, a product of more than one distillery. However, beware of vatted malts whose names imply a single distillery, such as names beginning 'Glen'. Malt whisky labels usually carry the name and address of the company and the distillery somewhere in the small print, as well as giving the distillery name in the headline. A vatted malt will not be able to give a distillery address.

Let us look at some examples of malt whisky labels and consider the significance of what they actually say.

This is a distiller's standard bottling – J & G Grant's ten-year-old Glenfarclas.

The whisky's name. This will usually be the name of the distillery itself, although there are exceptions such as The Singleton (from Auchroisk), Glen Deveron (from Macduff), and Longrow (from Springbank).

Single: the product of a single distillery.

Scotch: Scotch whisky must be distilled in Scotland.

The distillery's name and address.

Bottle contents. The standard bottle is now 70cl, or 700ml.

Malt: whisky made entirely from malted barley.

Age statement. The age of the youngest whisky in the bottle. Do not forget that single malts are usually bottled from a vatting of many casks at a time and the youngest cask in a bottling run must be at least this age.

It says that it is distilled and bottled in Scotland. It may also say that it is 'matured' or 'aged' there too. Some labels simply use the phrase 'Product of Scotland' instead; many use it in addition, as here.

Alcoholic strength. The legal minimum strength for Scotch whisky is 40 per cent volume, or 70° proof.

This is an independent merchant's bottling – Bowmore,
from Wm Cadenhead's Original Collection.

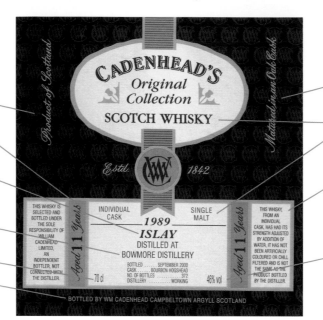

It says 'Product of Scotland'.

Age statement. Notice that Cadenhead's also quotes the dates of distillation and bottling.

The region of production, in this case Islay.

The distillery name.

Quantity.

The merchant's details.

The phrase 'Matured in an Oak Cask' is superfluous. This is a legal requirement for Scotch whisky.

It says 'Single Malt Scotch Whisky'.

Cadenhead's makes the point on the labels that its bottlings are different from the distillers' own.

Alcoholic strength. Cadenhead's Original Collection malts are bottled at 46% vol. Their Authentic Collection malts are bottled at cask strength and will vary from distillery to distillery, and from cask to cask.

Independent merchants often provide the opportunity to obtain whiskies from distilleries which are now closed, such as this bottling of St Magdalene from Gordon & MacPhail's Connoisseurs Choice range.

It says 'Single Malt Scotch Whisky'. In this case the region of production is also given, and more distillers are now quoting this detail.

The company to which the distillery was licensed.

The merchant's details.

Quantity.

The name of the distillery – St Magdalene.

The Connoisseurs Choice range quotes the year of distillation, rather than an age. This is qualified on a separate, smaller, label which gives the year of bottling.

It says 'Product of Scotland'.

Alcoholic strength.

Independent bottlings

It is difficult to say for certain whether independent bottlers serve a niche market or create one, but thanks to them enthusiasts are able to sample, if at a price, many examples of whisky which would otherwise be unavailable. When the trade was in its infancy merchants began to sell whisky first from the cask, then in bottle. The adoption of branding was inevitable and some of the biggest names in the industry emerged at this time and from these activities. Modern independent bottlers are simply carrying on a tradition which dates from the early nineteenth century.

Merchants will buy stocks of whisky which may be left to mature at the distillery, or matured in their own bonds, and are bottled when the merchant feels the time is right. For this reason their whiskies may not necessarily correspond to the versions bottled by the distillers themselves. Some merchants are also blenders and so their activities are not limited to the supply of single malts.

There are three main attractions to independent bottlers' ranges: the chance to try versions of single malts which are different in terms of age or maturation from the distillers' own; the possibility of obtaining from these merchants supplies of whiskies from distilleries which are no longer operating; and the availability of particularly rare malts such as those not bottled by the distillers themselves, or ones which have been left to mature for far in excess of the normal period.

The best-known independent merchants are probably Gordon & MacPhail of Elgin and Wm Cadenhead of Aberdeen. Gordon & MacPhail offers different ranges of malts, one including some of the big names bottled in a choice of ages and strengths, another known as the Connoisseurs Choice range, which also includes a selection of miniatures. They also offer a selection of rare old malts including 1936 distillations of Mortlach and Glen Grant, a 1939 distillation of Linkwood, and a particularly rare 1942 Mortlach distilled during World War II when most distilleries were closed. If you need to ask the price of these, you will certainly not be able to afford them! The company has recently diversified into distilling with the acquisition from United Distillers of Benromach Distillery at Forres, which has been mothballed

since 1983, and it is encouraging to see such a distillery awakened from its slumbers.

Cadenhead's is an old-established company dating from 1842 and offers an extensive selection of malts bottled at 46 per cent volume or cask strength. Theirs is a very traditional method of working, all whiskies being bottled from single casks, and the company has an almost religious avoidance of chill filtering. When whisky becomes cold it throws a haze which will disappear when it warms up again, if the alcoholic strength is 46 per cent volume or above. Most distillers prefer to filter out this haze by artificial means, although the fact is not publicised. The use of single casks also makes tasting notes on Cadenhead's malts highly specific, as no two casks will be the same. It must also be borne in mind that single casks yield a limited number of bottles, often less than 300, and so these bottlers' product ranges are constantly changing.

A number of other merchants have also appeared in recent years, including Signatory and the Adelphi Distillery Ltd, both of Edinburgh, The Vintage Malt Whisky Co. of Milngavie, James

MacArthur of High Wycombe and Murray McDavid. The managing director of Adelphi is the great-grandson of the last owner of the original Adelphi Distillery, which was founded in 1826 in the Gorbals area of Glasgow. The company bottles its malts directly from single casks with no chill filtering. Signatory has quite an extensive range which includes malts from distilleries often ignored by the independents. The Vintage Malt Whisky Co. was founded in 1992 and offers a range of single-cask bottlings in its Cooper's Choice series. Murray McDavid was founded in 1995 and won two out of the three trophies for single malts at the 2000 International Wine and Spirit Competition. Following Gordon & MacPhail's example the company has already diversified into distilling with the purchase from JBB of Bruichladdich Distillery, which is to be run by former Bowmore manager James McEwan. Signatory, too, has recently taken a similar direction with its acquisition of Edradour, and has quite an extensive range which includes malts from distilleries often ignored by the independents. Some specialist whisky retailers have also undertaken their own bottlings, such as The Whisky Castle of Tomintoul and The Master of Malt at Tunbridge Wells.

One thing that must be accepted with independent bottlings is that the whisky may not have been matured under the same conditions, or even in the same area, as the distiller envisaged. You may therefore find that Mr Merchant's Brand X tastes different from the distillers' own equivalent Brand X and you may or may not like the difference. Some distillers also frown on merchants whose ideas on their whisky do not agree with their own, for instance a merchant who chooses to mature a sample of Macallan in plain oak (it has been done). Gordon & MacPhail has released versions of its Speyside Malt matured in port and brandy casks, but since the individual distillers are not named no one is in a position to complain. Other distillers simply object to others using their registered brand names. Wm Grant avoids both these problems by refusing to supply merchants or blenders with pure Glenfiddich or Balvenie, supplying instead a vatting of the two which neatly prevents its whiskies from being sold as 'independent' single malts.

The following are the main independent bottlers:

Gordon & MacPhail Ltd
58–60 South Street
Elgin
Moray
IV30 1JY

Telephone 01343 545111
www.gordonandmacphail.com
email mail@ gordonandmacphail.com

James MacArthur & Co. Ltd
20 Knights Templar Way
High Wycombe
Bucks
HP11 1PY

Telephone 01494 530740

Cadenhead's Whisky Shop
172 Canongate
Royal Mile
Edinburgh
EH8 8BN

Telephone 0131 556 5864

Adelphi Distillery Ltd
3 Gloucester Lane
Edinburgh EH3 6ED

Telephone 0131 226 6670
www.adelphidistillery.com
email
james@adelphiwhisky.demon.co.uk

Signatory Vintage Scotch
Whisky Co.
7–8 Elizafield
Newhaven Road
Edinburgh
EH6 5PY

Telephone 0131 555 4988

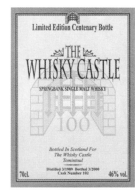

The Whisky Castle
Main Street
Tomintoul
Banffshire
AB37 9EX

Telephone 01807 580213
www.thewhiskycastle.co.uk
email
Thewhiskycastle@aol.com

Murray McDavid Ltd
56 Walton Street
London
SW3 1RB

Telephone 0207 823 7717
www.murray-mcdavid.com
email
malt@murray-mcdavid.com

The Master of Malt
96a Calverley Road
Tunbridge Wells
Kent
TN1 2UN

Telephone 01892 513295
www.masterofmalt.co.uk
email
shop@masterofmalt.co.uk

The Vintage Malt Whisky Co.
2 Stewart Street
Milngavie
Glasgow
G62 6BW

Telephone 0141 955 1700
www.vintage-malt-whisky.co.uk
email whisky@globalnet.co.uk

SCOTLAND'S WHISKY-PRODUCING REGIONS

In the days of the industrial revolution disparate legislation effectively placed Scotland's distillers in one of two categories, Highland or Lowland, and despite changes to the law since then this classification is still relevant today. However this distinction is becoming increasingly coarse, and when one considers in particular the decimation of the Lowland industry it is akin to categorising the wines of France as being simply red or white. The great wine-producing countries of the world work on a regional basis with each area having its own regional characteristics or specialities, France for instance with its red wines from Burgundy, Beaujolais and Bordeaux. In the same way Scotland makes its malt whiskies in certain distinct regions, each of which shapes its spirit according to many factors. Each region's malts follow a characteristic style, to which they are conformed by the local environment to a greater or lesser extent, for instance the power of the Islays, the delicacy and complexity of the Speysides, the spiciness of the northern Highland malts and the softer sweetness of the Perthshires.

The art of distillation probably came to Scotland with the early Christian missionaries, through Kintyre and Islay, and these are even now regarded as distinct regions worthy of separate consideration. The size, and diversity, of the Highland region demands that it be regarded in subdivisions of western, northern, eastern and southern areas. Speyside is officially regarded as a region on its own, and includes the famous Glenlivet. The industrial belt of the country comprises the Lowland region, in which sadly only three malt distilleries remain active.

The maps in the following chapters 'The Whisky Trail' and 'Lost Distilleries' show those distilleries whose single malts are still available in bottle. At the start of the new millennium there were about eighty-five malt distilleries actually working, and around a dozen mothballed or working sporadically. The remainder, although marked on these maps, have been closed down, and in some cases even demolished to make way for other buildings. For the time being their malts are still obtainable, usually in independent bottlings, and needless to say their rarity value means that they are expensive. Because such distilleries will never reopen, stocks of their malts are finite, and will one day be exhausted. Mothballed distilleries may reopen again at some point in the future when the stock situation and trading conditions allow.

Campbeltown

The royal burgh of Campbeltown is the smallest of Scotland's distinct whisky-producing regions and historically one of the most important. It was here in AD 503 that King Fergus established the first parliament of the Celtic Kingdom of the Scots, which was eventually to spread throughout the whole of Scotland. St Columba came here from Ireland on his Christian mission before moving on to Iona, where he founded a monastery in AD 563, and it is possible that he brought the practice of distilling with him. However, the first written account of whisky in this area is in the records of the Pursmaister of the Thane of Cawdor and refers to aqua vitae being sold in a village near Campbeltown in 1591.

As the distilling industry progressed Campbeltown built up a good smuggling trade with Glasgow, which later continued on a legal footing. Between 1817 and 1879 a total of thirty-four distilleries and twenty maltings were established in the town. It was said that a boat's skipper could find his way into the harbour in thick fog just by following the smell of the stills. Trade was good and confidence led to carelessness. In their greed to supply the Prohibition bootleggers many distillers adopted a 'quantity over quality' attitude which was to be their downfall. The reputation of Campbeltown whiskies fell alarmingly. To compound the disaster the local coal mine, which had supplied the distillers with cheap fuel, had to be abandoned after an underground fire in 1925, and the Depression left many distillers with vast stocks of whisky they could not sell.

Today, Campbeltown is no more than a shadow of its former self. Only clues remain as to the town's once-thriving industry, such as the pagoda roof on what is now a bus depot and streets whose names echo those of the old distilleries. Once well accessible by sea it has now become remote by road and, situated at the end of a peninsula, it has no passing tourist traffic that can be persuaded to stop by. Only two distilleries, Springbank and Glen Scotia, survived the collapse of the industry and kept their reputations intact. The demise of Gibson International in 1994 saw Glen Scotia mothballed, though it has since been acquired by Loch Lomond Distillery and is now working again.

The old Campbeltown whiskies were similar in character to the Islay malts, big, heavy and peaty, and Longrow and Glen Scotia still conform to this style but with a sweetness where the Islays are dry. Springbank is lighter and more complex, and in all three the influence of the sea is apparent.

Islay

Islay is a green and fertile island, and the most southerly of the Inner Hebrides. A quarter of the island, something like 35,000 acres, is covered with peat to a depth of up to 100ft. Driving from Port Ellen to Bowmore the Laggan peat bog stretches into the distance on both sides of the road and the view ahead is of the Paps of Jura. On an island where coal is prohibitively expensive peat is still the main domestic fuel. Many householders rent a strip of land from which to cut peat, which then has to be left stacked under covers to dry. In spring the landscape is dotted with these stacks.

The early Christians who visited Campbeltown also passed this way. Scattered around the island are the signs of their occupation: hundreds of standing stones, crosses and stone circles. Just beyond Ardbeg Distillery in the churchyard at Kildalton stands the finest Celtic stone cross in the whole of Scotland. Islay was the first of the Hebridean islands to have planned villages, of which the first was Bowmore. At the entrance to the village stands the round church of Kilarrow. Bestowed on the village in 1769 by the owner of Islay, who probably wanted to be more certain of his place in the afterlife, it was built circular so it would have no corners in which the Devil could hide.

Whisky distilling was already a big industry on Islay at the time of the Old Statistical Account in 1793, thanks to the abundance of local barley. The islanders found that if the grain was dried over a peat fire it was prevented from going mouldy. It also picked up a characteristic flavour. For a long time Islay whisky was exempt from duty on the island itself, a quirk which led to much carousing and farmers selling their barley to the distillers instead of using it for food. Illicit distilling and smuggling were both popular and easy, there being no shortage of hiding places on the lonely moorlands or amongst the cliffs and caves of The Oa.

The main industries today are sheep and dairy farming (Islay no longer grows its own barley), fishing, and of course whisky. Tourism is just beginning to make its presence known on Islay and the expensive visitor facilities which have been built by some of the distilleries could be taken as evidence of their confidence in seeing tourism increasing significantly. Whisky is almost a religion here, and many come to worship at its altar. Even the small village supermarkets have impressive collections of the island's malts with prices approaching the atmospheric, if not stratospheric, level. One hotel in Bowmore offers visitors a menu for its collection of some 400 malt whiskies, one of which carries a three-figure price for a single 35ml measure, and the bottles are all part empty!

There are no large factories on Islay, nor intensive farming. Its climate is surprisingly temperate, benefiting as it does from the Gulf Stream. Snow falls in winter but never lies long. Its water is very pure and soft, and perfect for distilling. Although by no means flat, Islay is not mountainous like the Highlands. Streams are slower-running and tend to seep through the peat, picking up more peat flavour. All the distilleries are coastal and mostly similar in appearance, collections of small whitewashed buildings with the distillery name in huge black letters on the warehouse wall facing the sea. All of them are lashed by the wind and rain and salt spray, Bowmore's warehouse even semi-submerged at high tide. Little wonder that Islay's malts are characterised by the sea and the peat-reek from both the water and the malt.

Since the mid-eighteenth century there have been twenty-three licensed distilleries recorded on the island. There are now only eight. Of these Port Ellen is not currently in production, and although it still stands it is debatable if it will ever distil again. The last permanent closure was that of Lochindaal, which was dismantled in 1929 after its acquisition by DCL. The taste of the whiskies follows a rough pattern. The south coast malts are the strongest – tangy and medicinal with definite hints of seaweed and iodine. Further north the flavour moderates and becomes rounder and softer as one progresses through Bowmore, Bruichladdich and on to Bunnahabhain. The theory can even be extended to encompass Jura, whose whisky bears more resemblance to a Highland, rather than an island, malt. This is probably attributable to the clearer water and the particularly tall stills at this distillery. The exception that proves the rule is Caol Ila, near Port Askaig, whose 'toasted malt' flavour is as characterful as anything that Islay's south coast has to offer.

Highlands

The Highland Line was defined by Act of Parliament in the Wash Act of 1784 and is an imaginary line drawn across Scotland, from Dundee to Greenock, which separates the country into two main areas, the Highlands to the north and the Lowlands to the south. The Highlands account for over half the area of Scotland and have the lion's share of virtually everything for which the country is best known, from its myths and legends to its sporting facilities, and of course its whisky distilleries.

Sportsmen are well catered for. There is shooting on the grouse moors and fishing on two of the finest salmon rivers in Britain, the Dee and the Spey, golf is enormously popular, and the Grampians and Cairngorms are home to the UK's only ski resorts.

Whole new chapters in Scottish history were opened by the clan wars, the Highland clearances, the Jacobite rebellion which culminated in the battle of Culloden and Bonnie Prince Charlie's escape across the sea to Skye, and endless tales of folk heroes and villains from Burns to Macbeth. There are stories of mythical creatures from the kelpies, or water spirits, to the most famous of all Scottish legends, the Loch Ness monster.

The whisky industry really began to grow in the 1750s when working methods improved and both the quality and flavour of aqua vitae began to change. Distilleries were slower to appear in the Highlands than they were in the more industrialised Lowlands, but even so some still survive which first saw the light of day in the late 1700s: Balblair, Oban and Strathisla for instance. In the late eighteenth and early nineteenth centuries Highland distillers were regarded very differently by the government from those in the Lowlands. The unfairness of the situation caused much antagonism and gave rise to the smuggling trade, out of which grew the basis of the Highlands' legitimate whisky industry. Many of the Highland distilleries surviving from this period can trace their roots back to an illicit still and the industry was gradually brought out into the open after George Smith's initiative following the Excise Act of 1823. Over 400 malt distilleries have been recorded as having legally operated in the Highlands, although some of those existed for maybe as little as a few months. There are now around seventy-six working malt distilleries in the region, out of a total working in Scotland of about eighty-five. The Western Isles (with the exception of Islay) counted as part of the

Highland region, had their own whisky industry with fifteen recorded distilleries scattered around the islands of Skye, Mull, Jura, Arran, Bute, Tiree, Lewis and Seil. Only three of the old distilleries remain: Jura (in a new guise created by Delmé Evans), Tobermory on Mull, and Talisker, the sole survivor of five distilleries to be built on Skye. Arran has recently re-entered the whisky industry with the opening in 1995 of the Isle of Arran Distillery at Lochranza at the northern tip of the island.

The Highland region can be thought of as being (unofficially) sub-divided into five areas, each of which has its own collection of distilleries: western; northern, including Orkney; eastern; southern; and Speyside, the area most densely populated with distilleries.

The western Highlands

There is some argument over which distilleries should be classed as being western Highland, some people maintaining that the island distilleries should be thought of separately. However the island malts do not conform to a uniform style. Some exhibit characteristics more usually associated with the northern Highlands, and there is no set pattern. For the sake of simplicity I will take this region as including the area from Oban to Fort William, and the islands of Arran, Jura, Mull and Skye. There is great variance between the malts produced in this region, and if they can be said to have a general character at all it is that they are fairly dry, round and malty, with some peat smoke.

The mainland area contains only two distilleries. Oban is one of the oldest surviving distilleries in Scotland, dating from 1794. Fort William has the other one, Ben Nevis, which was built by 'Long' John Macdonald and has been rescued from closure by Nikka Distillers of Japan, whose founder Masataka Taketsuru learned his craft at Hazelburn Distillery at Campbeltown. Also in Fort William was Glenlochy, which made a good example of a western Highland malt, but the distillery was closed by DCL in 1983. Although the site has since been sold for redevelopment the maltings and kilns have been preserved as listed buildings.

Arran, often described as 'Scotland in miniature', has not had a licensed distillery since the demise in 1837 of Lagg, on the island's south coast. The new Arran Distillery is the brainchild of former Chivas MD Harold Currie, and stands in a glen about a mile from Lochranza. The spirit is said to mature quickly, due to Arran's macroclimate, and has already been bottled at five years old. Of the three old-established island malts Talisker conforms best to the 'island' character. Some aspects of its working methods are similar to those of the old smugglers, scaled up of course, a factor which no doubt contributes to its traditional flavour. It is one of UDV's Classic Malts and rightly deserves its place in that range. Huge and powerful, it has been described by one taster as 'the lava of the Cuillins'. Four other distilleries were built on Skye between 1816 and 1833. None survived for more than a decade. Tobermory Distillery on Mull, also known as Ledaig, has a long and chequered history. Dating from 1798, it has seen many changes of ownership and protracted periods of closure in its two centuries of existence. It is now owned by Burn Stewart Distillers. Jura produces a subtle malt in which the island character is quite restrained. The distillery was rebuilt in 1963 with tall Highland-type stills, and as a result its malt now bears little resemblance to those of its Islay neighbours with whom it once shared many characteristics.

The northern Highlands

The northern Highland area can generally be defined as the immediate environs of the main A9 road from Dalwhinnie to Wick, and the mainland of Orkney, home to the two most northerly of Scotland's distilleries. The overall character of these malts is one of spiciness, tempered with tones of fruit or heather, and the coastal location of those distilleries furthest north is apparent. With one or two exceptions the influence of the peat is moderate, which is probably contrary to expectations for a region so well endowed with it. Some 13 million tons of peat are contained in bogs covering over 21,000 acres of Caithness.

The region contains twelve working malt distilleries, including one of the two on Orkney.

As the A9 enters the Grampians the first distillery you come to is Dalwhinnie, which makes one of UDV's Classic Malts. Fourteen miles further north is Kingussie. The Speyside Distillery was built near here in 1895 and lasted until 1911, when the company was liquidated and the distillery dismantled. The name was recently resurrected when a new distillery was built near to Tromie Bridge, opening in December 1990. The new Speyside Distillery is one of Scotland's latest, narrowly following Kininvie into production.

Beyond Aviemore the A9 comes to the village of Tomatin, on the River Findhorn. Tomatin Distillery is the largest malt distillery in Scotland and the second largest in the world, exceeded in size only by Suntory's Hakushu Distillery in Japan. Tomatin has been steadily enlarged since 1956, when it had only two stills. The stillhouse has been extended bit by bit as stills have been added, until twelve were installed together in 1974 giving it a total of twenty-three, one less than Hakushu.

Inverness had a thriving whisky industry with at least a dozen distilleries recorded in and around the town at various times, with possibly up to a further dozen whose locations have not been positively identified. The last three working distilleries were closed by DCL in the 1980s. Millburn can still be seen by the main road skirting the town centre. It was converted in 1985 into a restaurant but its origins are revealed by the distillery chimney, which has been left standing. Glen Albyn and Glen Mhor, which stood opposite each other by the Caledonian Canal, were demolished the following year. The site is now a shopping complex. A few miles to the east, at Cawdor, is Royal Brackla, which is one of four distilleries acquired by Bacardi following the Guinness-Grand Met merger. It stands in an area associated with some of Scotland's bloodiest history, including the battle of Culloden, a conflict in which the Pretender lost 1,000 of his men in the space of forty minutes.

Above Inverness the main road passes near Muir of Ord, birthplace of the geologist Sir Roderick Murchison, and the site of Glen Ord Distillery. Glen Ord is a smooth, characterful and underrated single malt which deserves to be better known, and probably will become so as it is made more widely available.

At the head of the Cromarty Firth lies the village of Alness. On the shore of the firth is Dalmore, once owned by a family whose friends James Whyte and Charles Mackay went on to form the company which owns the distillery today. Across the main road is Teaninich, whose one-time proprietor Innes Cameron went on to play an important part in the success of Linkwood. Nearby is Invergordon. The village dates back to the eighteenth century but the distillery which takes its name, the most northerly grain distillery in Scotland, only began production in 1961. A malt distillery, Ben Wyvis, was built within the complex four years later. In 1976 it closed, its single malt being one of only a handful which it was thought had never been bottled as such, until Invergordon discovered three long-forgotten casks tucked away in a warehouse. A limited edition 27-year-old was bottled from those casks in October 2000.

The next distillery is Glenmorangie. Now the biggest-selling single malt in Scotland, Glenmorangie bottles virtually all its production as a single malt and it has been sold in this form for nearly a century. After the distillers appointed a US agent the Mayor of Nashville declared that in that city 1 September 1991 would be 'Glenmorangie Day'. Glenmorangie has popularised the fashion of 'wood finishing', whereby the spirit completes its maturation in casks which have previously held sherry, port, wine or other spirits. Although the method is not unique Glenmorangie has vastly developed its range and is constantly experimenting.

A few miles further on is Edderton, known as the 'parish of peat'. In its beautiful setting Balblair appears as an archetypal Highland distillery, yet its malt is more fruity than earthy, as the village's nickname might suggest.

This far north the distilleries are much more isolated, there being only two others between Balblair and the tip of the mainland. The town of Brora was founded by crofters forcibly moved to the coast in the Highland clearances, and illicit distilling soon began in the town. The Marquis of Stafford, who played a part in the clearances, founded a distillery named Clynelish in an attempt to wipe out the area's illicit trade and provide local employment. The distillery was renamed Brora when the new Clynelish Distillery was built alongside in 1967. Brora closed in the 1980s but Clynelish continues in production, its coastal location evident in its powerful single malt.

The northernmost mainland distillery is Pulteney, at Wick, and is the only distillery in Caithness. Its tangy single malt is bottled as Old Pulteney and is said to be a fast-maturing whisky which resembles manzanilla sherry. The distillery was sold by Allied Distillers in 1996 to Inver House. Wick itself is also known for herring fishing and many years ago introduced prohibition in an attempt to curb drunkenness amongst its seasonal casual workforce.

The furthest-flung of Scotland's distilleries are on the mainland of Orkney, a group of over seventy islands whose history is rich in legends of the Norsemen who first settled there over 1,000 years ago, before sailing on to the Western Isles, Islay and Kintyre. Many monuments of the early settlers remain and today the islands attract increasing numbers of visitors from Scandinavia. The two distilleries are at the islands' capital town of Kirkwall. Scapa overlooks Scapa Flow, where the German fleet was scuttled at the end of World War I, and was once saved from destruction by fire by Royal Navy ratings billeted at the distillery. Now owned by Allied Distillers, Scapa is one of the few distilleries to use unpeated malt. In contrast, Highland Park uses the local heathery peat to imbue its malt with a smoky-sweet flavour. It also uses three yeasts, instead of the usual two, and a high proportion of sherry ageing. The distillery is built, rather eccentrically, on a hill, which means that its water supply has to be pumped up to it. The site was that of an eighteenth century illicit still operated by Magnus Eunson, who took full advantage of his position as a church minister to fool the local Excise officers, hiding his illicit whisky in his pulpit. Highland Park is Scotland's most northerly distillery, by a margin of about half a mile.

Speyside

The heart of Highland malt distilling, the 'Golden Triangle' of Speyside extends from Forres along the Moray/Banffshire coast to Banff itself, and down to Tomintoul in the foothills of the Cairngorms. The Spey is one of the country's foremost salmon rivers and rises at Loch Spey, at the north end of Glen Roy, some 14 miles from Dalwhinnie, an area at the southern limits of the region where mountain passes once provided smuggling routes to the main Lowland centres. The river then flows through Kingussie, Aviemore, Grantown-on-Spey and Craigellachie before reaching the sea to the east of Elgin. Speyside is probably something of a misnomer as the region extends eastwards from the River Findhorn to the Deveron and Bogie, and also includes the Lossie, the Avon, the Fiddich and the Dullan, and of course the Livet.

Glenlivet has long since been immortalised in the industry's history, with so many distilleries playing on its reputation in the early days that it gained the sobriquet of 'longest glen in Scotland'. The Glenlivet was popular with royalty even in the days when it was still being made illicitly and distillers jumped on the bandwagon, eager to capitalise on its success. The story of the Smiths' legal battle to establish their right to the name 'The Glenlivet' is well-documented but even today there are seventeen other distilleries which have used the Glenlivet suffix in their names, even though there are only three distilleries actually in the glen itself (The Glenlivet, Tamnavulin and Braeval, formerly the Braes of Glenlivet), with a further one in Glenlivet parish (Tomintoul). A glance at the map will reveal how tenuous some distilleries' links really are: Miltonduff and Glen Moray, for instance, are 20 miles away to the north and actually on the River Lossie.

Speyside has around fifty of Scotland's remaining malt distilleries, although not all these are currently working. Some fell prey to the economic problems of the 1980s, some to more recent rationalisation programmes. The distilleries are not scattered willy-nilly throughout the region but are distributed along Strathspey from Grantown to Craigellachie and thence to Elgin, and in particular centres – Glenlivet, Dufftown, Rothes and Keith. A few stragglers lie along, or near, the coast, with three outlying to the east of Huntly.

Dufftown is probably Scotland's whisky capital

and for many years has been the subject of a local adage comparing its seven stills to Rome's seven hills. Seven certainly seems to be the limit for Dufftown: Parkmore Distillery's place in the original seven was eventually taken by Pittyvaich, and Convalmore's by Kininvie. All Dufftown's distilleries lie within a mile of the clock tower in the town square. Rothes, to the north, has five distilleries of its own, including Glen Grant, and Keith has four, including the oldest working distillery in the Highlands, Strathisla. At the eastern end of the Speyside coast, the towns of Banff and Macduff straddle the mouth of the River Deveron. Banff Distillery itself no longer exists. Having survived being bombed in World War II it closed and demolished by DCL in the early 1980s, but in its heyday it supplied whisky to the House of Commons. Macduff Distillery was built in 1962 and is now owned by Bacardi. Its single malt is bottled by the independents as Macduff, but by the distillers themselves as Glen Deveron. To the south of Banff the eastern edge of Speyside is marked by two Teacher's distilleries, Ardmore and Glendronach.

The single malts of Speyside vary widely in character, although they are all generally complex but well balanced. This is especially true of those from Glenlivet, which have a particular delicacy. Elsewhere Speyside's malts range from the light and sweet, such as Glenfiddich, to the dark and sherried Macallan. Most of them are lightly peated, the peatiness in the flavour coming mostly from the water.

The eastern Highlands

This is basically the triangle of land to the east of a line drawn from Macduff down to Dundee, with an extension westwards along the Dee valley. The fertile coastal plain is one of Scotland's barley-growing areas and, as recently as the early 1980s, had a complement of nine malt distilleries. Only three of these are currently still in production, and each owned by different companies. Needless to say, some eastern Highland malts are becoming exceedingly rare, stocks being finite once the distilleries close. The single malts of this region do not conform to any one particular style. In general

they are dry and fruity, some being light and sweet, others quite aggressive.

Glenugie, at Peterhead, was once Scotland's most easterly distillery, Peterhead being the easternmost point on the Scottish mainland. The distillery was closed by Long John in 1983 and the process equipment dismantled, but its assertive malt is still available from independent sources. Further down the coast at Stonehaven was Glenury-Royal. This distillery was founded in 1825 by the local MP and got its 'Royal' suffix through his friend, a certain 'Mrs Windsor', and her influence on King William IV! Glenury closed in 1985 and its licence was revoked in 1992. The site has since been sold for redevelopment.

Glen Garioch, at Oldmeldrum, is the Highland distillery of Morrison's trio and is one of the oldest surviving distilleries in Scotland, dating from 1798. It had a profitable sideline in greenhouse tomatoes until it was mothballed in 1995. Happily, it has since resumed distilling.

Below Stonehaven, between the coast and the foothills of the Grampians, is the plain known as the Howe O' the Mearns. It is a rich barley-growing area which had five distilleries around its periphery, one at Fettercairn, two at Brechin and two at Montrose. Fettercairn is reputed to be the second distillery licensed under the 1823 Act and produces a malt with a nutty character. The two distilleries at Brechin made very different malts, both only available from the independents, Glencadam's sweet and buttery, North Port's dry and astringent. Glencadam was mothballed by Allied Distillers in 2000, but was acquired in May 2003 by Angus Dundee Distillers, the owner of Tomintoul, which plans to reopen it North Port closed in 1983, giving way to a supermarket and a funeral parlour. Only a plaque marks its passing. At Montrose are Lochside and Glenesk, both also closed. Formerly the Deuchar brewery, Lochside was converted for both malt and grain distilling in 1957 and has been owned by a Spanish company since 1973. Glenesk, which was also once a grain distillery, was last licensed to Wm Sanderson, the blenders of Vat 69.

The last of the eastern malts is Royal Lochnagar. The distillery is situated at Crathie, near Balmoral Castle, and is the only distillery on Deeside. Its whisky was said to be Queen

Victoria's favourite, so much so that she used to add it to her claret, and it was she who granted the distillery the first of its three royal warrants.

The southern Highlands and Perthshire

This is the area from the southern edge of the Grampians down to the Highland Line and incorporates the burgh of Perth, home town of Arthur Bell. Perth is an ancient city, at least 1,000 years old, and was once Scotland's capital. In fact there is evidence of much older settlement there, excavations having revealed traces of habitation going back to 4000 BC. The eight distilleries in this region are an intriguing mixture of ancient and modern, two dating from the eighteenth century, one from 1949 and two from 1965. Their malts are generally light and fresh, the exceptions being Edradour and Tullibardine which are darker, heavier and sweeter.

Pitlochry, the 'gateway to the Highlands' has two distilleries, Blair Athol at the southern end of the town and Edradour at the hamlet of Balnald, a mile or so away. Blair Athol calls itself 'the home of Bell's whisky' and was bought by the company in 1933 when it diversified from blending into distilling. Edradour is Scotland's (and probably the world's) smallest distillery and is operated by only three men, in much the same way that it would have been in the nineteenth century. Legend has it that it was once taken over by a leading American Prohibition bootlegger, and it did brisk business with the States during that period.

Aberfeldy is the only distillery on the River Tay and was built by Dewar's to ensure a steady supply of malt whisky for its blending operations. To the south, near Crieff, is Glenturret. A contender for the title of oldest surviving distillery in Scotland, Glenturret claims to have been founded in 1775. Its single malt is bottled in a wide range of ages and strengths and has won a number of awards.

Beside the A9 at Blackford is Tullibardine. This distillery opened in 1949 on the site of a former brewery and was designed, like Glenallachie and Jura, by Delmé Evans. The distillery is about 3 miles from the famous Gleneagles Hotel. At Doune, a few miles north of Stirling, Deanston is another newish distillery. It is also an unusual-looking one, converted from a cotton mill in 1965. The mill dates back to 1785 and was designed by Richard Arkwright, the inventor of the spinning frame, a successor to the jenny. The River Teith, which runs past the building, supplied the mill's power. Deanston now has its own hydroelectric generating station and draws process water from the Trossachs.

On the northern fringes of Glasgow are the two southernmost Highland distilleries. Glengoyne, at Killearn, and Loch Lomond, at Alexandria, stand almost right on the Highland Line. Glengoyne is an attractive distillery which is a popular tourist attraction for visitors to Glasgow. Loch Lomond Distillery was converted from a dye works at Alexandria in 1965–6 by the owners of Littlemill. Loch Lomond uses a combination of pot stills and rectifying stills, the latter incorporating dephlegmators, or reflux condensers, to adjust the level of reflux and alter the character of the distillate. It makes altogether seven different malts, not all of which are bottled as such, and also has a grain distillery on site. Its best-known malt is called Inchmurrin, named after an island in Loch Lomond itself. It parted company with Littlemill in the early 1980s after the take-over by Amalgamated Distilled Products, but by coincidence the two were reunited under the ownership of Glen Catrine Bonded Warehouse Ltd.

Lowlands

The industrial revolution led to great expansion of the main Lowland trade centres. Glasgow and Edinburgh grew rapidly both in size and importance with the influx of people arriving from the Highlands and Ireland. An upsurge in distilling was the consequence, fuelled by the availability of cheap labour and the size of the ready market, people regarding drink as an essential commodity. Some of the distilleries founded during this period were amongst the largest industrial concerns of the time and their proprietors, in particular the Haig and Stein families, wielded a great deal of power.

New legislation led to changes in the nature of

the whisky being made, the malt tax leading to distillers mixing unmalted grain with their malted barley to offset the effects of the tax, and the Wash Act with its tax on still capacity placing the emphasis on throughput rather than on quality. The introduction of the patent still changed the face of the industry and some distilleries gained a new lease of life by abandoning their pot stills in favour of making patent-still grain whisky, which itself was to lead to the appearance and subsequent growth of the blending trade. By 1870 twelve patent stills from a total of 123 distilleries were responsible for producing 55 per cent of Scotland's whisky. The blending, bottling and distribution side of the industry was all, as it still is today, Lowland based.

It is now highly unlikely that even a specialist shop will have more than a dozen Lowland malts on sale, and distillery closures made since the mid-1970s mean that some of these whiskies are exceedingly rare. Five Lowland malt distilleries were built within grain-distilling complexes, ostensibly to supply malt whisky for their parent companies' blending operations, but it was inevitable that someone, if not the distillers themselves, would make these malts available in bottle. The last of these distilleries to close, Inverleven, was also the longest-lived, closing in 1991 after a working life of fifty-three years within Ballantines' Dumbarton distilling complex. Others were Glen Flagler, within Garnheath (Moffat) grain distillery; Kinclaith, within Long John's Strathclyde complex; and Wm Grant's Ladyburn Distillery, at Girvan. The fifth was also the shortest-lived: Strathmore. Converted from Knox's brewery at Cambus, and reputedly haunted by a former brewer, it was unusual in making malt whisky in a patent still, but this lasted for only two years before the plant changed over to grain distilling. No Strathmore malt is known to exist, and Glen Flagler and Ladyburn are rare, but Inverleven and Kinclaith are not too difficult to find, and are even sold in miniatures.

This leaves the enthusiast with a choice of a further six Lowland malts: Auchentoshan, Glenkinchie, Rosebank, Bladnoch, Littlemill and

St Magdalene. Rosebank and Bladnoch have suffered recently from rationalisation, being closed in 1993. Littlemill was mothballed the following year after the failure of Gibson International and, though acquired by Loch Lomond Distillery, has since been partly demolished. Rosebank, beside the Forth–Clyde canal at Falkirk, was one of the few distilleries still using triple distillation. Bladnoch, at Wigtown, is the most southerly distillery in Scotland, being further south than Newcastle. It was sold by United Distillers and its new owner began by operating it as a visitor attraction. The good news is that he has since succeeded in buying back the plant from UDV and recommenced distilling in December 2000. Although the distillery has only a small capacity it is good to see another Lowland distillery in production. All three distilleries were still maturing stocks in bond at the time of closure, so hopefully there will be some continuity of supply. St Magdalene was at Linlithgow, the birthplace of Mary, Queen of Scots, and a town which once had five distilleries. It was one of the longest-surviving Lowland malt distilleries, founded in 1798, but was closed by DCL in 1983 and subsequently converted into flats. Its malt can still be found, albeit at a price.

Bladnoch's reawakening now leaves three malt distilleries in operation south of the Highland Line. Auchentoshan is the only one still maintaining the Lowland tradition of triple distillation. It stands in the shadow of the Erskine Bridge at Duntocher and is the Lowland partner in Morrison's trinity of distilleries. Glenkinchie, on the northern fringes of the Lammermuir Hills, is the Lowland representative in UDV's Classic Malts range, and has its own bowling green and museum.

Since the first imposition of the malt tax the Lowland area has seen the establishment of over 200 legally licensed malt distilleries. No other region of Scotland, not even Campbeltown, has seen its malt distilleries disappear as they have in the Lowlands. It is to be hoped that further depression in the industry can be avoided – it is unthinkable that the remaining ones should suffer the same fate.

THE WHISKY TRAIL

The Distilleries

Islay & Campbeltown

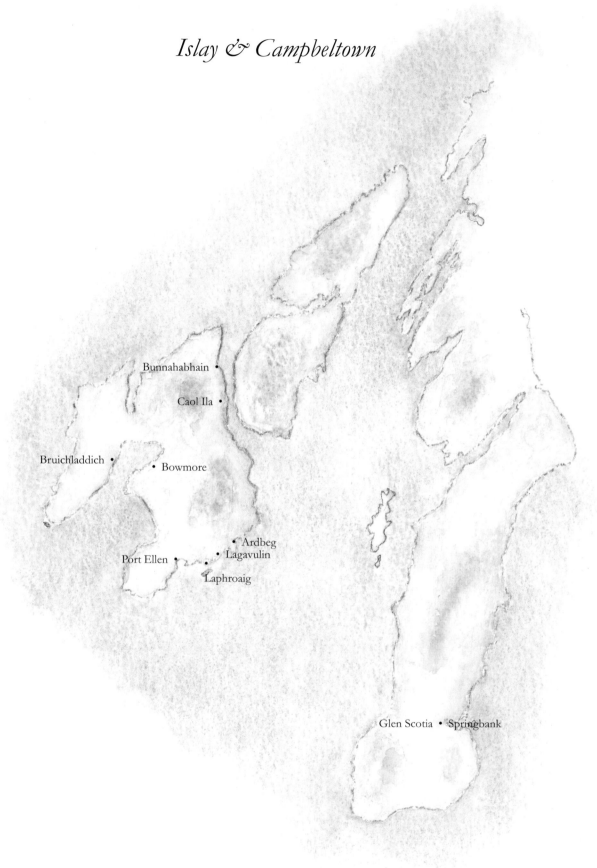

SPRINGBANK

Springbank Distillery is in many ways unique. It is the only distillery which makes three completely different whiskies, by differing methods, in the same, single, set of stills (other distilleries have made two or more malts on the same premises but using more than one set of stills, for instance Tobermory and Loch Lomond, or in different apparatus, such as Inverleven). It is the only distillery whose total malt requirements are met by its own floor maltings. It is the only distillery in Scotland built before the mid-nineteenth century which is still in the hands of the original founder's family, and it is the only malt distillery which is not a member of the Malt Distillers' Association of Scotland. Sadly, at times when Glen Scotia is closed, it is also Campbeltown's only remaining working distillery, although this situation may change as the company

The brothers, who were also farmers, fell out after a quarrel (evidently over sheep!), and William left Springbank to join his other brothers, Hugh and Archibald, at Rieclachan Distillery. John Mitchell took his son into partnership, creating the company of J. & A. Mitchell which owns Springbank today. The distillery stands near one of the best-known local landmarks, the prominent Longrow Church. It not only retains the original buildings but also encompasses parts of five of the old Campbeltown distilleries: Rieclachan itself, Argyll, Longrow, Springside and Union.

A unique and rather strange system of distillation is used which prompted one writer to declare

(incorrectly) that Springbank is triple-distilled, in the manner of some Lowland malts. The low wines are divided into two portions, one of which is distilled into feints by the second still before the whole batch is fed to the third still for final distillation. This use of an intermediate, or doubling, still maintains the strength of the spirit charge and is seen as a major factor in contributing to Springbank's mellowness. The company describes it as distilling 'two and a half times'. The whisky is lightly peated, allowing the briny, almost kippery taste to come through. Springbank's second product, Longrow, is distilled conventionally in two of the stills and uses malt which is entirely peat-kilned, giving it a heavier, almost Islay quality. The wash still is heated by oil fire and steam coil simultaneously, the direct firing giving a 'toasted' character which would not be present with straightforward steam-coil heating. In 1997 the company began to distil a third malt, an unpeated, triple-distilled malt called Hazelburn.

The distillery is one of only three in Scotland which bottle on site, and it prides itself on not chill-filtering its whisky at the bottling stage. Springbank itself is bottled in many different forms, from ten to fifty years old. A 1966 distillation made from locally grown barley malted at the distillery was bottled in 1998. Two versions of Longrow are bottled at ten years old, one from bourbon casks, the other exclusively from sherry wood. Hazelburn will be bottled at eight years old, commencing in 2005.

has bought the old Glengyle Distillery (formerly owned by the Mitchell family) and plans to reopen it

Springbank was founded in 1828, the fourteenth of the thirty-four known distilleries to be built in Campbeltown. It was built by the Reid family who were in-laws of the present owners. The Reids found themselves in financial trouble and were bought out by John and William Mitchell in 1837. During the first year's trading the ledger records the sale of 112 gallons of whisky at 8s 8d (43p) per gallon to a certain John Walker of Kilmarnock, who was later to become one of the biggest names in the business.

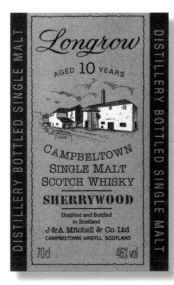

GLEN SCOTIA

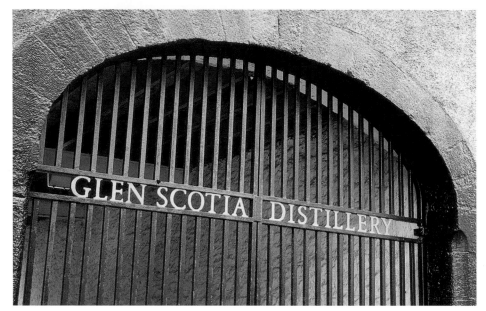

The early legal distilling industry in Campbeltown was an incestuous one, with the same few family names cropping up time and again on the licences of many of the distilleries, in particular the names of Colville, Greenlees, Ross and Beith. These families were shrewd business people who made the town a success. They lobbied parliament through a trade association that was ahead of its time, and pioneered the processing of draff for cattle feed. Yet with the advent of Prohibition the industry there became the architect of its own demise, as quality went out of the window and Campbeltown Loch became increasingly polluted by the millions of gallons of pot ale unthinkingly dumped into it. By the time Prohibition was repealed in 1933 there were just three distilleries working in Campbeltown, and of these Rieclachan closed the following year to be converted into a car showroom. Today Campbeltown's past lies buried beneath housing estates, contractors' yards, supermarkets and bus depots, and whilst Glen Scotia spent some years closed Springbank was left alone to keep Campbeltown's distilling heritage alive.

Glen Scotia stands at the junction of High Street and Saddell Street in the centre of town and was founded in 1832 by Stewart, Galbraith & Co., later owner of Glen Nevis Distillery on Glebe Street. In fact, Glen Scotia was to develop a further connection with Glen Nevis when it was later acquired by that distillery's founder. Stewart Galbraith held Glen Scotia's licence until 1919, when it sold the distillery to West Highland Malt Distilleries Ltd, a consortium led by Robertson & Baxter, which also acquired Campbeltown's Ardlussa, Dalintober, Glengyle, Glen Nevis and Kinloch distilleries at the same time. Ardlussa closed in 1923 and the consortium went into receivership, with Glen Scotia and Kinloch being sold in 1924 to the founder of Glen Nevis, Duncan MacCallum.

MacCallum's business career was chequered: he founded Glen Nevis only to sell it, buy it back, then sell it again, this time to Stewart Galbraith, then owner of Glen Scotia. MacCallum died after being swindled out of a large sum of money by a conman he met on a cruise, committing suicide by drowning himself in Campbeltown Loch, and it is said that his ghost still prowls the malting floors at Glen Scotia.

The distillery subsequently passed through the hands of Bloch Bros, the owner of Scapa Distillery, Hiram Walker and the romantically named Amalgamated Distilled Products, until a management buy-out resulted in the formation of Gibson International in 1989. Gibson also bought Littlemill and announced an optimistic business plan for the two distilleries, only to see the company fail in 1994. Both distilleries were acquired by Glen Catrine, and although Littlemill has been partly demolished, Glen Scotia resumed production in 1999. Production is not yet back to the levels achieved in the early 1990s but is at least steady under the guidance of its parent Loch Lomond.

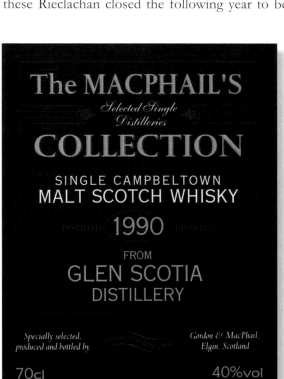

The MACPHAIL'S
Selected Single Distilleries
COLLECTION
SINGLE CAMPBELTOWN
MALT SCOTCH WHISKY
DISTILLED 1990 DISTILLED
FROM
GLEN SCOTIA
DISTILLERY

Specially selected, produced and bottled by

Gordon & MacPhail, Elgin, Scotland

70cl   40%vol

SIGNATORY VINTAGE
Vintage 1991
Single Campbeltown Malt Scotch Whisky
Distilled at Glen Scotia Distillery
on 11th February 1991
70CL   Matured in an oak cask for 9 years   43%VOL
Bottled on 29th November 2000   Natural Colour
Cask No. 218 · Bottle No.   of 398
This whisky has been selected, produced and bottled in Scotland for and under the sole responsibility of Signatory Vintage Scotch Whisky Co. Ltd. Edinburgh EH6 5PY Scotland.

PORT ELLEN

As the ferry approaches the pier at Port Ellen the most conspicuous sight is the huge maltings built alongside the distillery, and the most conspicuous smell that of burning peat, which pervades the entire village. Port Ellen grew up around the pier which was built to serve the distillery to which it gave its name, and quickly came to supersede Bowmore as the island's main port. Although it is now closed and unlikely to reopen, Port Ellen is significant for a number of reasons.

At the time of its foundation the distillery was used by Customs and Excise to test a new innovation – the spirit safe. Its use was to become law with the introduction of the Excise Act, but it could not be forced onto the industry without first checking that it would have no detrimental effect on the spirit. Robert Stein also carried out some of his early research work at Port Ellen, which resulted in the invention of the patent still.

Port Ellen's history is chequered, and its founder went bankrupt within months of officially starting up the business in 1825. After eleven years the licence had passed to its sixth proprietor. John Ramsay was a Glasgow sherry importer and became one of the earliest pioneers in the export of Scotch whisky to the USA, shipping directly from the distillery. He also inaugurated the first passenger ferry between Glasgow and Islay (which ran once every two weeks), and became a major landowner in the southern area of the island, contributing greatly to the farming community. By 1930 the distillery was a subsidiary of DCL, which closed it down at the onset of the Depression. For the next thirty-seven years it was used only for malting and warehousing, a fate that continued to the present day except for a brief revival from 1967 to 1984.

By the early 1970s it was obvious that the three DCL distilleries on Islay were producing between them only a third of their total malt requirements, and so the decision was made to build a centralised maltings alongside the distillery at Port Ellen. The new facility opened in 1973 and now supplies all the working distilleries on Islay and Jura. It is a drum maltings, each of the seven drums holding 46 tons of barley. Germination takes five days, after which the green malt is dried in one of three kilns. The size of the charge means that kilning takes about thirty hours, twice as long as in an average drum maltings on the mainland. A combination of peat smoke and hot air is used to dry the grain and the exact amount of peating given depends on the distillery at which the malt will be used. Lagavulin, for instance, uses heavily peated malt yet surprisingly there is one distillery on Islay for which the malt is not peated at all.

Her Majesty the Queen visited the maltings on 11 August 1980 and a special bottling of Port Ellen whisky was made to mark the occasion. Other than this, Port Ellen is only available from independent bottlers, but its single malt is typical of Islay's south coast and well worth trying should the chance present itself. The distillery is closed and unlikely to go back into production, although the warehouses are being used by Lagavulin.

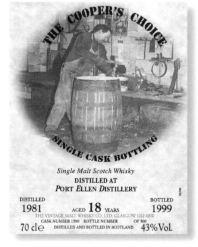

LAPHROAIG

Laphroaig is one of the most, if not the most, distinctive of all malt whiskies and many adjectives have been used to describe it – medicinal, phenolic, tangy, oily and peaty being just a few. For many it is an acquired taste, but one which rewards persistence.

Alexander and Donald Johnston were farmers at Laphroaig and set up a small distillery which became 'official' in 1826. Donald bought out his brother ten years later to become sole owner. He died in somewhat bizarre circumstances in June 1847 after falling into a vat of burnt ale. Following his death Laphroaig was leased to a trustee of his estate, Alexander Graham of Lagavulin. Johnston's son, Dugald, was only eleven years old at the time and did not take over until 1857. Even then Lagavulin continued as agents until 1907, when Laphroaig was being run by Dugald's brother-in-law Alex. After Alex died the new owners decided to terminate Lagavulin's agency as they considered the terms to be unfair. By this time Lagavulin was owned by Peter Mackie and the Johnstons took Mackie to court. He

was so annoyed that he responded with a little landscaping work at the lade, which cut off Laphroaig's water and resulted in another court case. As a parting shot, and following his experiments with the Malt Mill Distillery, Mackie made two unsuccessful attempts to buy out Laphroaig when its lease came up for renewal. The owners fought off the bids with the help of their new agents, Robertson & Baxter.

The distillery became a limited company in 1950 and from 1954 to 1967, when it was taken over by Long John, it was run by Bessie Williamson, who was in effect the only lady distiller in Scotland. She retired as chairman in 1972, having started at Laphroaig as the manager's temporary secretary nearly forty years previously. In 1990 Long John

sold Laphroaig to Allied Distillers. Refurbishment is in evidence in the stillhouse, and the tun room has stainless steel washbacks and a lauter mash tun. Some 90 per cent of production goes for blending, yet in the world single malt market Laphroaig ranks in the top ten.

The name is said to be a contraction from the original Gaelic meaning 'the beautiful hollow by the broad bay', yet this assertion is causing argument amongst students of the language. It now seems possible that the name came from Norse origins and became 'gaelicised' (in both culture and spelling), something which happened to the language throughout the Isles, creating hybrid words which later became anglicised. The distillery stands on the shore of Loch Laphroaig on Islay's south coast. The warehouses are right at the water's edge and between them hold in bond some 55,000 casks. The site now incorporates that of Andrew and James Stein's Ardenistle Distillery, which flourished briefly from 1837 to 1842, and included amongst Laphroaig's buildings is a hall where the local villagers hold their ceilidhs.

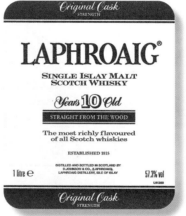

LAGAVULIN

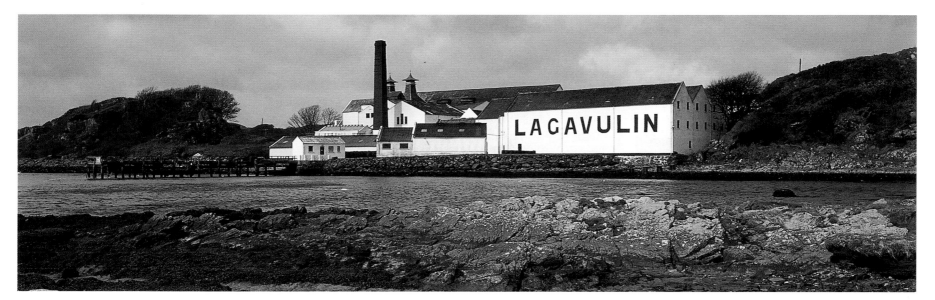

In the twelfth century, Islay became the domain of the Lords of the Isles and saw the foundation of the clan Macdonald. The clan seat, Dunyvaig Castle, stands sentinel over Lagavulin Bay and it was from here in 1314 that over 1,000 Islay warriors embarked to fight for Robert the Bruce at Bannockburn.

By the mid-eighteenth century illicit distilling was well established on Islay. Farmers saw it as a useful sideline and for some, such as crofters and fishermen, it was the only living available when winter came. By 1740 there were ten stills on Lagavulin Bay. These gave way to two fully fledged distilleries which had combined by 1837 to form the basis of the Lagavulin that the visitor sees today. The name comes from the Gaelic *lag a' mhuilinn*, meaning 'mill in the hollow'.

Its history is inextricably entwined with that of its near neighbour Laphroaig and on occasions the rivalry has been far from friendly, resulting in more than one court case. Lagavulin was jointly owned by the Graham family and James Logan Mackie & Co., a partner in which was Peter Mackie who went on to build the Craigellachie Distillery and establish the White Horse brand. As an experiment Mackie set up the Malt Mill Distillery in 1908 within Lagavulin itself, the aim being to recreate old traditional working methods. The kiln had a haircloth floor and was heated by

open chauffers fired entirely with peat. Malt Mill had its own washbacks but shared Lagavulin's mash tun, and heather was added to the mash (Mackie believed this to be the original practice). The two pear-shaped stills were the same as those at Laphroaig. Mackie even poached Laphroaig's brewer to work on his new venture. However, if he was secretly trying to duplicate Laphroaig's product (Lagavulin lost the agency for Laphroaig in 1907) the experiment was a failure.

Mackie's family line ended in 1917 when his son James was killed outside Jerusalem, but Malt Mill survived until 1962, its maltings now converted into Lagavulin's visitor centre.

In 1924 the company commissioned a small coaster to transport barley, coal and empty casks from Glasgow to Lagavulin and deliver the whisky to the mainland. The SS *Pibroch* (a pibroch is a phrase, usually a lament, played on the

bagpipes) remained in service until 1972 and also served Caol Ila and Talisker distilleries. On two separate occasions in 1937 the little puffer was called upon to rescue crewmen from Fleetwood trawlers which had run aground, earning her the nickname 'the Fleetwood lifeboat'.

Inset into a wall of the distillery building is a gravestone. It was intended as a headstone for the grave of a local man, buried on the nearby island of Texa. The stone never made it to the island however, as when it was being loaded onto the boat a chain snapped, and the superstitious boatmen took this as an omen and refused to make the crossing. The distillery has remained a memorial to him ever since.

Lagavulin is virtually a statement of the Islay character and many factors are held to be influential on the spirit, from the larch washbacks to the particularly steep angle of the lyne arms atop the stills. Peter Mackie attributed its flavour to the burns which supply the distillery's water and which fall over almost 100 waterfalls on their way down the peat-covered slopes of Beinn Sholum. It is pungent and assertive and, at sixteen years old, quite a good age for a standard bottling. A 1980 distillation finished in Pedro-Ximénez wood (Pedro-Ximénez is a grape used to make sweet wines which are used in the blending of the sweeter sherries) was recently released.

ARDBEG

Following the main A846 from Laphroaig and Lagavulin the road, barely wide enough for two cars to pass, suddenly makes a sharp right turn and you find yourself at the water's edge right in the middle of Ardbeg Distillery. The road which continues another 4 miles to Kildalton Church seems almost an afterthought.

Ardbeg was founded by the MacDougall family in 1815, which makes it the second oldest distillery on Islay (its claim as the oldest arises from the fact that Bowmore was re-established in 1825). The area was used by a gang of smugglers whose activities were only curtailed when the Excise watchers seized a large quantity of illicit whisky, a coup which led to the break-up of the gang and the start of a legitimate operation. The distillery was privately owned until it was taken over by Hiram Walker in 1979, but its future became uncertain when Walker's merged with Allied Vintners and it closed in 1983. It reopened in the late 1980s, although operating below capacity, was mothballed again in August 1996, and subsequently sold to the owner of Glenmorangie.

Peat plays an important part in Ardbeg's flavour and in this part of Islay it is particularly good, being free of sulphur and other undesirable minerals. Until its closure the distillery was able to make all its own malt, the last distillery on Islay to be able to do so, and the kilning was done exclusively over peat fires (most distillers only kiln for part of the time over peat). With no fans in the pagodas to draw the peat smoke upwards it would diffuse slowly through the malt, infusing its reek into the grain. The malt had to be turned regularly during the kilning to prevent it from stewing. The water too picks up its own flavour, flowing over peat and heather on its 3-mile journey to the distillery from Loch Uigeadail.

Ardbeg has never worked to an enormous capacity. It has only six washbacks and a single pair of stills. Fermentation takes longer than normal, at about sixty hours, and only one type of yeast is used. The spirit still has a purifier fitted. In its early days it could make only 600 gallons per week. By the time of its closure this figure had risen to an annual output of about 300,000 gallons, still way below that of most other Islay distilleries. Perhaps understandably, Ardbeg Single Malt has never been widely available and was at one time only sold in a couple of local hotels and to company shareholders. Most of its production went to blenders, although its pungency may have made its market a limited one, which in turn could have accounted for the distillery's temporary closure. It seemed that Ardbeg was destined to stay in the background of Allied Distillers' operations as a poor relation of its sister Laphroaig, with whom it shared many of its characteristics. Its acquisition by Glenmorangie has given it a new lease of life.

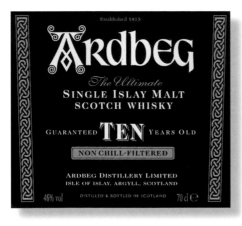

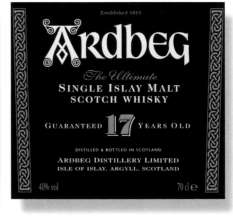

BRUICHLADDICH

Bruichladdich was founded in 1881 and had a succession of owners before being acquired by Invergordon in 1968. It was built the year previous to Bunnahabhain by the Harvey family, who already owned two Glasgow distilleries, Yoker and Dundashill, the latter being Scotland's largest malt distillery at the time. They decided to use in its construction a revolutionary new building material – concrete. The building contractor was John MacDonald of Tollcross, Glasgow, who held a patent on the material. It was one of the first distilleries in Scotland to be built this way and the various buildings are blocky in appearance, whitewashed, and grouped around a courtyard. It stands facing Bowmore on the western shore of Loch Indaal, only separated from the sea by the coast road.

After Prohibition the distillery was acquired for the National Distillers of America and the Glasgow blending company Train & McIntyre was appointed as manager. The deal was orchestrated by Joseph Hobbs who owned the ship *Littlehorn* and acted as principle liaison between Teacher's and its clients in Prohibition San Francisco, to whom he delivered cases of Highland Cream wrapped in hessian. There were in all seven distilleries included in this deal, the others being Benromach, Fettercairn, Glenesk, Glenlochy, Glenury-Royal and Strathdee, of which only Fettercairn and Benromach are now working. The National Distillers of America withdrew from Scotland in 1954.

Invergordon extended the distillery in 1975, enlarging the mash house and tun room and adding a second pair of stills to bring Bruichladdich's annual capacity to 800,000 proof gallons. Despite this modernisation, some of the original equipment installed by the Harveys remains, including the mill and the washbacks. The mash tun dates from 1900 and came from Bunnahabhain. An old riveted wash still was replaced at the end of the 1980s. Like Jura, Bruichladdich has tall stills which produce a relatively clean spirit and Bruichladdich is certainly light-bodied in comparison to most of the other Islay malts. It has usually been bottled at ten years old, but older versions are also available from time to time and it is beginning to prove

popular with the independents.

Since the closure of Lochindaal Distillery at Port Charlotte in the 1920s, Bruichladdich has been Scotland's westernmost distillery, at a longitude of 6° 22' W. Travelling west from here the next distillery you would come to would be (appropriately enough) in Nova Scotia.

Before the management buy-out of Invergordon in 1985 Bruichladdich was indirectly a subsidiary of Hawker Siddeley Aviation, a strange and probably unique alliance between such traditional and new technology.

The distillery was mothballed after the Whyte & Mackay take-over of Invergordon but was sold on 19 December 2000 by Invergordon's parent company JBB (Greater Europe) plc to the independent bottlers Murray McDavid. Brought in as a founding partner of the new Bruichladdich Distillery Co. is James McEwan, formerly a

manager of Bowmore and three-times winner of the title 'Distiller of the Year'. Amongst his plans for Bruichladdich is a unique 'centre of excellence', a teaching facility which will enable people to learn about whisky, whether by simply enjoying an unhurried afternoon in the library or by actually mucking-in on a 'get-your-hands-dirty' course in the craft of traditional whisky distilling. The company has been quoted as saying that 'if we could not have bought an Islay distillery we would not have bothered at all', and restarted distilling in May 2001. In addition to the regular Bruichladdich spirit, two other malts are being distilled: Port Charlotte, peated to a level between that of Bowmore and Lagavulin, and an occasional distillation called Octomore which is more heavily peated still. A new bottling hall was commissioned in 2003, making Bruichladdich the only Islay malt to be distilled, matured and bottled on the island itself.

BOWMORE

Bowmore is the oldest legal distillery on Islay, dating from 1779, and was founded by a local merchant named Simson. It was unusual in being run by the founding family, whereas subsequent Islay distilleries were often leased out to their operators by the proprietors. Although Simson founded and ran the distillery, he was acting as agent for Daniel Campbell of Shawfield, an entrepreneurial character who was also a Member of Parliament. Campbell was one of the first Scottish MPs to vote for the introduction of a malt tax following the Act of Union in 1707, a tax whose ramifications were obvious to both the distillers and the public. A measure of his unpopularity came from the good citizens of Glasgow, who burnt his house to the ground. The government were kind enough to compensate him for this inconvenience to the tune of £7,000 which he used to buy the island of Islay.

The distillery had passed by 1852 to the German Mutters family who expanded it and purchased a small coaster, similar to that owned by Lagavulin, to transport whisky and raw materials between Glasgow and Islay. William and James Mutter operated Bowmore until the end of the nineteenth century, when the Bowmore Distillery Co. Ltd was formed. James Mutter, in addition to his job as distiller, also held the post of the Ottoman, Portuguese and Brazilian vice-consul in Glasgow! The distillery was purchased by Sherriff's Bowmore Distillery Ltd in 1925, which itself was taken over in 1950 by William Grigor & Son Ltd of Inverness. In 1963 Bowmore was acquired by Stanley P. Morrison Ltd, now Morrison Bowmore Distillers Ltd, which is in turn owned by the biggest distilling company in the world, Suntory.

Bowmore stands on the shore of Loch Indaal, literally at the water's edge, and at high tide the sea encroaches some 4 or 5ft up the warehouse wall. One of the original eighteenth-century buildings is still in use. It is one of the few distilleries to maintain its own floor maltings and produces about a third of its malt requirements, using Chariot and Prisma barley from the Scottish mainland. It has its own peat bog and, in the interests of conservation, has developed a method of burning chopped and moistened peat in the kiln. Not only does this produce more smoke, it cuts the amount of peat needed for kilning to 20 per cent of that used previously. Waste heat from the condensers is used to heat the public swimming pool next door, built in one of the old bonded warehouses.

During World War II the distillery was used as a base for the Coastal Command flying boats engaged on anti-submarine duty in the Atlantic and the visitor centre still displays a collection of photographs showing the Catalinas and Sunderlands flying over the village. Bowmore has

an impressive visitor centre which says much for the company's confidence in Islay's growing tourist industry.

One of Islay's best-known characters was Bowmore's head cooper, Davie Bell. Apprenticed as a cooper in Glasgow, Davie came to Islay to work first at Bruichladdich before moving to Bowmore in 1936. He did not retire until he was seventy-four years old, and even at the age of ninety-five would still visit the distillery almost daily to keep an eye on the precious casks.

Bowmore's flavour lies somewhere between that of the pungent south coast Islays and those of the island's northern region, and a bewildering array of bottlings at up to forty years old is available. The 21-year-old was the gold medal winner in its class in the 1992 International Wine and Spirit Competition and also won the Scotch Whisky Heritage Centre Trophy, beating over 1,000 other entries. The 17-year-old won the silver and the 10-year-old (now superseded by Legend, itself a trophy winner in its class) the bronze! The trophy for best special edition was won by Black Bowmore, a 1964 distillation bottled at twenty-eight years old in 1992. Further limited bottling runs were also made in 1993 and 1994. The distillers have also experimented with 'finishing' the malt in different woods. Bowmore Darkest is finished in oloroso sherry butts after twelve years in bourbon casks. Bowmore Dusk is finished in Bordeaux wine casks, and Voyage is finished in port wood and bottled at 56% vol. Recently released is a 40-year-old 1955 distillation, filled on 22 November of that year into bourbon casks where it spent twenty years maturing before being racked into sherry wood, where it has rested for a further twenty years. Its maturation has been monitored by seven distillery managers! In 1995, Bowmore achieved the ISO 9002 accreditation for quality management.

About 60 per cent of Bowmore's production goes for blending and Japan is an important market. The malt is a valuable component in Suntory's blends, and there are bars in Japan called 'Bowmore malt houses' which sell nothing but Bowmore whisky!

CAOL ILA

Caol Ila stands on the most sheltered bay in Islay and takes its name from the strait which separates the island from Jura, which it overlooks. Through its massive picture windows the stillhouse has arguably the best view of any in Scotland. Since it was built by Hector Henderson in 1846 the distillery has had a number of owners, including in its early days the Isle of Jura Distillery. Since 1927 it has been under the control of DCL and its successors.

Like nearby Bunnahabhain, Caol Ila is a community in itself with workers' housing on site. Up until the 1930s the distillery also had its own mission hall where a local minister would preach in winter, and in summer services would be held by divinity students from Glasgow and Edinburgh. For a long time distillery workers have served in the crew of the lifeboat based at Port Askaig.

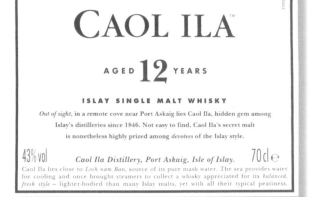

It is a big distillery, certainly one of the largest in the Hebrides, yet is run by only sixteen employees. The original Victorian production buildings were replaced in 1973 with rather functional-looking structures finished in a pale cream render. It also lost its pagoda roof at this time, its malt now coming from the centralised maltings at Port Ellen. Sixteen mashes are made each week using 11 tons of malt at a time, and the eight wooden washbacks each hold 10,000 gallons of wort. The size of the stills can be appreciated when seen from outside the stillhouse through its wall of windows. The wash stills have a capacity of 7,775 gallons, the spirit stills being slightly smaller at 6,500 gallons. Distillation of the spirit from the low wines takes around seven hours. The peaty water supply comes from Loch nam Ban about a mile away and arrives at the distillery in a narrow waterfall which was once also the distillery's source of power.

Caol Ila is one of the more 'droppable' names in whisky circles, being relatively unknown outside Islay. Although it has been available in the past in independent merchant's bottlings the distillers' 'official' version only appeared on the market in 1988–9, and was rarely seen outside specialist stockists off the island. However, it has now found its way into UDV's 'Hidden Malts' range, a range which also includes Glen Ord, Clynelish and Glen Elgin, which is intended to complement the Classic Malts series. Caol Ila has a characteristic toasted flavour which is not shared by any other Islay malt, and is largely aged in sherry wood. It is sought after by blenders and finds its way into, amongst others, Buchanan's Black & White, Johnnie Walker's Red Label and Bell's 8-year-old.

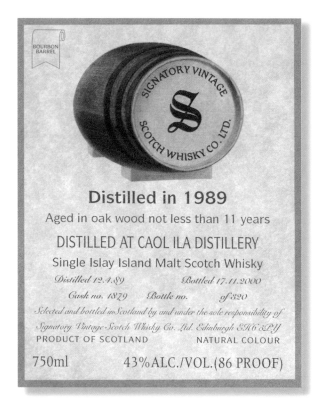

BUNNAHABHAIN

Bunnahabhain was the last of the surviving distilleries to be built on Islay, and in fact only Peter Mackie's Malt Mill Distillery, within Lagavulin, was built on the island subsequently. It was built by the Islay Distillery Company, which was formed by the Greenlees brothers, who were local farmers. The site was no more than bare moorland at the time but the partners were particularly attracted to it because of its supply of good-quality water from the Margadale spring, and its commanding position at the north end of the Sound of Islay. Only 300 yards away the Margadale River flows into the sound, giving the distillery its name, which in Gaelic means 'mouth of the river'.

Because of its remote location the contractors had to build not only the distillery itself but also housing for the workforce, a reading room and schoolroom, a pier and a road to Port Askaig. The estimate for the project was £30,000. During the construction one of the foremen found a box on the beach, inside which were a number of decaying human bones. The superstitious workmen were told that the box had once belonged to a doctor who had gone abroad.

Shortly after, a hurricane struck the island, damaging the partly finished buildings. Two large steam boilers, left on the beach whilst awaiting installation, were swept across the sound and onto the shore of Jura.

The distillery was built with all mod cons and was much admired when it was completed in 1882. Robertson & Baxter were appointed sales agents with a commission of 2d (1p) per gallon. In its first six months' trading Bunnahabhain yielded a profit of £5,000 – a return on the capital of 23 per cent. The success was repeated the following year with profits of nearly £10,000. The directors were greatly impressed with the manager, Mr Smith, who was able to name his own terms to stay in the job. He demanded, and got, a salary of £350, free house, fire and lighting, keep for a cow, removal expenses and 'not less than £30' to be spent on furniture!

The Islay Distillery Company lasted little more than five years before amalgamating with the Glenrothes Distillery to become the Highland Distilleries Co. Nearly all production went for blending until the late 1970s when Bunnahabhain 12-year-old Malt was launched. The label depicts a sailor at the helm of his vessel, and the legend 'Westering Home'. The phrase comes from a Scottish folk song and it could well be Islay that the sailor is 'westering home' to. There are 250 recorded wrecks around Islay and an ocean-going trawler has lain off Bunnahabhain since 1974.

The Northern & Western Highlands

Highland Park • • Scapa

• Pulteney

• Clynelish

Balblair • • Glenmorangie

Teaninich • Dalmore
Glen Ord • • Royal Brackla

Talisker •

Tomatin •

• Speyside
• Dalwhinnie

• Ben Nevis

Tobermory •

• Oban

• Jura

• Arran

ARRAN

The Isle of Arran is situated in the Firth of Clyde between the Ayrshire coast and the Kintyre peninsula and is known as 'Scotland in miniature'. Its history is ancient, and it was bought by the Scots from its Viking landlords after their defeat by Alexander III in 1263 at the Battle of Largs. The island has distinct highland and lowland halves, separated by the same Highland Boundary Fault which divides the mainland. It is a popular holiday destination, especially for golf, fishing and hillwalking, despite the locals' assertion that summer attire on Arran is 'shorts and wellies'!

From Brodick the A841 curves away around the bay, hugging the coastline so closely that the sea laps to within a few yards of the road. At Corrie rows of attractive cottages, all with immaculate gardens, rise from the very roadside up a steep hillside overlooking the tiniest harbour imaginable, then at Sannox the road abruptly turns inland and snakes along Glen Chalmadale to Lochranza, along bracken-covered hills down which a 'mare's tail' waterfall seems to appear every few hundred yards. A mile outside Lochranza, at the foot of Gleann Easan Biorach (which means 'the valley of the little cascade'), stands the new Arran Distillery, only the second legally licensed distillery recorded on the island. Its predecessor was built in the south of the island, at Lagg, and survived from 1825 to 1837.

The distillery was founded by Harold Currie, a former MD of Chivas. He preferred to build his distillery from scratch, rather than take over an existing one, so it could be built to his specification, and he chose to site it on Arran as his family has links with the island. The exact site was determined after the company tested numerous water sources before settling on Loch na Davie, some 3 miles south. Capital for the project was raised in part by selling 'bonds', new spirit pre-sold for the customer's own private bottling six years later. The distillery opened in 1995 after taking a year to build. The work was interrupted for two months by a pair of nesting eagles!

As at Edradour and Speyside the process takes place in one building. Malt is bought in, using Chariot and Optic barley from Aberdeenshire, mashed in a full lauter mash tun, fermented in four wooden washbacks and distilled in a single pair of small stills. The initial plan was to bottle the malt at six years old in 2001, the distillers reckoning that due to Arran's macroclimate the spirit matures more quickly than it would on the mainland. In 2000 a few sherry butts were discovered to have matured particularly quickly, and a run of some 3,000 bottles of 5-year-old Arran malt was made. The company also sells the Loch Ranza blend, which has a 45 per cent malt content.

The distillery also has an excellent visitor centre, opened by Her Majesty the Queen on 9 August 1997. There are interactive displays demonstrating each aspect of the process, and a particularly informative tour. Upstairs is a restaurant which serves a formal dinner in the evenings.

JURA

J ura is a wild and rugged hammerhead-shaped island which is separated from the Scottish mainland by the island of Scarba and the Strait of Corryvreckan, the most formidable tide race in the British Isles. It is officially deemed un-navigable by the Royal Navy due to its dangerous overfalls and whirlpools, although neither the Lords of the Isles nor the Norsemen who raided this part of Scotland in the eleventh century seemed to agree with the Royal Navy on this point and regularly sailed their galleys and longships along this passage, risking a one-way trip to *Tìr nan Òg*, the 'Land of the Ever Young'.

From Port Askaig a vessel resembling an ex-World War II tank landing craft ferries vehicles and passengers to Feolin Ferry, from where the only road in sight leads away around the island and after 7 miles passes by the Jura Distillery. The name Jura is supposed to mean 'deer island', and its human population is outnumbered twenty to one by its deer. One hamlet on the island was abandoned in the 1840s after its inhabitants were falsely accused of poaching the Laird's salmon.

Illicit distilling was once carried out on Jura in a cave near to the site of the present distillery. In 1810 a proper distillery, complete with maltings, was built at Craighouse at the south end of Small Isles Bay by the Campbell family, the owners of

the Jura estate. It passed through the hands of a number of licensees until 1876, when it was taken over by James Ferguson, who also built Ardlussa Distillery at Campbeltown three years later. Ferguson rebuilt the distillery at considerable cost, taking over ownership of the plant and running the business. In 1901 Ferguson fell out with the

Campbells and left the distillery, taking the plant with him. This effectively called a halt to the operation and the Campbells removed the building's roof to avoid paying rates (rates were only charged on completed buildings).

In 1958 two Jura landowners approached Scottish & Newcastle Breweries with plans for a new distillery to revitalise the island's economy. The distillery was designed by Delmé Evans, who also created Glenallachie and Tullibardine, and opened in 1963. The equipment is modern and includes a stainless steel semi-lauter mash tun and six stainless steel washbacks similar in size to those at Caol Ila. The first Isle of Jura Single Malt was sold in 1974. It is technically a Highland malt and comes from stills which have very tall necks, producing a relatively light spirit. The distillery's water comes from Market Loch and feeds a massive waterfall which can be seen from the road on the approach to Craighouse. It is so pure that some of the distillery's employees bottle it to use at home in preference to tap water. To the north are the Paps, or breasts, of Jura, said to be the home of a lovesick witch. On a clear day the Isle of Man is visible from their summits.

TOBERMORY

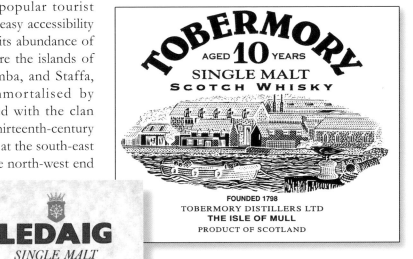

The island of Mull is a popular tourist destination, thanks to its easy accessibility by ferry from Oban and its abundance of attractions. Off the west coast are the islands of Iona, resting place of St Columba, and Staffa, whose Fingal's Cave was immortalised by Mendelssohn. Mull is associated with the clan MacLean and the clan seat, the thirteenth-century Duart Castle, stands on the coast at the south-east end of the Sound of Mull. At the north-west end of the sound lies Tobermory, in whose bay it is said that a galleon of the Spanish Armada is sunk.

The village is clustered around the sweep of the bay, the harbourside lined with brightly painted buildings. The story goes that a paint company offered to decorate the façade of one of the hotels, but the idea was vetoed by the local authority which preferred the buildings to remain plain grey stone. The villagers rebelled, and all the harbour-front buildings were painted bright contrasting colours! At the foot of a steep hill at the entrance to the seafront stands the distillery, the only legally licensed distillery ever recorded on Mull.

Tobermory is an old distillery, but has by no means enjoyed continuous success. A sign outside claims a foundation date of 1823, but records show it as having been licensed to its first proprietor, John Sinclair, in 1798. Since then it has had a number of owners and seen protracted periods of closure. The Depression forced its silence from 1930 to 1972, when it was reopened and renamed Ledaig Distillery by a company with Spanish and Panamanian backers. Their tenure was short-lived, as was that of its next owner, the Kirkleavington Property Company of Cleckheaton, Yorkshire, which changed its name back to Tobermory. In 1993 the distillery was acquired by Burn Stewart Distillers, the owner of Deanston, for a total investment of £800,000.

Tobermory, like Springbank, now makes two single malts. Tobermory itself is made from unpeated malt, a feature it shares with Deanston. Ledaig is made using malt which is peated to a similar level to that used by Lagavulin. Burn Stewart has changed the emphasis in recent times to making more Ledaig whisky, which now accounts for about 70 per cent of production. The distillery has two pairs of stills, the wash and spirit stills being of approximately equal size. The Steel's masher and underback are unusual in being made from copper, and there are only four Douglas fir washbacks of average size. The mash tun is a traditional type, with a copper dome. The distillery takes its water supply from the company's private lochan 2 miles away. There is no permanent bonded warehousing on the site, and the new spirit is stored only temporarily on the island before being sent by tanker every two weeks to Deanston for maturation.

OBAN

The pretty Victorian town of Oban is the capital of Scotland's western Highland region. It's a small and colourful town, its planners having apparently eschewed the uniformity normally beloved of their profession, and all the more attractive for it. It stands in a natural amphitheatre, the hills of Mull visible beyond the island of Kerrera which shelters the bay. On top of a 400ft high cliff overlooking the seafront stands McCaig's Folly, a replica of Rome's Colosseum built at the end of the nineteenth century by a philanthropic banker for no better reason than to give the town's unemployed something to do. At the foot of the cliff a cave was discovered in which were found remains of Oban's first inhabitants, Azilian man, dating from around 5000 BC, migrants who came to Britain from Europe. Shoehorned into the space between the cliff and the promenade shops is the distillery.

The first thought that occurs is why the distillery's founders should have chosen such a strange place to build their premises. In fact, the Stevenson family got there first. Oban Distillery is one of the oldest in Scotland, built in 1794, and actually predates its home town by a good few

years. At the time of its foundation Oban itself was nothing more than a fishing village and the distillery would have stood directly on the harbourside, an ideal situation for exploiting seaborne trade links with the Clyde ports. Gradually, the town grew up around the harbour and the distillery ended up seemingly squashed against the cliff in a back street.

For almost the first seventy years of its existence the distillery remained in the hands of the Stevensons. They had built the family residence adjoining the stillhouse, into which the sitting room partly projected, and a peep-hole door had been fitted which allowed the proprietor to keep an eye on the distilling operation. The peep-hole was retained by the next owner, who converted the Stevensons' rooms into offices. The company was a major supplier to Pattison's of Leith, and suffered a near-fatal blow when Pattison's collapsed in 1898. Altogether the distillery passed through seven changes of ownership, finally being acquired by Scottish Malt Distillers (a subsidiary of DCL) in 1930.

The present buildings date from the late 1800s and were modernised in the 1960s and early 1970s. Oban single malt is now bottled at fourteen years old and has become part of UDV's range of Classic Malts. It is a slightly oily whisky, lacking the influence of the sea which might be expected from its location. The label tells the stories of the discovery in the caves, the Stone of Destiny and the origin of the clan MacDougall, whose clan seat, Dunollie Castle, lies just to the north of the town.

BEN NEVIS

Ben Nevis is the sole survivor of the three recorded legally licensed distilleries to be built in Fort William and was founded in 1825 by 'Long' John Macdonald. Long John's heritage was a rich one: the branch of the clan Macdonald from which he came could trace its ancestry back to Alexander Macdonald, a son of the Lord of the Isles, and ultimately to Somerled, King of Argyll. Long John turned from farming to distilling and his new distillery quickly became successful. He named his whisky Long John's Dew of Ben Nevis, after the most prominent local landmark, and presented a cask to Queen Victoria when she visited the distillery in 1848.

Long John died in 1856 and was succeeded by his son, Donald Peter Macdonald. Ben Nevis expanded until it was making 3,000 gallons of spirit a week, and in 1878 Macdonald built an extension nearby to augment production. The new distillery was christened Nevis, and operated in tandem with its elder sister. The company built a pier on the shore of Loch Linnhe to serve its own fleet of steamers, and a continuous procession of some twenty horses and carts operated between the distillery and the harbour. Nevis survived until 1908, when Macdonald took it out of production, using only its warehousing to supplement Ben Nevis's own. By this time Fort William's third distillery, Glenlochy, had been established, and Macdonald may have doubted the ability of a small western Highland community such as Fort William to sustain three distilleries. Glenlochy's fortunes proved to be chequered, at best. The Macdonald family continued to run Ben Nevis until 1955, by which time they had long since sold off the Long John brand

name, although they continued to market Dew of Ben Nevis, which eventually became a blend.

Just before World War II a number of malt distilleries, including Glenlochy, were acquired by Associated Scottish Distilleries, a company run by Joseph Hobbs on behalf of the National Distillers of America. Hobbs finally sold ASD for £38,000 before moving to Fort William, where he bought Inverlochy Castle and established the Great Glen cattle ranch. Hobbs took over Ben Nevis in 1955 and installed a Coffey still, enabling the distillery to

make malt and grain whisky side by side, although his flirtation with grain distilling was short lived. The distillery closed around 1978, after Hobbs's death, and was bought from his family in 1981 by Long John International, who thus reunited Ben Nevis with the Long John brand name. However, despite refurbishing the distillery, Long John was unable to keep it open for more than two years and, after a further closure, sold it to the Japanese Nikka company in 1989.

Ben Nevis is now one of the very few malt distilleries where one can obtain a cask of whisky for a private bottling. The distillery's 10-year-old single malt has recently won two gold medals at the Brussels Monde Selection competition, and a 26-year-old is also bottled, so your private bottling will be in good hands! In spring 1990 a limited edition of ninety bottles from a 63-year-old cask sold at up to £2,000 a bottle.

TALISKER

The mystical Isle of Skye is the largest of the Inner Hebrides and owes much of its fame to its brief encounter with Bonnie Prince Charlie. Its scenery is spectacular, from the misty Cuillin Hills to the numerous, and sometimes huge, sea lochs which deeply indent its coast. As Islay was to the Macdonalds, Skye was the stronghold of the clan MacLeod and many places on the island feature in occult folklore.

Talisker was founded in 1830 and is the island's only surviving distillery. Built at a cost of £3,000 by Hugh and Kenneth MacAskill, it stands at the foot of Hawk Hill from where the burn which supplies its water tumbles the last hundred yards or so down a narrow waterfall. It has had more than half a dozen owners, one of whom was Roderick Kemp who moved on to Macallan in 1892, selling out to his partner for £12,000. Men from the Hebrides who joined up for World War I

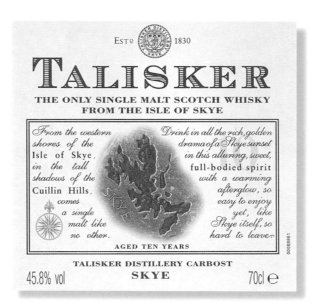

were promised their own crofts after the war and this corner of Skye was set aside for them. The farming community on the island is very tight knit and the distillery manager organises work to fit in with farming schedules. At times of lambing, shearing or dipping, distilling has to take second place.

Many of the workers have other jobs – or maybe distilling is their other job! One man farms oysters on Loch Harport, which are sold locally, and lobsters and velvet crabs which are exported to Spain. One of the stillmen is a shepherd and his three sheepdogs sit patiently outside the stillhouse waiting for him to finish his shift. The manager's own cow used to provide the villagers with fresh milk and at one time the distillery even used to issue its own currency – coins denominated in days' work which employees could 'spend' on the island. Most of the workers have long service records. One was still being referred to as the 'new man' after working there nine years.

The distillery is one of the few in Scotland whose stills are not paired. Talisker has five stills, two for wash and three for low wines, the extra still being there to cope with the volume of low wines generated in the first distillation. The wash stills are unique in having a bend in the vapour delivery pipe and although this must have an effect on the spirit, no one at the distillery is quite sure what. Unusually for a Highland malt (which it technically is) Talisker used triple distillation until 1928, a technique which was not, as is commonly believed, exclusive to the Lowland malt distilleries. The existing stillhouse replaced the original one which was destroyed by fire in 1960.

Skye is known colloquially as *Eilean a' Cheò*, 'isle of the mist'. The visitors' book for 1898–1903 records two visits by the same person. Each time he comments on the 'rainy weather'. The warehouse windows are not glass but wire mesh, to allow the damp sea air to reach the casks. The flavour of this whisky is not just peat and smoke but also brine and bladder-wrack. It is rightly included in UDV's Classic Malts range, and has been partnered with a version finished in amoroso wood.

HIGHLAND PARK

Orkney comprises a group of some seventy islands, the closest of which lies within 10 miles of the north-east tip of the Scottish mainland. The Norsemen arrived in Orkney around a thousand years ago on their way to the Western Isles, and the islands are scattered with antiquities. About twenty of the islands are inhabited, and the North Sea oil industry now plays a big part in their prosperity. Like Islay, Orkney benefits from the warming effects of the Gulf Stream and its climate, although windy, is surprisingly mild for an area on the same latitude as Stockholm.

There have been seven legally licensed distilleries recorded on Orkney, of which Highland Park was the first to be built. All seven were built around the Orkney capital, Kirkwall, or at Stromness. Stromness Distillery itself, or Man O' Hoy as it was later known, was the longest-lived of the 'lost' distilleries, being founded in 1817 and finally falling silent in 1928. The demise of its neighbours has left Highland Park as Scotland's most northerly distillery, by a margin of about half a mile. Orkney's only other surviving distillery, Scapa, was mothballed by Allied Distillers in the early 1990s, although recently it has been working sporadically.

Highland Park was founded by one David Robertson in 1795, making it one of Scotland's oldest surviving malt distilleries. It is reputedly built on the site of a smuggling bothy operated by Magnus Eunson, who was not only an illicit distiller but also a church minister! Stories abound of Eunson's exploits. It is said he hid his illicit whisky in his pulpit, and on one famous occasion when he was tipped off about an impending Excise raid, he and a few compatriots hastily rigged an impromptu funeral service in which the casks of whisky were concealed beneath the coffin! Excise men arriving at the scene were soon discouraged from mounting a search when the word 'smallpox' was heard whispered.

The distillery had many owners throughout the nineteenth century, the Eunson family name cropping up again in 1867. In 1895 the distillery passed to James Grant, whose father was manager of The Glenlivet. Grant enlarged the distillery from two to four stills and his family controlled Highland Park for forty years, finally selling out to the Highland Distilleries Co. in 1935.

The distillery overlooks the town of Kirkwall to the north and Scapa Flow to the south and is built, rather eccentrically, on a hill, which means that its water supply has to be pumped up to it. It still maintains its own floor maltings, has its own peat beds, and has two kilns, in which some heather is burned along with the peat. It also uses three yeasts, instead of the usual two, and a good proportion of sherry butts is used in maturation. Highland Park has been bottled for many years at twelve years old, and the distillers added 18- and 25-year-old versions in 1998. Its reputation also makes it popular with the independents.

SCAPA

Scapa Flow was the principal base for the British naval fleet in both world wars and saw drama in both conflicts. The German fleet was interned there after surrendering to the Allies in November 1918, and was scuttled on 21 June 1919 by the skeleton crews left aboard. On 14 October 1939, shortly after the outbreak of World War II, a German U-boat penetrated Scapa Flow's defences and sank HMS *Royal Oak*.

Scapa Distillery historically has many links with the Royal Navy. Ratings billeted there in World War I saved the distillery from destruction by fire, and officers quartered there built the wooden stairway in the mill room. The Italian chapel on Lamb Holm was built by prisoners of war and is now a tourist attraction.

Scapa Distillery lies to the south-west of Kirkwall on the A964 by the Lingro Burn. It was

founded by Macfarlane and Townsend in 1885 and later continued by J. T. Townsend alone, who also became a director of Linkwood. Alfred Barnard visited Scapa in 1886 and noted that the distillery was of an advanced design for its time. The stills, according to his report, were steam-heated and fitted with anti-collapse valves, devices which are now universally fitted to stills. Townsend was succeeded by the Scapa Distillery Co. Ltd, which was liquidated in 1934–6, after which the distillery was acquired by Bloch Bros, the owner of Glen Scotia Distillery at Campbeltown. Bloch Bros sold its distilleries in 1954 to Hiram Walker, which promptly disposed of Glen Scotia to A. Gillies & Co. Ltd, and licensed Scapa to its subsidiary company Taylor & Ferguson Ltd.

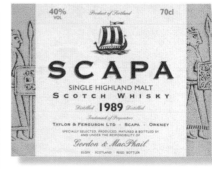

Scapa was rebuilt in 1959, when the wash still was replaced by a Lomond still, a type of cylindrical pot still surmounted by a water jacket which could control the degree of reflux. Walker's took to this device, which was invented by one of its employees, and installed similar stills in three of its other distilleries, Miltonduff, Glenburgie and Inverleven. At those distilleries the Lomond still was used in addition to the conventional pot stills to generate a second malt, distinct from the distillery's main product. At Scapa the Lomond still replaced the normal wash still in the conventional double distillation process. The distillery's water, from the Lingro Burn and local springs, is peaty enough for Scapa to use completely unpeated malt.

Hiram Walker became part of Allied Distillers in 1988 when it was acquired by Allied-Lyons. Scapa was mothballed shortly after its acquisition, although it is now back in sporadic production. Its malt is a component of Ballantine's blend and a 1989 distillation is bottled under licence by Gordon & MacPhail. At the time of its closure the distillery's warehouses held in bond some 23,500 casks, the oldest from a 1965 distillation.

PULTENEY

Pulteney is the most northerly mainland distillery and the only one surviving in Caithness, yet this was formerly a county with a surprisingly active distilling community. Some twenty-nine malt distilleries are recorded as having existed here since the mid-eighteenth century, mostly in or around particular centres such as Thurso, Halkirk and John o' Groats. Twenty-two of these pre-date Pulteney's foundation, although only half a dozen of them were still working by the time Pulteney was built. The fact that many appeared in the records for a single year, and on the map look to be in the middle of nowhere, suggests that they were attached to farms and run briefly by the farmer as a sideline. The more successful ones lasted thirty-odd years, and the last one to vanish was one of those to be built at Halkirk: Gerston. It was at this distillery that William Grant's second son, William

(Inver House Distillers Ltd)

junior, worked briefly as book-keeper. Sadly he never made it into the family business, as he died of typhoid at about the time Glenfiddich began production.

Pulteney was founded in 1826 by James Henderson and is the second distillery recorded at Wick, a town known mainly for its herring fishing. The first, Hempriggs, was built south of the town, near Loch Hempriggs, and worked very briefly at the end of the eighteenth century. Henderson was the distiller at the short-lived Stemster Distillery, founded in 1821, but he is thought to have been distilling illicitly for some years previous to that. The family name crops up at Brawlbin, at Halkirk, and at Clyth, further down the coast. Pulteney was also known as Pulteney Town, the name given to the southern environs of Wick which can be found marked on some maps, and stands on Huddart Street. The family carried on the business as James Henderson & Co. until 1920, when the distillery was acquired by James Watson & Co. of Dundee. Watson's itself was subsequently taken over by Dewar's, and hence passed to DCL in 1925. DCL formed a new subsidiary, Scottish Malt Distillers, in 1930 to handle the business of all its malt distilleries, and Pulteney was promptly closed down.

It remained closed until 1951, when it was revived by Robert Cumming, who had recently acquired Balblair. Cumming sold Pulteney to Hiram Walker in 1955, although he kept Balblair until he retired in 1970, and it was licensed to J. & G. Stodart Ltd, hence passing to Allied Distillers. In June 1995 the distillery was sold to Inver House, which then also acquired Balblair the following year.

Pulteney makes what is said to be a fast-maturing whisky which resembles manzanilla sherry, with a tangy, salty character drawn from the distillery's coastal location. It was one of those malts bottled for Allied by Gordon & MacPhail, in this case as an 8-year-old sold as Old Pulteney. Inver House now bottles a 12-year-old, a 15-year-old single cask version and a whisky liqueur.

CLYNELISH AND BRORA

Clynelish is a name which has been used at one time or another by two distilleries which share a common site. The original distillery was founded in 1819 by the Marquis of Stafford, later the Duke of Sutherland, who played a part in the Highland clearances. Crofters were moved to the coast, to allow landowners the use of the Highland terrain for large-scale, and highly profitable, sheep farms. The crofters were allotted smallholdings on the coastal strip, and it was decided that a distillery would afford them a legitimate market for their grain. The marquis was keen to see an end to illicit distilling in the area, a practice described by his lands commissioner, James Loch, as having 'nursed the people in every species of deceit, vice, idleness and dissipation'.

The distillery was built on Clynelish Farm at a cost of £750 and was purpose-built, as opposed to being converted from farm outbuildings as were many distilleries of the time. Spent grains from the distillery were used to feed pigs, which in turn fertilised the land. The local mine at Brora provided coal to fire the stills. The distillery was first licensed to James Harper, who commenced distilling with a 200-gallon wash still and an 87-gallon spirit still. In the season 1821–2 Harper made 10,015 gallons of whisky, on which he paid duty of £2,774. He was succeeded as licensee by Andrew Ross, then by George Lawson, who extended and improved the distillery. Lawson was a proficient farmer, his cattle and sheep winning prizes at the 1894 Smithfield Show. His whisky was also highly thought-of. His customers throughout the country took so much of his production that for a long time he refused trade orders.

Lawson sold Clynelish to Ainslie & Co., a Leith blending company, in 1896. In 1912 Ainslie's went bankrupt and Clynelish was taken over by its trustee, John Risk, previously owner of Bankier Distillery in Stirlingshire, who brought in DCL as partner to found the Clynelish Distillery Co. This company bought Coleburn in 1916 bringing in as a further partner Johnnie Walker, thus paving the way for Clynelish's absorption into DCL when DCL and Walker's finally merged.

The Depression forced Clynelish to close in 1931. It reopened in 1938, just in time for the onset of the war, which shut it down again, this time until November 1945. It was not until the 1960s that mains electricity supplanted the old steam engine and the stills were converted to steam heating. The last consignment of coal from the Brora mine was delivered on 4 November 1966.

The following year a new distillery was built alongside and named Clynelish. The old distillery closed for rebuilding, after which it reopened as Brora Distillery in April 1975. Recession forced the closure of Brora in 1983, and its buildings are now used by the new distillery for warehousing and for a visitor centre. Clynelish makes a powerful, spicy, briny malt which evinces the distillery's coastal location and has appeared in UDV's Flora & Fauna range at fourteen years old.

BALBLAIR

(Inver House Distillers Ltd)

Balblair is one of the oldest distilleries in Scotland and one of two in the area of the Dornoch Firth. It dates from 1790 and is often confused with an earlier illicit still at the village of Balblair in the Black Isle, founded some forty-one years before. The distillery was originally further up the hill and moved to its present location after the lease changed hands in 1894. The name Balblair means 'battlefield' and was probably coined when the Vikings raided this part of Scotland about a thousand years ago.

The distillery is in the village of Edderton, known as the 'parish of peat', in the county of Ross-shire. The surname Ross is prevalent in this area. The distillery was founded by John Ross and remained in his family until it was sold by his grandson James in 1894. When operations were restarted after World War II one of the first employees was Hugh Ross, who eventually retired from the distillery after forty-two years' service.

Balblair's lease was taken over from the Ross family by Alexander Cowan, a wine merchant from Inverness. It was Cowan who moved the distillery to its new site and constructed many of the present buildings, including the dunnage

warehousing. Until fire regulations dictated the building of a dividing wall part-way along, Balblair had the longest bonded warehouse of any distillery in Scotland. All its warehousing is earth-floored except for No. 3, which has a concrete floor left there by the army, which commandeered the buildings for the duration of World War II and built its canteen there.

After the war the distillery was purchased by Robert Cumming, a solicitor from Banff. One night, after a few too many drams in a public house in Tain, Cumming told the landlord that he would buy the place and promptly signed a cheque on the spot. The landlord returned it to him the following day when he returned a little more sober!

Cumming had high hopes for the distillery and embarked on a successful programme of expansion. The stills were converted to steam heating and a new wash still installed. The old riveted wash still remains and is the only one of its type left in the industry. A new boilerhouse was built, the tun room extended and two more washbacks added. Hot water for mashing is derived from the condensers, where the cooling water is heated by the distillate as it runs through. The distillery's maltings closed in 1975 and the malt barn is now used as a hospitality suite for entertaining large groups of the company's visitors.

In 1970 Cumming retired, selling out to Hiram Walker which is now a subsidiary of Allied Distillers. Allied was on the verge of mothballing the distillery when it was bought in 1996 by Inver House Distillers. Balblair's malt was being bottled for Allied under licence by Gordon & MacPhail, but Inver House now bottles a 16-year-old and a version without age statement known as Balblair Elements. The oldest cask in Balblair's warehouse is from a 1952 distillation and would be highly prized for a limited edition.

GLENMORANGIE

On the outskirts of Tain, the oldest royal burgh, Glenmorangie backs onto the Dornoch Firth. It takes its name from its location in the Glen of the Morangie Burn, which in Gaelic means 'great tranquillity'. It stands on a site which has been used for brewing purposes since the Middle Ages and, like its sister Glen Moray, started life as a brewery, being converted for distilling in 1843.

Over recent years the distillery has been refurbished, with particular attention being paid to the stillhouse. Converted from an existing duty-free warehouse, it is beautifully panelled and fitted in natural wood. The eight stills are the tallest in Scotland at 16ft 10¼in and of these four are new, built to the original design by McMillans coppersmiths of Edinburgh. Before use they had to be 'sweetened' (to remove any remaining copper residue) by boiling a mixture of water, peat, heather and herbs in each one. Glenmorangie is one of the few distilleries to have hard water and this has caused a few

problems in the past, the water pipes in the condensers becoming so clogged with limescale that it has had to be drilled out.

Locked away in one of the warehouses is a unique piece of furniture, an antique oak desk which used to occupy the office of the resident Excise officer, or gauger, as he was called. These days, every dram of whisky in the warehouses is recorded and accounted for. In the early days, it was accepted practice for both manager and gauger to have their own private supply. The gauger kept his bottle in the right-hand drawer of his desk. The left-hand drawer belonged to his superior, a government surveyor, and the centre drawer was kept locked. Whenever the surveyor paid one of his regular visits the gauger simply pushed his illicit bottle through a hole into the locked centre drawer to be retrieved later when the coast was clear. Now that the law has become

much tighter, candidates for a gauger's post must prove that they are teetotal.

Apprentices in any distillery traditionally started in the maltings. Floor malting is a long, tedious and back-breaking job, and apprentices would spend a full eight-hour shift tending the grain. In the warmth of the maltings a tiring job such as this could easily lead to them losing concentration, even falling asleep, and left unturned the malt would be ruined. To avoid this, a new apprentice would be taken aside on his first day and the manager would warn him about the ghost known as the White Lady, said to haunt the maltings. The mere sight of her had driven men mad, he would be told. Strangely, Glenmorangie has no record of any of its apprentices ever falling asleep during a shift! The distillery no longer operates its own maltings and apprentices now start their careers in the cooperage which, the manager tells them, is haunted by the ghost of the White Lady…

DALMORE

Fifteen miles due north of Inverness is the old naval base of Invergordon, now the site of the most northerly of Scotland's grain distilleries and repair yards for the North Sea drilling rigs. Whilst the oil industry was in the doldrums redundant rigs would be anchored in the firth, incongruous against the huddle of Dalmore's old stone buildings at the edge of the marsh.

The distillery was founded in 1839 by Alexander Matheson on the site of Ardross Farm and later passed to the Mackenzies, a distinguished local family. Their distinctive stag's head logo comes from the coat of arms of the Mackenzie clan, arms granted to the clan chief by King Alexander III some 700 years ago after the chief saved the king from a charging stag whilst hunting. The Mackenzie family were friends of James Whyte and Charles Mackay, who in 1882 founded the company which is now Dalmore's parent. The name Dalmore probably comes from a combination of Norse and Gaelic words taken to mean 'great meadow', an apt description of the surrounding area. The site was carefully chosen: it was well supplied with locally grown barley and the company secured the exclusive right to draw water from the River Alness, a source still in use today.

The distillery is said to resemble a country railway station and the offices, which overlook the firth and the Black Isle beyond, are partly furnished in oak panelling taken from a shooting lodge. During World War I it was commandeered by the Admiralty on behalf of the US Navy and used as a base for the manufacture of deep-sea mines. Towards the end of the war the inevitable happened, and some of the distillery buildings were destroyed in an explosion. Miraculously the stills were undamaged, but the rebuilding work took four years and Dalmore did not begin distilling again until 1922.

Subsequent expansion has doubled the number of stills to eight, the four new ones being of a smaller design than the originals. Each of the spirit stills has a 'boil ball' at the base of the neck, and is surmounted by a water jacket which partly cools the raw spirit before it enters the condensers. Although, as in any distillery, the stills have had sections replaced over the years, one of them still has a mid-section remaining from when it was built in 1874. The distillery operated its own malt floor until 1956, when it changed to a Saladin box system. The maltings closed for good in 1981, and all Dalmore's malt now comes from commercial maltsters.

Dalmore is regarded as a premium malt by blenders and is an important component in Whyte & Mackay's own blends. The spirit is aged in sherry wood and American oak, with a good proportion of sherry butts being used, and the company bottles it at twelve years old as its flagship single malt.

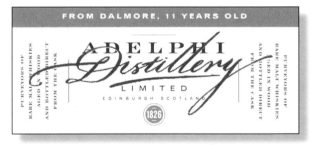

TEANINICH

Not far from Dalmore, just west of Alness, stands Teaninich Distillery. Founded in 1817 by Captain Hugh Munro, the owner of Teaninich estate, it was built at a time when many Ross-shire parishes were using their entire barley crops in illicit distilling, and landlords were being encouraged by the authorities to build legal distilleries in order to stamp out the illicit trade and improve the quality of the end product.

The distillery subsequently passed to Lieutenant General John Munro who, despite his long absences on service in India, was highly respected for his charitable work amongst his tenants, visiting them in person to distribute medicines, provisions and fuel. His army commitments led the general to lease out Teaninich, first to Robert Pattison in 1850, then in 1869 to John McGilchrist Ross, who was lessee when Alfred Barnard visited the distillery. Barnard noted that the distillery was the only one north of Inverness to have electric lighting, and that it was connected to the proprietor's house and Excise officer's quarters by telephone. In 1895 John McGilchrist Ross transferred the lease to Munro & Cameron, an Elgin company formed by John Munro, a spirit merchant, and whisky broker Robert Innes Cameron. Munro & Cameron purchased the assets outright in 1898 and embarked on a programme of improvements which cost the company around £10,000. Innes Cameron became sole proprietor of Teaninich in 1904, by which time he also had interests in other distilleries including Benrinnes, Linkwood and Tamdhu, and was an influential figure in the industry. When he died in 1932, prime minister Ramsay MacDonald sent a wreath to his funeral. A year later Cameron's trustees sold Teaninich to Scottish Malt Distillers Ltd.

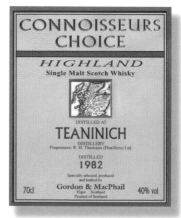

The distillery closed in 1939 for the duration of World War II. It had impressed one visitor as being rather primitive, with clay malt floors and two pairs of stills, one pair of which were particularly small. When it reopened in 1946 the small stills were removed. Milling and mashing were powered by a steam engine, backed up by a waterwheel. A smaller waterwheel, fed from the worm tubs' overflow, powered the rummager. Electric power took over when the stillhouse was refitted in 1962. Two more stills were installed and the coal furnaces gave way to steam heating. A new stillhouse, containing a further six stills, was commissioned in 1970. It became known as 'A side', the original part of the distillery becoming 'B side'. The milling, mashing and fermenting parts of 'B side' were rebuilt in 1973, and a dark grains plant was built two years later. Process and cooling water is drawn from Dairywell spring on the Novar estate, about 2 miles to the west.

Teaninich was mothballed from 1985 to 1991, when 'A side' resumed production. Its single malt now appears in UDV's Flora & Fauna range, bottled at ten years old. The label features the porpoise, which can be seen in the Cromarty Firth, one of its few natural habitats in the British Isles, and part of the shore of the firth near the distillery is a designated nature conservation area.

GLEN ORD

Glen Ord is another of those malt distilleries which lie within a stone's throw of the A9, Scotland's main arterial road which runs from Falkirk to John o' Groats, and it is the site of one of UDV's regional maltings. Muir of Ord is an unremarkable place which none the less has two claims to fame, or rather one claim to fame and one to infamy.

Its most famous son was Sir Roderick Murchison, a noted geologist. Murchison was one of the founding members of the Royal Geographical Society and also founded the Chair of Geology and Mineralogy at the University of Edinburgh.

Ord's claim to infamy goes back to the seventeenth century. It is the site of the chapel of Cilliechriost, or Christchurch, where one of the most inhuman acts of the clan wars was perpetrated. The Macdonald and Mackenzie clans were bitter rivals, and one Sunday morning the Macdonalds seized their chance to attack their enemies whilst they attended Mass. Barricading the church, the Macdonalds set it alight. Everyone inside perished in the flames. The surviving members of the Mackenzie clan exacted a poetic revenge. Finding thirty-seven of the Macdonalds celebrating their victory at an inn near Inverness, they imprisoned them inside and razed it to the ground.

Ord Distillery was founded in 1838 and at the time was one of ten licensed stills in the parish. It shared the site with a meal mill, to which the rights to the estate's water supply belonged. After its

(United Distillers & Vintners)

first two owners went bankrupt, the widow of the second was sensible enough to marry a banker from Beauly, who became the distillery's third owner. In 1923 Glen Ord was acquired by John Dewar & Sons Ltd. Dewar's became a subsidiary of DCL and, following a period of closure during World War II, DCL set about the task of bringing Ord up to date. Until it gained a mains electricity supply in 1949 the distillery was lit by paraffin lamps, a perilous method in premises awash with highly flammable spirit (as was discovered at Dalwhinnie). Experiments were conducted to determine the relative merits of heating the stills by coal, oil or steam, experiments which resulted in many of DCL's distilleries converting their stills to steam-coil heating. By 1966, the distillery had been entirely rebuilt and re-equipped.

The floor maltings was converted in 1961 to a Saladin box system and heather was mixed with the peat during kilning, a method also used by Highland Park Distillery on Orkney. A new maltings was completed in 1968 which supplies seven other distilleries in the north of Scotland and Skye. It is a drum maltings having eighteen drums, each with a capacity of 30 tons. Barley is delivered to Ord sidings in trainloads of around 600 tons at a time, and conveyed on to the maltings by road. A dark grains plant, working alongside the maltings, converts by-products into animal feedstuffs.

During the period of its existence the distillery seems to have suffered something of a recurring identity crisis. Only recently has it shared the same name as its whisky, being known at various times as Ord, Muir of Ord and now Glen Ord. Its single malt started life as Glen Oran and is now bottled at twelve years old as Glen Ord.

TOMATIN

Sixteen miles south-east of Inverness the village of Tomatin lies beside the main A9 road in the valley of Strath Dearn, which carries the River Findhorn from the foothills of the Monadhliath Mountains on its journey to the Moray Firth. The village is ringed by peaks which exceed 2,000ft, and near the distillery is the 'Hill of Parting', which marks the location of the disbanding of the clans following their defeat at Culloden. Three miles south of the village the A9 passes over Slochd Summit, the highest point on the main road between Inverness and Strath Spey. Tomatin Distillery is one of the highest in Scotland, at 1,028ft above sea level.

The distillery was founded in 1897 by the Tomatin Spey District Distillery Co. Ltd, and has grown like Topsy since its modest birth. Its first owner lasted only a decade before going into liquidation, and the distillery was reopened in 1909 by the New Tomatin Distillers Co. Ltd. Tomatin had but a single pair of stills until 1956, when the company began an ambitious expansion programme which was to span eighteen years, beginning with the addition of a second pair of stills. Another pair was added in 1958, four more in 1961, another one in 1964, and finally twelve were added together in 1974, taking the total to twenty-three. Over this period the company invested £5 million, including the purchase in 1967 of the first lauter mash tun to be installed in a Scottish distillery. Further funds were raised in 1981 when a new share issue was sold to a subsidiary of Heineken, giving it a 20 per cent stake in the company. In 1985 the company was liquidated and Tomatin was subsequently sold to the Japanese consortium Takara, Shuzo Co. Ltd, making it the first Scottish distillery to come entirely under Japanese ownership.

Tomatin now has a production capacity of some 5 million proof gallons per annum, but it has never operated at anything like its full capability. Six wash stills and six spirit stills, each of 3,700-gallon capacity, are in use, and the stillhouse can be controlled by a single stillman from the ground floor level. A good job too, as it has been extended bit by bit as more stills have been added, making it a rabbit warren of copper pots, charger tanks and pipework which makes it difficult to see clearly from one end to the other. Process water comes from the Allt-na-Frithe burn, a tributary of the Findhorn, which rises in the Monadhliath Mountains. Tomatin's sixteen warehouses hold some 215,000 casks and the distillers bottle its single malt at twelve years old.

SPEYSIDE

Scotland grain distillery at Cambus, who bought the site at Drumguish, by the River Tromie, in 1956. The distillery building was erected on the estate for other purposes by dry-stone dyker Alex Fairlie, who worked on it virtually single-handedly for about seventeen years. Christie decided that it was too expensive to buy out an existing distillery, but the new building suited his needs perfectly. Work started on the conversion in March 1990 and the distillery was up and running that November, narrowly following Kininvie into production. The distillery stands alongside the original Tromie Mill, which is used as the office and mill room, and the old milling machinery and water wheel are still in place. There are no warehouses on site – spirit is tankered to the company's bonds at Glasgow – and, as at Edradour and Arran, the process takes place in a single building which houses a 4-ton-capacity semi-lauter mash tun, four stainless steel washbacks and a single pair of small stills. The stills were supposedly designed to mimic the shape of a bottle once used by George Christie for his blends!

Speyside's single malt was first sold as Drumguish, after its location, and went on sale without age statement as soon as it reached the legal minimum age of three years, certainly the youngest single malt currently bottled by a Scottish distillery. Now that the distillery has a few years' production under its belt Drumguish continues to be bottled alongside a 10-year-old malt which is sold as Speyside. The company also sells a vatted malt called Glentromie. George Christie retired to Old Milton, the nearby residence of the MD of the original Speyside distillery, and the company was acquired in September 2000 by a consortium which numbers amongst its members Christie's son.

K ingussie is a small town on the River Spey some 10 miles north-east of Dalwhinnie, and confusingly has seen two distilleries built there which share the same name. The original Speyside Distillery was built in 1895 and stood near the junction of the main street with what is now the B970. It was founded by Sir George MacPherson Grant, the Laird of Ballindalloch, who was also involved with the company which built Tomatin, and run by another George Grant, who had retired in 1893 from Glen Grant due to ill health. The

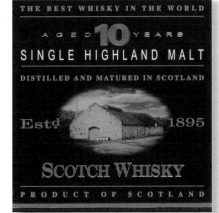

distillery never seemed to find its feet, despite help from Charles Doig, and George Grant left in 1897, passing away a few months later at the tender age of forty-seven. The company was wound up in 1911 and the distillery, which had cost £20,000 to build, was sold for £750 and promptly largely demolished. The worm tub was sold to Dalwhinnie, where it survived until 1986.

The new Speyside Distillery stands in spectacular countryside near to the confluence of the Tromie and the Spey, with the ruin of Ruthven Barracks to one side and an RSPB nature reserve on the other. It was the brainchild of blender George Christie, former owner of the North of

DALWHINNIE

D alwhinnie stands at the entrance to the Drumochter Pass on the main A9 road from Inverness to Perth and is the highest distillery in Scotland at 1,164ft above sea level. An inscribed stone at the summit of the pass marks the spot where General Wade's road-building troops met, one team working from Dunkeld, the other working south from Inverness. The roads from Inverness and Fort Augustus also mark the original routes taken by drovers on their way to the cattle fairs in the Lowlands and Dalwhinnie is where they would have rested the herds.

It is a desolate and lonely place. Besides the distillery, the village itself is little more than a couple of hotels, a tea room and a petrol station. The moorland behind the distillery was the site of the encampment of Prince Charles Stuart and his army in 1745 and also the scene of a great clan battle between the followers of Athol and the Macphersons of Cluny, in which the Macphersons were badly beaten.

Dalwhinnie began production in February 1898 and was at that time called Strathspey. This would seem to be stretching a point a little considering its distance from Speyside, but a look at the map will show that the Spey rises in the Monadhliath Mountains to the west and passes within a few miles of the distillery. The first venture was not a success and in 1905 the distillery was sold for £1,250 to Cook & Bernheimer of New York, the largest distillers in the US at that time. The name was changed to Dalwhinnie just before the sale. Their involvement ended with the enactment of Prohibition in 1919 and Dalwhinnie changed hands three times, finally joining DCL.

Until 1934 the village had no electricity and no telephone. Steam engines were used for power and paraffin lamps for lighting, and it was perhaps due to these that an outbreak of fire caused extensive damage which resulted in the closure of the distillery. Rebuilding and refitting took four years. The stills were converted to steam heating in 1961 and further modernisation took place in 1970 and 1972.

The distillery is Station 0582 of the Meteorological Office and the manager's job also entails taking records of temperatures, wind speed, sunshine and snow depth. It is a well-chosen station for this purpose as it is not uncommon for the village to be snowbound for four or five days at a time in winter. Records from the bad winter of 1937 tell of snowdrifts 20ft deep, and the only way for the villagers to leave their houses was through a first-floor window.

Dalwhinnie is now licensed to James Buchanan & Co. Ltd, and its malt is a major component in the company's well-known Black & White blend, as well as being bottled as a 15-year-old single malt as part of UDV's Classic Malts range. The distillery also features a heritage centre, built in 1992 at a cost of some £½ million.

ROYAL BRACKLA

The coastal plain between Nairn and Inverness is an area steeped in some of the richest of Scotland's history and legends. The battle of Culloden was fought here in 1746, and Shakespeare set much of Macbeth in the area around Cawdor. Indeed, the play is based on historical fact: Macbeth was Thane of Cawdor and succeeded to the throne by murdering his cousin, King Duncan, in 1040 and was himself murdered by Duncan's son Malcolm after a successful reign of seventeen years.

A plan of Cawdor estate dating from 1773 shows the distillery site as that of a 'malt brewhouse', and was probably the site of the original Cawdor Castle. Legend has it that when the thane wanted to build a new tower, he chose the present location after it was shown to him by a magician in a dream. He was told it would be by a hawthorn tree, and visitors can still see the dried-up stem of the tree (which has since been proved to be a holly, radiocarbon dated to the fourteenth century) in the castle's ground-floor guard house.

Brackla was established in 1812 by Captain William Fraser and given its 'Royal' prefix in 1835 by William IV, who obviously liked its product. Fraser was forced to compete on rather unequal terms with Speyside's many illicit distillers and had to develop markets further afield, sending whisky by land transport to Aberdeen and the Lowlands. When the Excise Act of 1823 reduced duty to realistic levels his sales increased substantially, from 5,660 gallons in 1822 to nearly 37,000 gallons in 1833. However, Fraser was not the most law-abiding of distillers and was fined five times between 1827 and 1844, the fines rising to a hefty £600.

Fraser was justifiably proud of his royal warrant, the first to be granted to a whisky distiller, and crowed about it in an advert placed in a London newspaper, *The Morning Chronicle*. The 'king's own whisky', it said, could be obtained from the sales agent, Graham & Co., opposite the Marylebone workhouse! A second royal warrant was granted by Queen Victoria in 1838. For much of the second half of the nineteenth century Brackla's sales agent was Andrew Usher, who also became a partner in the distillery, and it is a fairly safe bet that Brackla would have been a constituent of the very first brands of blended Scotch whisky to be sold.

The distillery was rebuilt in 1890 and subsequently changed hands a number of times, passing to John Bisset & Co. and finally to DCL in 1943. It was modernised in the mid-1960s and new warehousing was built in 1975. Brackla was mothballed in 1985 and was reopened by United Distillers in 1991. Its single malt appeared in the Flora & Fauna series at ten years old, until the distillery was sold to Bacardi following the Guinness-Grand Met merger. It has also appeared in both Cadenhead's and Gordon & MacPhail's Connoisseurs Choice ranges, and is described as a classic.

Speyside

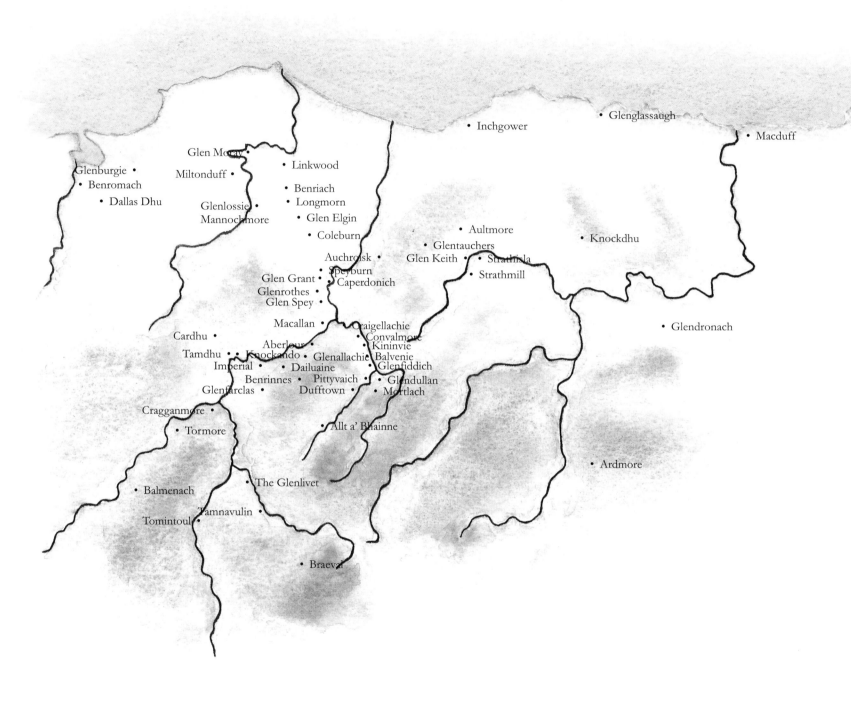

BENROMACH

Benromach Distillery is sited at Forres, and stands right beside the main A96 which bypasses the town. Its brick chimney, almost 100ft tall, makes a prominent landmark. The distillery is now owned by Gordon & MacPhail, a company whose story parallels that of some of the whisky industry's pioneers – a blending and bottling company treading the seemingly inevitable path to the ownership of its own distillery.

Benromach was founded in 1898 and was built at about the same time as Dallas Dhu. The founding partners were Duncan MacCallum, founder of Glen Nevis in Campbeltown, and whisky broker F. W. Brickmann, who was also a director of Oban and Aultmore Distilleries Ltd. It was designed by Charles Doig, architect of a number of Speyside distilleries, and was in the process of having its roof installed when the Pattison crash occurred. Brickmann was closely associated with Pattison's and his own firm failed a few months later. The opening of Benromach was postponed, and it seems possible that it remained silent until 1909. MacCallum was in dispute with the Inland Revenue over a rates assessment, claiming that the distillery had not commenced operations. The taxman was unimpressed, pointing out that all its equipment was installed, and the claim was dismissed. MacCallum sold out.

After World War I Benromach was acquired by John Joseph Calder, who had interests in various food- and drink-related companies. He sold it to the Benromach Distillery Ltd, whose main shareholders were Macdonald, Greenlees & Williams Ltd, a company controlled by his brother James (and the owner of Glendullan Distillery in Dufftown), and six England-based brewery companies. They in turn sold it to Joseph Hobbs's Associated Scottish Distilleries Ltd. Hobbs flitted around the whisky industry, both in Scotland and in America, building

up ASD to the ownership of seven distilleries before selling out and moving to Fort William, where he took over Ben Nevis Distillery. ASD was acquired by the National Distillers of America, which sold Benromach, together with Glenesk, Glenlochy and Glenury (Bruichladdich and Fettercairn found other buyers and Strathdee probably remained closed after World War II) to DCL in 1953.

DCL licensed Benromach to J. & W. Hardie Ltd, blenders of The Antiquary, which operated it until it closed in 1983, the last filling being made on 24 March, marked by the signatures of the workmen on the filling store wall. Gordon & MacPhail

acquired the site in 1993 and began refurbishing it. The new stills were specifically designed to yield a rich spirit and so are smaller than the original pair, which were believed to be the first stills to be heated by direct oil firing. The new stills are steam heated. The four larch washbacks had to be reassembled, like some gigantic jigsaw, from their component staves. In 1998, its centenary year, the distillery came back into production. Gordon & MacPhail has bottled Benromach's malt for some time now and produced a 17-year-old Centenary bottling by way of celebration. A 15-year-old malt was selected and finished for a further two years in three sherry casks dating from 1886, 1895 and 1901. On 15 October 1998 Benromach was officially reopened by HRH the Prince of Wales, Duke of Rothesay.

GLENBURGIE

L ike nearby Brackla, Glenburgie stands in an area of countryside scattered with the ruins of castles and abbeys and rich in myths of the occult, and in particular the legend of Macbeth. About a mile to the east is a hill called The Knock. It is now marked by the York Tower but is said to have been the site of Macbeth's meeting with the three witches. Shakespeare rather misrepresented Macbeth in the name of art, but there were allegedly witches in this area, back in the days when witch-hunting was a popular pastime, and three were executed at Forres in AD 965 for the murder of King Duffus.

The distillery is in a small valley in the Monaughty Forest between Forres and Elgin, and is only about 3 miles from the sea. It was founded as the Kilnflat Distillery in 1829 and had a still capacity of 90 gallons. Some years later it fell into disuse but was revived in 1878 by Charles Kay and renamed Glenburgie. It passed through the hands of three further owners, each of whom increased its capacity, until it was acquired by Ballantine's in 1936. It is now operated by Ballantine's parent company, Allied Distillers.

Like many distillers Ballantine's attempted to keep the operation as traditional as possible, but economics forced it to discontinue floor malting in 1958 and the distillery's weekly malt requirement now comes from Allied Distillers' central maltings, Robert Kilgour & Co., at Kirkcaldy. There are now seven steel washbacks in addition to the six old wooden ones, and two pairs of stills of 3,000 gallons capacity each. The distillery's current annual

capability of around 1 million gallons is twenty-five times its capacity a century ago.

In 1958 Glenburgie became one of the four Ballantine distilleries to have Lomond stills fitted. This was a variant of the pot still designed by a former Hiram Walker employee, the late Fred Whiting, and was cylindrical in design, with an 8ft column in place of the normal swan neck and a water jacket on top of that which controlled the degree of reflux (the amount of spirit vapour condensing and running back down into the still). A separate condenser followed. It produced a characteristic heavy, oily spirit which matured into a powerful single malt. The product of the Lomond stills was different enough from Glenburgie's

usual single malt to be sold as a separate whisky and was named Glencraig, after Bill Craig, the general manager of Allied Distillers' Malt Distilleries. Mr Craig, who retired in June 1993 after forty-nine years' service with the company, has the honour of being one of the very few people to have a malt whisky named after him and it is still possible to find it in independent bottlings, but supplies will be finite as the Lomond stills were removed in 1981. The bulk of Glenburgie's single malt goes into Ballantine's blends but when it is available, it is bottled by independent suppliers and has somehow managed to acquire the appellation of 'Glenlivet'.

DALLAS DHU

People's natural reaction is to laugh when told that Dallas, Texas, was named after a tiny hamlet in the Scottish Highlands, yet this is not far from the truth. The village was acquired from the Crown in 1279 by William de Ripley and Dallas, Texas, was named after one of his descendants, then US vice-president George Dallas, in 1845.

The distillery was originally to have been called Dallasmore and was built on Alexander Edward's Sanquhar estate, some 6 miles from Dallas, by Wright & Greig Ltd, a Glasgow blending firm. It sits in a hollow, which was considered an advantage in that the water supply would come in under pressure. However, the ground turned out to be boggy and some of the walls began to sink almost as soon as they were built. Construction work was finally completed in April 1899, just in time for the recession which followed the Pattison crash. In November that year, the company invited orders for its Dallas Dhu whisky. No explanation for the name change was given.

Dallas Dhu changed hands twice before its owner was acquired by DCL in 1929. On the night of 9 April 1939 farm workers were awakened by a loud crackling noise to find flames leaping through the stillhouse roof. It took the Forres Fire Brigade four hours to control the blaze and prevent it from spreading to the rest of the distillery. The damage was estimated at £7,000. The distillery remained closed for the duration of World War II and it was not until 1950, when it was connected to the national grid, that any degree of modernisation took place. The wash still rummager was powered by a waterwheel up until 1971.

Despite the relatively small production of its single pair of stills, and its lengthy periods of closure, Dallas Dhu nevertheless achieved a high reputation and although it closed for good in the early 1980s its single malt is still bottled by Gordon & MacPhail.

In 1988 it was reopened by Scotland's Historic Buildings and Monuments Directorate as a time capsule of the distilling industry, and is now part of Speyside's Whisky Trail. It is a 'hands-on' museum, where visitors can try their hand at operating the spirit safe, peer into the stills and climb inside the mash tun. Although guided tours are available, it is far more fun to follow the white footprints painted on the floor and wander through the buildings at your own pace. The workers' various tasks are explained by a number of wax dummies, whose prerecorded 'voices' are activated by the press of a button. Visiting on a quiet day is a very strange sensation, as if the entire workforce had just mysteriously vanished and been replaced by these effigies.

It is an interesting concept for a museum, and all the more so for allowing visitors free rein to explore. Following closures forced by the 1990s recession Bladnoch, the most southerly malt distillery in Scotland, has succeeded in gaining a new lease of life in a similar manner.

MILTONDUFF

The first mention of whisky in official records referred to a certain friar John Cor making aqua vitae from malt, and monasteries have always made their own liquor in one form or another. Miltonduff stands on land that once belonged to the Benedictine Priory of Pluscarden, originally one of the wealthiest monastic settlements in Scotland, whose estate stretched from Elgin to Rothes. One New Year's Day in the fifteenth century, a ceremony took place in the grounds of the priory. The old abbot led the monks to the banks of the Black Burn and, kneeling on a stone, blessed the waters of the stream. From that day, the spirit distilled with water from that stream would be known as aqua vitae – 'water of life'.

It is said that there were fifty illicit stills on the Black Burn and Miltonduff was built on the site of one of them, legally licensed in 1824. The priory's original brewhouse became the stillhouse and tun room of the new distillery and the stone on which the abbot knelt, some 400 years before, was built into the wall of the malt mill. The work was carried out by Andrew Pearey and Robert Bain, who acquired the site from one of the original smugglers. Nearby was the home of Enoch Arden. Arden was something of a local celebrity, having bigamously married whilst abroad. The whole thing was due to a lack of communication which led him to believe that his wife had died. On returning to Scotland, he not only found her alive and well but willing to accept his new wife and family into her home!

The distillery later passed to William Stuart and thence to Thomas Yool, who sold out to Hiram Walker in 1936. It is now owned by Allied Distillers. Walker's expanded the distillery shortly after acquiring it, and again in the 1970s. From the 2-acre site it occupied at the time of Stuart's ownership, it has grown to cover 185 acres and has an annual capacity of 2 million proof gallons. Walker's also installed a Lomond still, a special type of column-shaped still which worked on the same principle as a conventional pot still and produced a heavy, oily spirit. The company seemed to take to this invention and installed it in a number of its distilleries, usually using it to make a second malt which would be sold under a different name from that of the distillery itself. The whisky made in Miltonduff's Lomond still was sold as Mosstowie, named after a hamlet about a mile away. It is no longer made, but it has appeared in Gordon & MacPhail's Connoisseurs Choice range and limited stocks may still be available.

Miltonduff is one of eighteen distilleries which class themselves as Glenlivets, despite being a good 20 miles from the nearest point of the Livet Water. In the nineteenth century it became a selling point to claim the use of the Glenlivet suffix, although Allied prefer to think of it as an appellation, or regional definition. It would be more accurate, perhaps, to call it a Glenlossie.

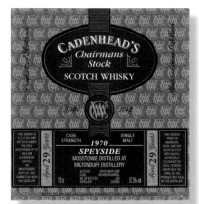

GLENLOSSIE AND MANNOCHMORE

Glenlossie was built in 1876 by John Duff, the tenant of the Fife Arms at Lhanbryde and one-time manager of Glendronach. It is situated at Thomshill, to the south of Elgin, and some 2 miles from the Millbuies nature reserve.

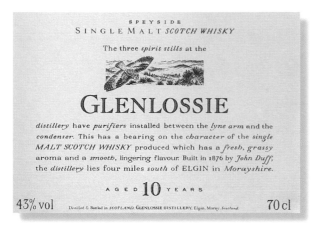

Duff was joined in the venture by two partners, Alexander Grigor Allan, Procurator Fiscal of Morayshire, and H. M. S. Mackay, burgh surveyor of Elgin. Duff himself drew up the plans for the distillery in collaboration with Elgin architect A. Marshall Mackenzie. There was a fall of some 70ft between the dam and the 8hp waterwheel which ensured that there was plenty of water power for driving the machinery without having to resort to buying a steam engine. The distillery was built of cement made from sand and gravel taken from the nearby River Lossie.

By 1887 the Glasgow blending company John Hopkins & Co. were sole agents for the sale of Glenlossie's malt, and Hopkins himself had become a partner in the business. After Duff's departure (he founded Longmorn in 1894) the company was liquidated and reformed in 1896 as the Glenlossie-Glenlivet Distillery Co. The share issue was more than three times over-subscribed. The company extended the distillery and built a siding to Longmorn station to reduce cartage costs. After a brief closure by government order during World War I, Glenlossie was acquired by Scottish Malt Distillers, a subsidiary of DCL, and it is still owned by their successor, United Distillers & Vintners.

Glenlossie suffered a serious fire on 6 March 1929 which caused some £6,000 worth of damage and resulted in the closure of the distillery for the rest of that season. The fire was fought by the distillery's own horse-drawn Shand Mason fire engine, which was built in 1862 and won a prize at the International Exhibition at Crystal Palace in that year. The engine was never used again.

Scottish Malt Distillers began to expand the distillery in the mid-1950s. Electricity came to Glenlossie as late as 1960, and two more stills were installed in 1962, making a total of six. The three spirit stills have purifiers installed between the lyne arms and the condensers. In 1971 the company built Mannochmore Distillery on the same site. Like Glenlossie, Mannochmore also has six stills, but without purifiers. All six are steam heated, and Glenlossie's stills were converted to steam heating after Mannochmore was built. The two distilleries take their process water from the same source: the Bardon Burn. A dark grains plant built in 1969 serves both distilleries.

Although not well known, Glenlossie appears to have a good reputation. Mannochmore has only recently appeared as a bottled single malt, and both malts now have a place in UDV's Flora & Fauna range, perhaps reflecting the distilleries' proximity to the nature reserve, Glenlossie's at ten years old and Mannochmore's at twelve years old. Both distilleries are licensed to Haig's and their products form components of that company's blends.

GLEN MORAY

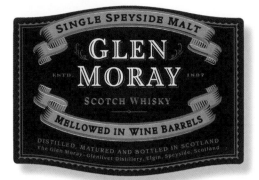

The royal burgh of Elgin is an elegant medieval city which nestles in the loops of the River Lossie and is the administrative capital of the district of Moray. The town centre is bordered by Lady Hill to the west, atop which was the castle, and the cathedral to the east. Over the centuries, this once-magnificent building has

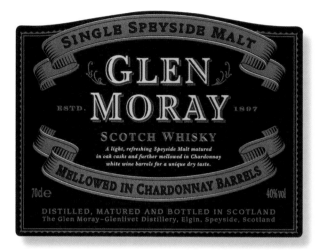

suffered many indignities: it was burned by the 'Wolf of Badenoch', the illegitimate son of King Robert II, and had the lead stripped from its roof by the Regent Moray who sold it to pay his army's wages.

Below Gallow Hill, the city's original place of execution, the old road into Elgin passes through the grounds of Henry Arnot's West Brewery which, in 1897, became the second of Elgin's two distilleries. The old brewery arch still exists, appearing as a huge stone face which silently contemplates you as you enter the courtyard. The whisky boom ended shortly after the distillery began production and its owner, R. J. Thorne, eventually went into liquidation. In 1920

it was acquired from the liquidator by Macdonald & Muir Ltd, which had been a regular customer for its single malt for use in its blending operations (it is still used in its Highland Queen blend). It is a coincidence that Glen Moray's sister distillery, Glenmorangie, also started life as a brewery.

In 1958 the distillery was refurbished and expanded but the temptation to increase the size of the stills was resisted and the original designs holding 2,000 gallons of wash and 1,400 gallons of low wines were retained. This is perhaps smaller than would be the current average, but two of each of these stills now give Glen Moray an annual production capacity of around 700,000 proof gallons. All four stills are heated by steam coil, and the wash stills have in addition steam cans, or kettles, attached to the coils. These are

simply stainless steel cylinders projecting upwards from the steam coil which help to distribute the heat from the coil more evenly through the wash, which being a milky liquid takes more effort to heat. Since the widespread introduction of steam-coil heating in the late 1950s, these cans are becoming a standard addition.

Glen Moray is the furthest-flung of those distilleries which call themselves Glenlivets. Its single malt is usually bottled at twelve and sixteen years old, along with a 'non-age' version at around eight years old. Glen Moray became the first Speyside distillery to use white wine barrels to 'finish' maturation and at the end of their normal maturation period the older versions are mellowed (as the company puts it) for a further six months in Chenin Blanc barrels. The non-age version is similarly mellowed in Chardonnay wood. A Centenary Edition finished in port wood has also been released.

LINKWOOD

This classic distillery was actually the first of the two in Elgin to be built and was established in 1821 by Peter Brown. Brown came from a prominent family; his father surveyed most of Telford's roads through the Highlands and his brother was commander of the Light Division in the Crimean War. Peter Brown was an influential farmer and it is possible that Linkwood drew all its barley from his estate. It is also fairly certain that the distillery's waste was processed for cattle feed, a practice common today.

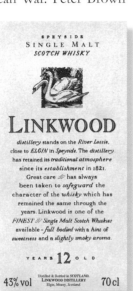

From 1842 Linkwood was operated on Brown's behalf by James Walker, who had previously been managing Aberlour in partnership with his brother and John and James Grant. Walker moved to Linkwood after the lease on Aberlour expired and the Grant brothers moved to Rothes to establish Glen Grant. The distillery was rebuilt in the early 1870s, by which time Linkwood had established quite a reputation in the district. In 1897 the premises were extended and Linkwood was floated as a limited company. The board of directors included J. T. Townsend, co-founder of Scapa Distillery, and later Innes Cameron of Teaninich. Cameron became the company's managing director and main shareholder, and was responsible for seeing Linkwood successfully through periods when many distillers found themselves in financial difficulty. When he died it was decided to sell the distillery and wind up the company, and consequently Linkwood was sold to Scottish Malt Distillers, a subsidiary of DCL, in 1933 for £80,000.

When Linkwood reopened after World War II, a new manager was appointed from the employees. Roderick Mackenzie was the stuff of which legends are made, and supervised

Linkwood with a vigilance bordering on fanaticism. He was a firm believer in the theory that a malt whisky was shaped not only by the equipment in which it was made, but also by the entire environment within the distillery. Consequently, he refused to allow anything to be changed unless absolutely necessary, even forbidding the removal of spiders' webs from the stillhouse!

In 1962 the distillery was rebuilt

again, with Mackenzie directing the operation. The new stills were exact replicas of the ones they replaced and the new equipment was finally commissioned shortly before Mackenzie retired the following year. A second stillhouse was added in 1971, bringing the total number of stills to six. However, Linkwood remains a peaceful place with a maturity that belies all the relatively recent modifications. The dam looks more like an ornamental lake, although the swans are there for a reason: they keep the weeds down.

UDV now bottles Linkwood at twelve years old and it deserves a far wider audience, as it is generally thought to be one of the finest of single malts. It is elegant and complex, yet perfectly balanced. It is popular with the independents, with Gordon & MacPhail providing the widest range of distillations, including one from 1939.

INCHGOWER

The eastern side of Spey Bay is crowded with picturesque little fishing villages, with names such as Findochty and Portknockie, all nestling in the cliffs as if hanging on by their fingernails. The only town in the bay is Buckie, an important fishing centre and the home of one of only three distilleries which can class themselves as being both Speyside and coastal (the others being Glenglassaugh and Macduff).

Inchgower is a descendant of Tochineal Distillery, which was established by Alexander Wilson a couple of miles further along the road near Cullen. Its exact year of foundation is debatable although, in his book *The Whisky Distilleries of the United Kingdom*, Barnard claims it to be 1822. Tochineal supposedly moved to its present location because of problems with its water supply, although by the time it moved it had been in production for forty-odd years and any problems with the supply would surely have been apparent before then. The distillery

was built on land owned by the Countess of Seafield and it is said that, not liking the idea of having a distillery on her property, she doubled the rent!

Whatever the reason, Wilson built Inchgower in 1871 and moved his business there. The water supply was drawn from the Hill of Menduff, the source of all Buckie's town water, and in particular the Letter Burn, which flows over vast peat mosses on the hillside and past the distillery to the sea. Considering that it had only a single pair of stills, Inchgower was built on a grand scale. The main buildings are in the form of a quadrangle which covers almost 4 acres. The maltings was 400ft long and lit by forty-five windows, and the warehousing was so extensive that space was rented out to other distillers in the area. Barnard commented on the workforce being mostly middle-aged or elderly men. Most of

them of course had come from the old Tochineal Distillery and had worked for the company all their lives.

Wilson's descendants sold the distillery in 1933 to Buckie Town Council, which operated it for only three years before selling it to Bell's for £1,000. Since then it has been extensively updated, although the main courtyard still looks largely as it did when Barnard visited about a century ago. A heat-recovery system supplies hot water for mashing and also for an on-site dark grains plant, fed from heat exchangers on the stills, with aftercoolers condensing the spirit. Five new bonds enable Inchgower to store 44,000 butts, making it the third largest warehousing facility in UDV's entire malt division.

Inchgower seems to have been largely passed over by the independents, which is a shame, as older vintages would surely be interesting to sample. Fortunately the distillers bottle a highly individual 14-year-old malt which evinces the distillery's coastal location and which is often described by tasters as 'assertive', an adjective usually reserved for Islay malts. Its sea-salt tang stands it well apart from Bell's other malts: Blair Athol and Dufftown.

SPEYSIDE
SINGLE MALT
SCOTCH WHISKY

The *Oyster Catcher* is a common *sight* around the

INCHGOWER

distillery, which stands *close* to the *sea* on the mouth of the *RIVER SPEY* near *BUCKIE. Inchgower,* established in 1824, produces *one* of the most *distinctive single* malt whiskies in *SPEYSIDE.* It is a malt for the *discerning drinker ~ a complex* aroma precedes a *fruity, spicy* taste ⁓ with a hint of *salt.*

AGED 14 YEARS

43% vol   70cl
Distilled & Bottled in SCOTLAND.
INCHGOWER DISTILLERY.
Buckie, Banffshire, Scotland.

GLENGLASSAUGH

The Banffshire village of Portsoy built up a thriving farming and fishing industry in the nineteenth century, which owed much to the efforts of one man, James Moir, the owner of the general store in the High Street. Moir originally came from Aberdeen but lived for a time in Turriff, where he met his wife, the sister of the original owner of the store, which he would eventually inherit. The couple moved to Portsoy, shortly after which Mrs Moir died. Moir threw himself into the affairs of the community, where in addition to running the general store he also became the local agent for the North of Scotland Bank. He encouraged the development of the railway, and was a strong advocate of the fishing industry, eventually owning three boats and a stake in a salmon fishery at Macduff. The telegraph line connecting Portsoy, Buckie and Portgordon was erected at his own expense. As if all these enterprises did not keep him busy enough, he was also a member of the battery of artillery volunteers.

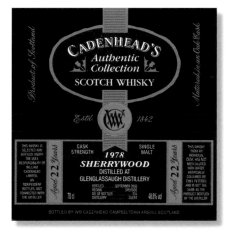

The general store built up a good trade in wines and spirits, and his need for supplies of whisky led Moir to the decision to build his own distillery, a venture which would also benefit local farmers, giving them a market for their barley. Moir recruited his two nephews and a Portsoy coppersmith, Thomas Wilson, as partners in the business. A site was found on the Glassaugh estate and land leased from R. W. Duff, the MP for Banff, in 1874. The lease, which imposed a rent of £95 a year, demanded that the partners also farm the attached 80-acre Craigmills Farm, and that they should keep the land 'in good heart'. The distillery was designed by Elgin architects Reid & Melvin. The sloping site made it possible to arrange the workings to take advantage of gravity, so cutting down on manual labour. Thomas Wilson, in collaboration with William Sellar of Keith, who was experienced in building distilleries, laid out the

plant. A 4,000-gallon wash still and a 2,000-gallon spirit still were installed, giving the distillery an annual production capacity of about 100,000 gallons. Process water came from the Fordyce Burn. The new distillery was completed in December 1874 at a cost of some £10,000 and took the name of the farm, which the partners had renamed Glenglassaugh.

It had been planned from the start that Glenglassaugh's whisky should be sold as a single malt and the partners found customers as far afield as Salisbury, Gosport and Weymouth. Robertson & Baxter was also a major client, supplying the make in turn to Teacher's. By 1892 three of the partners had died, and the remaining partner, James Moir's nephew Alexander Morrison, offered Glenglassaugh for sale to Robertson & Baxter. A price of £10,000 was agreed after some deliberation, and immediately after the sale had gone through Robertson & Baxter resold the distillery to the Highland Distilleries Co. at a £5,000 profit. Highland still own Glenglassaugh, but since it took over production has been sporadic. It was almost totally rebuilt in 1960 but closed in 1986. After a brief revival it is again mothballed.

MACDUFF

The town of Macduff dates from 1783, when the hamlet of Doune had burgh status conferred on it by the second Earl of Fife. Together with Banff it enfolds Banff Bay at the mouth of the River Deveron, and marks the upper, easternmost, point of Speyside's 'Golden Triangle'. The main A98 coast road enters Banff, *en route* to Fraserburgh, passing the Banff Springs Hotel, a somewhat less ambitious establishment than its namesake in the Canadian Rockies. In the town centre the side streets drop precipitously from the main road down to the harbour. The road skirts the bay and passes into Macduff itself, where the distillery stands overlooking the golf course at the edge of town. Like Inchgower and Glenglassaugh, Macduff has the distinction of being one of the few distilleries which can be classed as both Speyside and coastal.

Banff Distillery was closed by DCL in 1983 and subsequently demolished. It was established on a different site as Mill of Banff in 1824 and lasted until 1863, when the company was dissolved and the distillery closed. The owner, James Simpson, then built a new distillery at the hamlet of Inverboyndie, on the western edge of Banff. It was known to the locals by that name, although it was officially registered as Banff. Simpson's company sold out to Scottish Malt Distillers in 1932. Three other distilleries were recorded in the area around the town at the beginning of the nineteenth century. The longest lived only lasted sixteen years, the shortest only appearing on the Excise records in a single year.

Macduff Distillery was built in 1958–60 by a consortium comprising James Stirrat, George Crawford, Brodie Hepburn and Morton (Marty) Dykes, and made its first fillings in early June 1960. The consortium sold out to Block, Grey & Block in 1964. The distillery was extended between 1966 and 1968, a time when Stanley P. Morrison had an interest in the company, and now has five stills – two for wash and three for low wines. Shortly afterwards the company installed its own bottling line, one of the first to be installed in a malt distillery. This was used until 1972, when the distillery was acquired by Wm Lawson Distillers Ltd.

The Lawson trademark had been used from the 1890s by E. & J. Burke Ltd of Dublin. In October 1958 Clan Munro Whisky Ltd was formed as a subsidiary of Martini to supply blended whisky to various Martini companies worldwide. The company began operating firstly in Liverpool before moving to Coatbridge in January 1967. Clan Munro acquired the Lawson brand in 1969 and changed the name of the company to William Lawson Whisky Ltd, finally becoming Wm Lawson Distillers Ltd when it purchased Macduff Distillery and a quantity of maturing stocks. To supplement its facilities at Coatbridge the company acquired from Allied Distillers in 1993 the Westthorn production plant at Glasgow, the same year in which Bacardi acquired a controlling interest in Martini.

Following the Guinness-Grand Met merger Bacardi has emerged as a new force in the industry, having expanded its portfolio of distilleries from one to five, with the acquisition from UDV of Aberfeldy, Aultmore, Craigellachie and Royal Brackla. The company bottles Macduff's malt as Glen Deveron.

LONGMORN

There are a number of malt distilleries strung out along the main road from Elgin to Rothes, and Longmorn and its sister Benriach are the first ones the traveller comes to. Longmorn is tucked away down a side track by the old Elgin–Rothes railway line, now dismantled.

The distillery was founded in 1894 by John Duff, who had earlier built Glenlossie Distillery at Thomshill a little way to the west. Various theories have been put forward for the origin of the name Longmorn, but it is thought to be derived from Lann Marnoch ('the church of St Marnoch', *lann* being Gaelic for 'church' and St Marnoch a missionary who died in AD 625), and it is the former site of this church on which it is said that the distillery warehouses now stand.

Certainly, the place has a definite air of calm and serenity. Duff was joined in the new venture by two local businessmen, George Thomson and Charles Shirras, and after three years in business amended the name of the company to incorporate the Glenlivet suffix, yet another example of a Glenlossie masquerading as a Glenlivet. The following year, Longmorn passed to James R. Grant and subsequently to his two sons. It is a coincidence that they were to become associated with another family of Grants, namely those of Glen Grant, when Longmorn became a part of The Glenlivet Distillers Ltd in 1970.

Today, whilst still being very much a conventional distillery, Longmorn has seen many changes to bring it in line with modern working methods. Its floor maltings and kiln are no longer used and all its malt now comes from commercial maltsters. There are two stillhouses and a total of eight steam-heated stills. The four wash stills were coal fired until 1993 and are all in the first stillhouse, whilst the spirit stills are in the second stillhouse next door. Originally, the malt mill and washback switchers were also steam powered and the 1910 steam engine is preserved in working order. All the raw spirit is sent to Keith Bond for filling.

Longmorn has the capacity to make about 1 million proof gallons annually but is only now becoming more readily available as a single malt. It is regarded by blenders as being a 'top malt' and said to be equal in quality to The Glenlivet and Glen Grant. It is bottled by the distillers at fifteen years old and 45 % vol, as part of their Heritage Selection. Different ages and strengths have been bottled by the independents who usually give it its original title, Longmorn-Glenlivet.

BENRIACH

supplying malt to Longmorn from its floor maltings. Benriach came back into production in 1965 and still maintains its single malt floor, one of the last few traditional maltings still working in Scotland. It now provides only a small percentage of the distillery's requirements and with a capacity of only 700 tons per year, is no longer able to supply malt to Longmorn.

Both distilleries take their supplies of spring water from the same source: Mannoch Hill. Both also originally took peat from the same place, although it is now bought in for Benriach's maltings from commercial peat cutters. In a way, Longmorn and Benriach are similar to Glenfiddich and Balvenie: sister distilleries occupying adjacent sites and using raw materials from the same sources, yet producing quite different whiskies. Benriach's stills are smaller than those at Longmorn, the spirit stills particularly so, yet all the tasting guides agree that Benriach makes a lighter spirit than Longmorn (small stills usually contribute to a heavy spirit). In the early 1970s an extra pair of stills was installed, increasing capacity by 85 per cent to about 800,000 proof gallons annually. All four stills are steam heated.

As seems to be the current practice amongst Chivas distilleries, Benriach sends its production to Keith Bond for filling. Its whisky has a reputation for maturing quickly once in the cask and this has made it sought after by blenders. Chivas now bottles Benriach as part of its Heritage Selection at ten years old and 43% vol, and a variety of bottlings are available from the independents.

The distillery passed to Pernod-Ricard after they and Diageo jointly acquired Seagram's wine and spirits business at the end of 2001.

When John Duff, prompted by the booming growth of the whisky trade in the closing years of the nineteenth century, decided to expand his company's operations, his optimism was such that he built not one but two new distilleries. On adjacent sites to the south of Elgin, Longmorn opened for business first and Benriach followed it into production in 1898. Unfortunately Benriach has not shared Longmorn's record of continuous production and Duff cannot have foreseen the regression of the industry following the collapse of Pattison's of Leith. After a mere five years of existence, Benriach closed down. It was to remain closed for sixty-two years.

Pattison's took many distilleries down with them but Benriach was lucky in being associated so closely with Longmorn next door, and it was occupied at least to a certain extent in

GLEN ELGIN

Glen Elgin was founded in 1898 and is not actually in Elgin at all but in the parish of Longmorn; it lies beside the A941 Rothes road between Longmorn and Coleburn. It was still under construction when the Pattison crash occurred and its fortunes largely went downhill from there.

It was, as its architect Charles Doig predicted, the last distillery to be erected on Speyside for over fifty years. The venture was initiated by William Simson, a former manager of Glenfarclas. Simson was already in financial trouble before his new distillery opened and, like Glenrothes, it was built on a smaller scale than originally planned. Even so, it was rumoured that none of the contractors was paid in full, with the exception of the steeplejacks who threatened to pull down the chimney if payment was not forthcoming! The distillery began working on 1 May 1900, using a curious process which allegedly combined some stages of production, but by November that year it was up for sale.

Glen Elgin had cost Simson over £13,000 to build but was sold at auction in February 1901 for just £4,000. The names of the buyers were never disclosed but the following year the Glen Elgin-Glenlivet Distillery Co. was formed with a board of directors comprising the usual people with money but no previous experience in the industry – a banker, a solicitor, an advocate and a merchant – although they at least had the sense to include a distiller. The company lasted only four years before the distillery changed hands again and its existence was marked by long periods of closure until it was acquired by DCL in 1936.

Some of the distillery's problems were attributable to its siting, which was not ideal. Its process water came from the Glen Burn, which still runs behind the distillery, and which was used for power and cooling by Coleburn, about a mile upstream. The company was forced to find an alternative water supply and leased springs at Whitewreath from the county council. Transport was another problem. The distillery had been built alongside the railway in the hope of bringing in a private siding. The Board of Trade vetoed the idea as the gradient was too steep and as a result all goods had to be carted to and from Longmorn station. Even as late as 1948 a new manager found to his despair that the distillery had no boiler or electric lighting, and one employee was almost fully occupied in maintaining its paraffin lamps.

Glen Elgin was entirely rebuilt in 1964, when DCL was busily renovating many of its properties, and water power finally gave way to electricity. Production capacity was increased by installing four more stills, taking the total to six. DCL assigned the distillery's licence to White Horse and Glen Elgin still forms a component of that blend. It has been bottled as a single malt by Gordon & MacPhail and Signatory, and has finally found its way into UDV's Hidden Malts range.

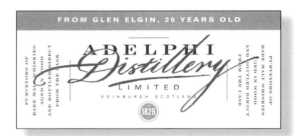

COLEBURN

oleburn is a mere mile from Glen Elgin on the A941 and, apart from a little trouble in building the Excise officer's house, seems to have had none of the problems that the latter had to face.

The distillery was built in 1896 by the Dundee blending company John Robertson & Sons Ltd. It too was designed by Charles Doig and was fortunate where Glen Elgin was not: it had first claim on the water of the Glen Burn and was looked on kindly by the North of Scotland Railway, which built a goods station and sidings especially to serve it. In fact, the railway delivered supplies right into the distillery buildings and remained in use until 1966. The problems in construction came with the Excise officer's cottage, which was in an awkward spot, and provision of suitable sanitary arrangements for the Excise office itself took eighteen months to resolve. During the building work the Excise officer had to lodge at the manager's house, a situation which caused the manager to remark on more than one occasion that the Excise man seemed 'a trifle hard to please'. The first manager, John Grant, looked after Coleburn for over thirty years.

Under these less than ideal circumstances the distillery began production in January 1897, and it was thanks to savings made possible by the proximity of the railway that Coleburn survived the depression which followed the Pattison crash. The distillery was absorbed into DCL in a roundabout way, being bought in 1916 for £5,000 by the Clynelish Distillery Co., of which DCL and Johnnie Walker each owned a third share. When the latter two companies merged Clynelish entered DCL, taking Coleburn with it.

DCL made gradual improvements to Coleburn, and the original plant lasted well: the spirit still until 1950, the wash still until 1955, and the mash tun until 1959. The worm tubs gave way to condensers along with the small waterwheel which, fed from the overflow from the worm tubs, powered the rummager. The maltings fell

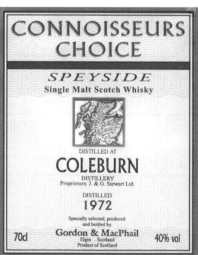

into disuse in 1968. The smaller of the two kilns was used for drying barley at a controlled temperature. The distillery had a team of horses, which gave rise to the local saying 'as hard worked as a distillery horse' – distillery horses only worked when there was work for them whereas farm horses worked all day long.

DCL transferred the licence for Coleburn to J. & G. Stewart Ltd, a company whose take-over by DCL was one of the biggest transactions in the industry, involving some 8,000 butts of maturing whisky. Stewart's was a pioneer in the export trade and once held two royal warrants, as supplier of Scotch whisky to Her Majesty the Queen, and to the late King Gustaf Adolph VI of Sweden. In Stewart's name DCL also acquired the famous blending company of Andrew Usher, and Coleburn was a constituent of Usher's blends until the distillery was closed in 1985.

SPEYBURN

Speyburn sits in a deep, wooded valley at the north end of Rothes and was founded by John Hopkins and three partners in 1897. Hopkins's company was eventually to become licensee of Oban Distillery, but he was earlier a partner in Glenlossie and owner of Tobermory on Mull. With the benefit of local knowledge, Hopkins chose the site for Speyburn to take advantage of its access to the Elgin–Aberdeen railway line and more importantly, a previously unused water supply, the Granty Burn.

The distillery, like a number of others in this area, was designed by Charles Doig. Hopkins was adamant that it should be in production by 1 November, so that the first fillings could carry the date of Queen Victoria's diamond jubilee. He was unlucky; Speyburn did not start distilling until the last week in December and just one cask was bonded with an 1897 date. Even then, the building work was incomplete. The stillhouse had no doors or windows, and with a violent snowstorm blowing, the employees had to work in their overcoats.

The architect's job was not made any easier by the distillery's location. Because of the high valley sides enclosing the site, the buildings had

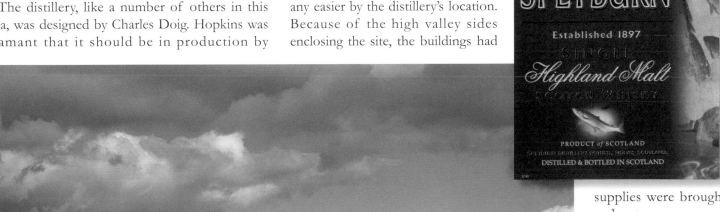

to be tall rather than wide. The main block and the maltings were all three storeys high, and the warehouses two. The foundations and most of the walls were made with stone taken from the bed of the Spey, and the maltings was built of concrete, a material pioneered a few years earlier at Bruichladdich. The maltings itself used Henning's pneumatic drum system, only the second of its kind installed in any distillery in Scotland, and the first in a malt distillery, yet it was to remain in use for seventy years. The malt was dried in two stages in a double-decker kiln. Hopkins's original plans to build a private rail siding fell through, and supplies were brought to the distillery by horse and cart.

Speyburn closed for the duration of World War II and was used as a base for two Scottish artillery regiments, which parked their guns in the courtyard. Production resumed in 1947 and, shortly after, the distillery was connected to the national grid. Despite this, the head maltman insisted on keeping the old steam engine, his pride and joy, in working order and it could take over in a matter of minutes in the event of a power failure. A new manager, who took over in 1950, noted that it was so highly polished it could have been used as a shaving mirror.

For many years Speyburn was licensed to John Robertson & Sons Ltd, a result of John Hopkins & Co. being absorbed into the expanding DCL. United Distillers had only just begun to market Speyburn as part of its Wildlife (now Flora & Fauna) series, when in January 1992 the distillery was sold to Inver House Distillers. Inver House continued to bottle Speyburn at ten years old, and this bottling has already won an award.

GLEN GRANT

One of the most successful distilleries in Scotland, Glen Grant owes its prosperity to the acumen of its founders. John Grant began by smuggling illicit Highland whisky to the Lowlands, even selling legally distilled Glenlivet as hooch because his customers preferred illicit liquor. His brother James used to obtain credit from his suppliers by offering to pay his bills with a £100 note, knowing that no one could change it!

The Grants began distilling at Aberlour in 1832, in partnership with John and James Walker. After the lease expired in 1840, James Walker moved to Linkwood and the Grant brothers established Glen Grant at Rothes where John Grant later held the lease on Drumbain Farm. The distillery was originally known as Drumbain and the name is still marked on some Ordnance

Survey maps of the region. Right from the start, Glen Grant was built to distil 1,500 gallons of spirit per week from its large and small pairs of stills, and at the time of John Grant's death in 1864 it was paying £30,000 annually in duty.

Both Grant brothers were philanthropists, particularly James, who is credited with pioneering the railway in the north of Scotland, and was four times Provost of Elgin. The town declared a day of mourning on his death in 1872. Glen Grant then passed to his son, James junior, otherwise known from his army days as Major Grant. He appears to have been well-liked by his workforce, although he was a strict employer and something of a tyrant to his children. A notice posted in the distillery warned that any man found drinking the wash would be dismissed on the spot, but Grant ensured that all the workmen received a dram 'to see them home'. Each man was also given a bottle of Glen Grant every month. At one time all distillery workers received a daily dram of new make spirit, or 'clearic' as it was known, at the start of each shift. The practice ended with the introduction of the Health and Safety at Work Act in 1974, and concerns of alcoholism raised by doctors working in the main distilling centres.

The major outlived all his sons and, with no immediate family involved with the distillery, appointed his grandson Douglas Mackessack to take his place.

Mackessack started his new job with no pay and when the major was too ill to go fishing, he was forced to take his beat on the Spey so as not to waste the licence fee! Mackessack eventually retired on 31 January 1978, the day on which Glen Grant was taken over by Seagram and 138 years of the Grant family's direct control of the distillery ended.

Expansion has been the order of the day at Glen Grant. The distillery now has ten huge washbacks, each with a capacity of 20,000 gallons. There are four pairs of stills, some of which used to be coal fired. During refurbishment which was completed in June 1996, all the stills were converted to gas firing. The gas pipes were still in place following a previous flirtation with gas firing prior to the Seagram take-over. The result is a far quieter stillhouse than before, when the chain rummagers clanked in the wash stills. The wash stills have an unusual mid-section, shaped like a German army helmet, and the spirit stills are of two different designs. Both sets of stills are fitted with purifiers which remove the heavier alcohols before they reach the condensers, contributing to a clean spirit. The oldest stills used waterwheel-driven rummagers up until 1979, yet paradoxically Glen Grant became the first industrial premises in the north to have electric lighting.

In 1897, the Grants decided to build a second distillery, imaginatively titled Glen Grant No. 2, just across the road. The two distilleries were linked by a pipeline, at the insistence of Customs and Excise, and their products were vatted together as Glen Grant whisky. Spirit only flowed through this pipe during the daytime. At night it was washed out with water, thus foiling the attempts of any opportunists to help themselves to a free dram. The Pattison crash forced the closure of Glen Grant No. 2 in 1901. It remained mothballed until 1965, when it was reopened and rechristened Caperdonich, after the well which originally supplied Glen Grant. Both distilleries are run by a combined workforce of twelve men.

Glen Grant has thus progressed from being founded by two smugglers to being capable of distilling 2 million proof gallons per year. A 5-year-old version, bottled for export, is the best-selling malt whisky in Italy, and Gordon & MacPhail bottles it in a wide range of ages up to fifty years old, some aged exclusively in sherry wood. Only 20 per cent of production goes for blending, and along with Caperdonich it is a component of Chivas Regal. Caperdonich is slightly smokier than Glen Grant and is bottled as a single malt only by the independents.

GLENROTHES

D own a side street in the centre of Rothes, on the banks of the Burn of Rothes and opposite the town cemetery, stands Glenrothes Distillery. Now owned by the Highland Distilleries Co. it produces a highly regarded malt whisky, yet thanks to the financial problems of the syndicate that built it, it was lucky to survive its formative years at all.

Glenrothes was built by a consortium of businessmen who were in partnership with the then owner of the Macallan Distillery, James Stuart. Unable to fund his expansion plans alone, Stuart had taken on as partners the agent for the Rothes branch of the Caledonian Bank, Robert Dick, and an accountant and solicitor from the Elgin branch of the same bank. The expansion at Macallan was successful and the partners optimistically turned their ambitions to the building of a new distillery on the site of a sawmill in Rothes.

By the summer of 1878, the worst economic crisis for almost a century had brought the Caledonian Bank to the brink of collapse and it was forced to close pending an investigation into its affairs. This was catastrophic for Stuart's partners, who were not only shareholders in the bank but had financed their business venture by arranging their own overdrafts. They dissolved the partnership, leaving Macallan to James Stuart, and formed a new company to run Glenrothes after the bank's problems had been solved. Although the bank inspectors were not impressed with their employees' financial arrangements they did not press for immediate repayment, and encouraged by this the partners went ahead with the new distillery.

They were forced by their reduced circumstances to build the distillery much smaller than had originally been planned, but rather than admit this to the press they preferred to point out all the areas of the plant where they had left 'room for future expansion'! The recession kept business at a very low ebb and the company was forced to borrow more and more money to keep afloat. The bank advanced them £2,000, followed later by another £800. Two local businessmen each loaned them £1,000, another £2,000 came from Rear-Admiral Crombie-Gordon, and when they were particularly strapped for cash they borrowed £600 from the Presbyterian minister in nearby Archiestown.

As if these problems were not enough, James Stuart had decided after all to build a second distillery in Rothes and in 1883 began work on Glen Spey on the other side of the burn. There followed a predictable wrangle over the water rights, which took the best part of a year to resolve. Fearing for the company's survival, the partners proposed a merger with Bunnahabhain Distillery and the Highland Distilleries Co. was born. During the negotiations Robert Dick, still the bank's agent in Rothes, had been busy organising a new venture for a certain William Grant and had arranged his purchase of plant from Cardhu with which he would equip Glenfiddich.

Highland has steadily improved Glenrothes over the years. A huge new stillhouse was built in the 1980s, its smooth red granite facing matching that at its sister distillery, Tamdhu. The ten stills have an annual capacity of almost 2 million proof gallons and produce a malt whisky which finds its way into many blends, in particular Cutty Sark. Glenrothes single malt is not bottled at a particular age but as a vintage, and is increasing in popularity. The year of distillation is given on the label, which has a hand-written look intended to imitate those used on blenders' sample bottles.

GLEN SPEY

A PREMIUM SINGLE CASK SCOTCH MALT WHISKY

The MASTER of Malt

SPECIALLY SELECTED BY THE MASTER OF MALT TN1 2UN

12 YEAR OLD
SINGLE MALT WHISKY

Distilled in 1985 at
GLEN SPEY DISTILLERY

N—

GLEN SPEY

SPEYSIDE

PRODUCT OF SCOTLAND
70cl
43% vol.

to make the best of their plans. For its first few years Glenrothes merely ticked over as its owners struggled with their financial problems, then to their considerable consternation Stuart turned his attention to the conversion of the mill, bringing Glen Spey into production in 1885. Not only did this embroil Glenrothes in a legal battle with Stuart over its water rights, but its owners were now forced to seek a merger with Bunnahabhain in order to survive. The competition probably affected Stuart just as badly, as in the same year that Glenrothes and Bunnahabhain amalgamated, 1887, Stuart sold Glen Spey to W. & A. Gilbey.

Gilbey's history goes back to 1857, when it was founded by Walter and Alfred Gilbey as a wine merchant and gin distiller. The company entered the whisky trade with the purchase of Glen Spey, following with its acquisition of Strathmill in 1895 and Knockando in 1904. It also later acquired the Aberdeen-based blending company James Catto, which began exporting whisky with the help of two of Catto's former school friends who had founded the White Star shipping line, the owner of the *Titanic*. Gilbey's merged in 1962 with United Wine Traders Ltd to form IDV – International Distillers & Vintners. It in turn was acquired by Watney, Mann & Co. Ltd, shortly before that company was itself taken over in 1972 by Grand Metropolitan, which merged in 1997 with Guinness to form United Distillers & Vintners (UDV).

Glen Spey was rebuilt in 1970 and extended from two to four stills. The stills are fitted with purifiers, the spirit stills having a reflux pipe from the purifier. The condensers are equipped with after-coolers, which are necessary to increase their efficiency, as the cooling water taken from the Burn of Rothes has already done duty at other distilleries further upstream, and by this time is not as cold as it could be! Glen Spey is another of those distilleries reputed to be haunted, in this case by the ghost of a soldier electrocuted whilst billeted there in World War II.

It is easy for the visitor to overlook Glen Spey as it is tucked away off the main street through Rothes at the foot of a hill beneath the castle, the former home of the Earls of Rothes, the Leslie family. At the time of Barnard's visit it was the newest distillery in the district, and had started life as a meal mill called Millhaugh, which was owned by James Stuart, described on contemporary documents as a corn merchant and distiller, and at the time the owner of Macallan.

Stuart, together with partners from the Caledonian Bank, had successfully expanded Macallan, and decided to build it a sister. Glenrothes Distillery was erected opposite Stuart's mill, on the other side of the Burn of Rothes, a project which almost collapsed from under them as a crisis mounted at the bank. The partnership dissolved, leaving Stuart to run Macallan alone whilst his compatriots continued

CRAIGELLACHIE

The village of Craigellachie lies beside the A95 between Rothes and Aberlour, and marks the point where the River Fiddich joins the Spey. Victorian in character, it grew five-fold in the latter part of the nineteenth century when distilleries began to spring up around the area. It was here that Telford built his famous single-span iron bridge beneath the precipitous Rock of Craigellachie, and locals still tell the (untrue) story that the wrong components were delivered to the village from the foundry in Wales.

The Craigellachie Distillery Co. was founded in 1888 and the distillery itself was in full production by the summer of 1891. The company's major shareholders were Alexander Edward, the owner of Benrinnes Distillery, and a man who was to become one of the industry's legends, Peter Mackie. Mackie was already a partner in his uncle's firm, which owned Lagavulin, and incorporated the company as Mackie & Co. in 1890. He was known to his employees as 'Restless Peter' and was a workaholic with interests in half a dozen enterprises including the weaving of Highland tweed, the manufacture of concrete slabs (in which he employed only ex-soldiers, his late son having been an army man), and the production of 'BBM' (bran, bone and muscle) flour. The flour was mixed to a secret recipe by machinery under the floor of the boardroom in the company's office, and all Mackie's staff were compelled to use it at home. After his death most of his ventures were dropped, reportedly to the relief of all concerned.

Mackie devoted considerable energy to selling his blended whisky, Mackie's White Horse Cellar Scotch Whisky, a name he took from the White Horse Inn in Canongate, Edinburgh, which formerly occupied the site of his family home. He took sole control of Craigellachie in 1900, leaving Alexander Edward to other distillery ventures. Mackie had strong views on everything and chairmanship of the company gave him a prominent platform from which to express them. The company changed its name to White Horse Distillers Ltd after Mackie died in 1924, and three years later joined DCL.

In common with a number of other DCL distilleries Craigellachie was refurbished in the 1960s and its stillhouse, with its huge picture windows displaying the stills, was the first of a design used for the new stillhouses built at Ord, Clynelish, Teaninich, Glendullan and finally Caol Ila, between 1966 and 1973. All that remains of the old Victorian distillery are the kiln and parts of No. 4 warehouse. Process water comes from Little Conval hill 3½ miles away, just outside Dufftown. The wash still rummagers were powered by a waterwheel which was only removed when the new stillhouse was built.

From the outset Mackie promoted Craigellachie as a single malt, and continued to do so after introducing the White Horse blend. It has also been bottled in the past by the independents, sometimes as Craigellachie-Glenlivet. The distillery was acquired by Bacardi in 1998 after the merger of Guinness and Grand Metropolitan.

ABERLOUR

also had the longest-serving manager in the industry, Ian Mitchell, who spent forty-seven years there. Mitchell followed his father and grandfather into the company. His father started at Aberlour in 1936 and became brewer; his grandfather worked there during the distilling seasons and was also the town crier and greenkeeper at the local golf course. Mitchell's starting salary in 1945 was about 12s 6d (62½p) a week!

During his tenure Mitchell saw many changes at Aberlour. The distillery was water powered until 1960, and the mill used steam power until 1973 when Mitchell masterminded a £½ million refit which doubled production capacity. His place as manager was taken by Kenny

Fraser, probably the district's most famous piper. The bagpipes are not instruments which can be practised quietly, and for many years Kenny practised during night-shifts, playing to the casks in the warehouses and declaring that the music was the magic ingredient which made Aberlour so special!

The village of Aberlour was laid out in 1812 by the local laird, Charles Grant, hence its full name Charlestown of Aberlour, and marks the point where the Lour Burn enters the Spey. Today it is a resort village for the many fishermen who come to pit their wits against the Spey salmon; a pretty village with a tree-lined square, a park on the banks of the river, and small rose-covered cottages strung out along the long, arrow-straight main street.

There are stories from the early 1800s of an illicit still existing in the grounds of a mill about a mile from the present site, and the first legitimate distillery was established there in 1826 by James Gordon. The present-day distillery dates from 1879. It was destroyed by fire one winter night in 1898 and although the buildings were lost, all the villagers turned out to save the maturing casks of whisky! The distillery was subsequently rebuilt

and retains much of its Victorian exterior. In the grounds is Dunstan's Well, which supplies its water. Fed from springs on Ben Rinnes it is named after St Dunstan, a missionary and contemporary of St Columba, who established the first settlement here in AD 618, and who used the water for baptisms.

Many distilleries have long-serving workers (a job at one of the more remote distilleries is often a job for life) and Aberlour has men who have worked there for twenty-five years or more. It has

In 1974 the distillery's owner, The House of Campbell, was acquired by Pernod-Ricard and the company's whiskies have become big sellers in France. Aberlour was the first ever winner of the Pot Still Trophy for single malts, and the first malt whisky to win three gold medals in the International Wine and Spirit Competition. In 1989 the company bought the mothballed Glenallachie Distillery from Invergordon. Despite the hefty, but undisclosed, purchase price, the sale contract listed the distillery's complement of twenty ducks at £1 each, and the new owner received 286 applications for twelve jobs at the distillery.

BENRINNES

Ben Rinnes is the highest peak in the Speyside/Glenlivet region. Fishing boats in the Moray Firth use it as a landmark and from its summit can be seen nine counties. Its granite mass is a huge geological intrusion from which up to eleven distilleries have drawn their water. Benrinnes (note the spelling) was the first distillery to be built directly on its flanks and naturally appropriated its name.

The first distillery was recorded here in 1826 and was sited at Whitehouse Farm. It was swept away in the great flood of 1829 and rebuilt about a mile away, on the present site, in 1835. Many pure springs rise on Ben Rinnes which are ideal for distilling and there was an ample supply of peat for firing the distillery's odd tower-like kiln. Being on a hill it was built to take advantage of gravity: the tun room was unusual in being at the top of the mash house, and there was only one pump in the whole place. At nearly 700ft above sea level it was cool enough to continue malting all year round. The only disadvantage was that supplies had to be carted from Aberlour station, a distance of 3 miles.

In 1864 Benrinnes changed hands when its owner ended up in jail at Banff after going bankrupt. It was taken over by David Edward who, together with his son Alexander, was involved with a number of Speyside distilleries including Craigellachie and Aultmore. Alexander Edward made Benrinnes a limited company, buying the property, equipment and water rights for £78,930. One of his co-directors was Innes Cameron, who was also a director of Linkwood.

Benrinnes was rebuilt after a major fire in 1896 and three large stills were installed, giving rise to the distillery's use of semi-triple distillation. Less than three years later the company's sole agent went out of business and the whole industry entered recession following the Pattison crash, and Benrinnes found itself in trouble. After a few lean years it was acquired by Dewar's, which took it into DCL. Major reconstruction took place after World War II and the farmstead was demolished, obviating the need for visitors to negotiate a herd of cattle and a bull on their way to the office. On occasions the animals took fright and all the distillery workers would be roped in to help round them all up.

Benrinnes now has six stills, used in two sets of three, the two spirit stills in each set being different sizes. Strong feints are distilled in the big spirit still to produce the final spirit, whilst the small spirit still is used to increase the strength of the weak feints. The method differs from traditional Lowland triple distillation and gives a strong spirit of definite Highland character which is reputedly highly regarded by the independent bottlers, a fact which may have prompted UDV to include it in its Flora & Fauna range at fifteen years old.

MACALLAN

Not just Macallan, but The Macallan. Macallan pioneered this particular use of the definite article, a device now used by several of its rivals including of course The Glenlivet (although in this case it is used to show The Glenlivet's legal precedent, and that it is not just any old Glenlivet).

The distillery stands on Easter Elchies estate and the laird's manor house is now the company's headquarters. It dates from 1700 and the River Spey is literally at the bottom of the garden. In the eighteenth century, cattle drovers would have forded the river here on their way to the markets in the Lowlands. They would have provided ready business for the estate farmer who, like many others in the Highlands, was distilling as a sideline. This sideline became a legitimate operation in 1824. In 1892 Macallan was sold by its owner James Stuart, the founder of Glen Spey and co-founder of Glenrothes, to Roderick Kemp, formerly a partner in Talisker. Kemp's great-grandson, Allan Shiach, later became the company's chairman. After many years of supplying the blending trade with relatively young whisky the company decided to market a single malt, which would obviously involve ageing the spirit for a far greater time with no return on the investment for at least ten years. In order to do this, Macallan sought Stock Exchange listing and finally went public in 1968. All the distillery's workforce became shareholders, as did companies such as Suntory and Remy Cointreau. In 1996 Highland Distilleries purchased Remy's stake in Macallan and launched a hostile take-over bid for the company in a joint venture with Suntory. The deal was concluded later that year and a new company, HS (Distillers) Ltd, emerged, with Highland owning about 75 per cent and Suntory the remainder. Highland itself has since been acquired by The 1887 Company, a joint venture between the Edrington Group and Wm Grant.

All distillers pride themselves on the care that they take over their product but Macallan is fanatical. It is the only distillery to age all its malt exclusively in sherry wood. As a result of experiments carried out at the distillery, dry oloroso casks were deemed to have the best characteristics for ageing the spirit, and Macallan ensures its supply by buying new casks in Jerez and leasing them to a bodega for three years after which they are emptied and shipped intact to Scotland. The oak, freshly soaked in sherry, imparts a character so important to The Macallan that the casks will only be used twice. The company takes a dim view of independent bottlers that have different ideas about its maturation.

The full-bodied, estery spirit comes from the smallest spirit stills on Speyside, so small in fact that two have to be used for every wash still. A second stillhouse has been built alongside the first giving a total of seven wash and fourteen spirit stills capable of producing over 2 million proof gallons annually. The middle cut accounts for only 15 per cent of the distillation. Such is the demand for this whisky that a new high-tech warehouse has been built to cope with the company's expansion. It stands in a hollow scooped out of the hill behind the distillery and is the largest single-roofed whisky warehouse in Europe. Its handling systems can manage 66,000 casks yet it has traditional bare earth floors, damp and mouldy, ideal conditions for maturing whisky.

Macallan now ranks fifth in the world sales league and more than one distillery tour guide has confided to me that The Macallan is the whisky they drink at home, yet the success of The Macallan, as a bottled single malt, only really dates from 1980. Before that its main sales area only stretched from Elgin to Buckie, even though it has always been sought after by blenders as an important 'top dressing' in brands such as Chivas Regal, Bell's, Famous Grouse, Ballantine's, Cutty Sark and J & B Rare. It is now bottled at ten, twelve, eighteen, twenty-five and thirty years old, and there is also a 7-year-old bottled for the Italian market. Recently-introduced products include The 1874, a whisky intended to emulate one recently bought at auction which dated from that year, which is sold in a replica of the original bottle; and the 'Vintages' range, which includes a selection of malts from distillations going back to 1926 and bottled at up to 60 years old. Some years ago a limited edition 60-year-old, with a label by Peter Blake, sold for £6,000, and a Japanese businessman passing through Heathrow paid £10,000 for a similar bottle! The millennium has brought with it a rash of limited editions, Macallan's 50-year-old presented in a Caithness glass decanter and appropriately priced at £2,000!

Macallan are great believers in the personal touch and for a long time ran the company directly from the distillery. Visitors are accepted by arrangement only, but if you make an appointment you will be shown around by a member of staff, rather than a tour guide. No doubt The 1887 Company has plans for Macallan, but one thing is certain: the attitudes of 1974, when Macallan's advertising budget was £25, are long, long gone.

DAILUAINE

Dailuaine obviously impressed Alfred Barnard, as he devoted a seven-page article to it in *The Whisky Distilleries of the United Kingdom*. At the time of his visit the name was written Dail-Uaine, *dail* being derived from the Norse for 'meadow'.

The distillery stands at the foot of a steep hill on the road into Carron, and though out of sight of the main road its presence is marked by the steam-belching chimney and pronounced malty aroma of its dark grains plant. The location is marked by the confluence of three burns and the roughly triangular site is hemmed in by wooded hillsides. Beside one of the burns above the distillery Barnard discovered the ruins of an old smuggling bothy and heard the story of the shepherd who, attracted by the sight of a fire one winter's night, found the ghosts of the smugglers working their phantom still.

Dailuaine was built in 1851 by William Mackenzie, a local farmer. Mackenzie died in 1865 to be succeeded first by his widow, who leased Dailuaine to a banker from Aberlour, and then by his son Thomas, who went on to found Imperial further down the glen. Barnard found an efficient distillery. A new screening machine had been installed for removing foreign matter from the barley, and an automatic machine weighed the malt, measured the quantity and removed the culm before passing it on to the mill. The kiln, which was fired entirely by peat, had the steepest-pitched pagoda roof in Scotland, giving a 30ft space above the drying floor which resulted in better dispersion of the peat smoke and a more subtle flavouring of the malt. The Steel's masher was unique in being made of solid brass, and the water supply was piped all around the process buildings in an iron pipe fitted at intervals with hoses for cleaning or fire-fighting purposes. Barnard also noted that the office was in 'telephonic communication' with Carron station, and a private siding was laid to the distillery some time later.

Thomas Mackenzie died at Dailuaine House in 1915, leaving no family. His holding in what was now Dailuaine-Talisker Distilleries Ltd was put on the market and acquired by a consortium comprising DCL, Buchanan's, Dewar's and Johnnie Walker, at that time still separate companies. Improvements were made slowly and gradually. The distillery was not connected to the national grid until 1950 and a total of four steam engines, backed up by two waterwheels, powered various pieces of equipment until 1961. The waterwheels were 200yd apart but worked in tandem, connected by a steel cable supported on a Heath Robinson system of overhead pulleys.

Dailuaine was rebuilt in 1959–60 and still has similarities with the original construction, although the maltings and kiln have vanished and the configuration of the stills has changed, there now being six, paired as usual. The distillery's steam locomotive, Dailuaine No. 1, was donated to the Strathspey Railway Museum at Boat of Garten. Dailuaine's single malt has until recently only been bottled by the independents, the distillers preferring to use it for blending, although it has now found a worthy place in UDV's Flora & Fauna range.

SPEYSIDE
SINGLE MALT *SCOTCH WHISKY*

DAILUAINE

is the GAELIC for "the green vale". The *distillery*, established in 1852, lies in a hollow by the *CARRON BURN* in *BANFFSHIRE*. This *single Malt Scotch Whisky* has a *full bodied fruity* nose and a *smoky* finish. For more than a *hundred years* all *distillery supplies* were despatched by *rail*. The *steam locomotive* "DAILUAINE NO.1" was in use from *1939–1967* and is preserved on the *STRATHSPEY RAILWAY*.

AGED **16** YEARS

43% vol   Distilled & Bottled in SCOTLAND. DAILUAINE DISTILLERY, Carron, Aberlour, Banffshire, Scotland.   70cl

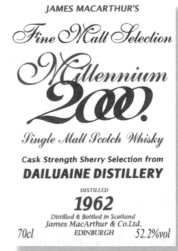

JAMES MACARTHUR'S
Fine Malt Selection
Millennium
2000.
Single Malt Scotch Whisky

Cask Strength Sherry Selection from
DAILUAINE DISTILLERY

DISTILLED
1962
Distilled & Bottled in Scotland
James MacArthur & Co.Ltd.
70cl   EDINBURGH   52.2%vol

IMPERIAL

I n the valley bottom below Dailuaine stands the tiny hamlet of Carron. Here, the Spey twists and turns on a course which bears an uncanny resemblance to that of the Thames as it flows through the east end of London. Unlike the Thames, however, the Spey is shallow and fast-flowing and tumbles over many rocks in its headlong rush to the sea. On the river bank, at the foot of a hillside of conifers, stands the knot of red brick buildings of the Imperial Distillery.

Imperial's history is entwined with that of nearby Dailuaine and also that of Talisker on the Isle of Skye. After the death in 1865 of William Mackenzie, the founder of Dailuaine, his son Thomas became a partner in the company and set about expanding the business by building a new distillery at Carron. Imperial was built in 1897, the year of Queen Victoria's diamond jubilee, and with empire fever at its height the new distillery was given an appropriate name. It even had a gilded replica of the imperial crown topping off the kiln roof.

Imperial was designed by Charles Doig, and apart from that one flight of fancy its design was very practical. Highland distilleries are usually built of granite, a material which is in plentiful supply, but Doig decided to build Imperial of red Aberdeen brick. The walls, which in places are 2ft thick to resist fire damage, are built within a framework of iron pillars and beams, and all internal doors were iron. The distillery was built literally alongside Carron station, so that cartage costs would be kept to a minimum.

In 1898 Mackenzie merged his company with that of Talisker, in which he had a substantial interest, to form Dailuaine-Talisker Distilleries Ltd, with himself as chairman and managing director. Imperial, newly finished, came under the ownership of the new company and began

40% Product of Scotland 70
vol. cl.

IMPERIAL
TRADEMARK OF PROPRIETORS: ALLIED DISTILLERS LTD

Single Highland Malt

Scotch DISTILLED Whisky
1990

IMPERIAL
Built in 1897, the year of
Queen Victoria's Diamond
Jubilee, the Imperial
Distillery stands
majestically among the
dark woods of Carron,
in a fold of the hills
which encompass the
glittering Spey.

Specially selected,
produced and bottled by
and under the
responsibility of
Gordon & Macphail,
Elgin, Scotland.
Regd. Bottler.

production that July. Six months later the boom ended with the bankruptcy of Pattison's Ltd and speculators lost interest in whisky. Mackenzie found that Dailuaine and Talisker could meet the reduced demand without assistance. After working for only one season, Imperial closed down for twenty years. Thomas Mackenzie died leaving no family and this, together with the recession, forced the company to seek a merger in order to survive. Mackenzie's shares were bought by a consortium of his customers, and when merged Dailuaine-Talisker became yet another DCL subsidiary.

Work restarted in 1919, using two of the biggest pot stills in Scotland, an 8,000-gallon wash still and a 7,500-gallon spirit still. The quantity of waste produced proved impossible to dispose of and again Imperial closed down. It spent the next

thirty years as a maltings until experiments at Aultmore led to the discovery of a process for making dark grains from distillery by-products, and Imperial was back in business. Over the next decade it was extensively refitted and the replica of the imperial crown, now rusted through, was demolished. After the Guinness take-over of DCL, Imperial was sold in 1989 to Allied Distillers, and its single malt is currently bottled under licence by Gordon & MacPhail.

In common with many distilleries, Imperial was requisitioned by the army for the duration of World War II as a billet for troops. Some of them used the dam for grenade practice and as a result it has leaked ever since. Before the war it had been used by the Caledonian Swimming Club of Aberdeen for their summer gala, which goes to show how hardy their swimmers must have been. Nowadays, distillery dams are usually surrounded by notices warning of the perils of swimming in the deep, cold water.

CARDHU

C ardhu, often marked on the map as Cardow, is the site of a distillery whose early days as an illicit still followed exactly the pattern of a farmer using his barley crop to make whisky, and selling that whisky for cash in the nearest available market.

The distillery was started by John Cumming, who took the lease on Cardow Farm in Upper Knockando in 1810. Its remote location in the hills, 4 miles from the nearest station, made it ideal for his purposes and there were abundant supplies of water and peat on Mannoch Hill nearby. Because of the absence of local inns, Excise officers visiting Knockando would lodge at the farm. One might expect someone running an illicit still to find this quite alarming, but Cumming's wife Helen's home baking served to mask the smell and smoke from her husband's still, and she would surreptitiously raise a red flag on the barn to warn her neighbours to hide theirs.

Cumming was convicted three times for illegal distilling and finally took out a licence in 1824. The distillery passed to his son after his death, but it was attached to the farm and the lease ran out every nineteen years. The buildings were primitive and much of the work was done by manual labour. Cumming's son died in 1872 and his widow took over, employing three men to run the distillery. In 1884 she bought land adjoining the farm and supervised the building of a new distillery complete with all mod cons, selling the old plant to William Grant. She adopted the name Cardhu as a trade mark and claimed to be the only Speyside distillery not to use the Glenlivet name, saying that the whisky was good enough not to need it. Blenders seemed to agree, reckoning

that a single gallon of Cardhu would cover 10 gallons of grain spirit, and it sold at a high price.

Elizabeth Cumming ran the business for seventeen years, handing over to her son, who sold out to Johnnie Walker in 1893.

Cardhu is still licensed to Johnnie Walker. It has been steadily upgraded over the years, and was largely rebuilt in 1960–1 when the waterwheels and steam engines were finally removed. It was the first Scottish distillery to have oil-fired stills, when one of the two pairs it then had were converted in 1922. It was an experiment far ahead of its time, but was abandoned after two years. Cardhu's workforce were also the first on Speyside to have electric lighting in their homes.

For many years Cardhu's single malt was bottled from bourbon wood at twelve years old. All sherry-aged spirit goes for blending, with two-thirds of production being taken by Johnnie Walker. However, in the distillers' efforts to keep pace with a soaring growth in demand from Spain, Cardhu has recently become a vatted malt, made with the addition of spirit from some of Diageo's other Speyside distilleries, one of which is Glendullan. To emphasise the change the distillery itself is set to adopt the name Cardow.

TAMDHU

Speyside first became accessible to tourists in 1863 when the Strathspey railway was opened, running from Boat of Garten to Craigellachie, and as more visitors were attracted to the area it drew the attention of the whisky blenders. Glenlivet-style whisky was already becoming popular and by the end of the century, when the industry was in its boom period, three new distilleries had been planned for the parish of Knockando: Tamdhu, Imperial and Knockando itself. It was a popular time for building distilleries. Within two years of Tamdhu's foundation, a further twelve malt distilleries were built on Speyside which are still working today.

Tamdhu was established in 1897 by a consortium of local businessmen headed by the agent for the Caledonian Bank in Elgin. He selected a site where the Knockando Burn enters the Spey, directly opposite that chosen for Knockando Distillery. The site was reputedly once used by smugglers who chose it for the exceptional quality of the water, the burn being fed by springs in the hills to the north. In common with numerous other distilleries at the time, it was far enough from civilisation to need accommodation for the workforce on site and a connecting road had to be built to link up to the main Grantown–Craigellachie road, now the B9102. The Strathspey branch line ran right past the distillery, which had its own station, named Dalbeallie. The railway closed in 1968; all that remains of it is a museum at Boat of Garten and its route is now the Speyside Way long-distance footpath. Dalbeallie station was converted into a visitor centre when Tamdhu was launched as a single malt in 1976, although at the time of writing the distillery has dropped from the tourist Whisky Trail.

The distillery's first manager, George Reid, was responsible for hiring the workforce and commissioning the plant. Altogether he employed twenty men, the highest-paid being the cooper, who was paid 27s (£1.35) a week. The first distillation was made in mid-July 1897 and produced 64.6 proof gallons, filled into port hogsheads for Robertson & Baxter. Samples of each distillation run were sent to each of the consortium partners for their opinions. The following year, on Robertson & Baxter's recommendation, Tamdhu was absorbed into the Highland Distilleries Co., in whose fold it has remained ever since. The distillery was expanded in the 1970s and was one of the first to have Saladin maltings. It now has ten Saladin boxes, each holding 22 tons of barley, and each located in separate (and very steamy) rooms within the maltings. Tamdhu uses 44 tons of malt every day and is the only distillery in the Highlands capable of satisfying all its own malt requirements. Surplus production may be supplied to other distilleries in the area, notably its sister Glenrothes.

Tamdhu single malt has been bottled at two or three different ages in the past, and the current bottling carries no age statement at all. It is a typical Speyside malt, light-bodied, fragrant and slightly sweet. It's also in demand from blenders and is a component of Famous Grouse.

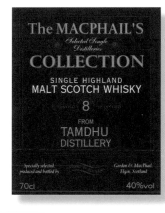

KNOCKANDO

Knockando is the flagship distillery of Justerini & Brooks, one of the first wine merchants in England to advertise Scotch whisky way back in 1779. The name derives from the Gaelic *Cnocan Dubh*, meaning 'little black hill'. It stands above a bend in the Spey, surrounded by trees above which only the pagoda roof is visible. The Speyside Way runs past the distillery, following the curve of the river, and on to Tamdhu a few hundred yards distant.

Knockando was built in 1898 by John Thomson. Despite being so close to Tamdhu its water comes from a completely different source, and Thomson secured the rights to the spring before building the distillery. He also established Knockando's tradition of 'seasonal' distilling. At the time of its foundation the distillery would only have worked during the winter, using barley sown in the spring. Subsequent owners have retained the idea of referring to each year of production as a 'season'. After all his work, Thomson only distilled at Knockando for a couple of years before the Pattison crash ended the whisky boom and he was forced to close down. The distillery was bought by W. & A. Gilbey in 1904 for £3,500. It has worked continuously since then, with breaks only during the two world wars when most distilleries were forced to close.

Although now over a century old, Knockando was quite advanced when it was built. It was the first distillery in Scotland to be built with electric lighting (although Cardhu's workforce were the first to have that novelty in their homes). Major reconstruction took place in 1969, when capacity was doubled. The site is beautifully kept, with rock gardens and lawns, and buildings in warm, yellow stone, the name 'Knockando' sculpted in relief on the stillhouse wall. The workers' cottages are still in use and the largest house, formerly occupied by the resident Excise officer, is now the home of the distillery manager. Manager Innes Shaw's great-grandfather was one of the carpenters who worked on the original distillery.

Knockando is almost unique in not being bottled simply when it attains a particular age, but rather when the master distiller considers it has matured to its peak. This is usually at around twelve to fifteen years old. Any casks which stand out as being extra special are kept for longer maturation, probably for twenty to twenty-five years, and this will become Knockando Extra Old. Knockando make a conscious effort to restrict the proportion of sherry ageing, so as not to dominate the flavour of the whisky. The season of distillation and the year of bottling are marked on the label, an interesting system also adopted by the independent bottlers Gordon & MacPhail for its Connoisseurs Choice range.

GLENFARCLAS

Glenfarclas is one of four distilleries on the flanks of Ben Rinnes and stands on the Rechlerich Farm on Ballindalloch estate. Established in 1836 by Robert Hay, it was acquired by the Grants in 1865 and has remained in their family ever since, although when John Grant first bought the distillery he sub-let it to John Smith, the brewer at The Glenlivet. The Grant family assumed complete control in 1870 after Smith moved on to Cragganmore.

When Alfred Barnard visited Glenfarclas in the late nineteenth century he found a small distillery isolated in wide open countryside. The single pair of stills produced around 50,000 gallons of spirit a year. Shortly after Barnard's visit, John Grant's two sons expanded the distillery to an annual capacity of some 300,000 gallons in response to the boom in demand for whisky. They also entered into an equal partnership with the ill-fated blending company Pattison's of Leith, whose failure in 1898 sent shock waves throughout the industry. The Grants retook full control of Glenfarclas and the company, as it is known today, was formed as a result of Pattison's collapse.

The distillery is now very advanced, and geared to high-volume production. It is functional rather than pretty, but its level of equipment is impressive. The 30ft diameter lauter mash tun is the biggest on Speyside and takes over 16 tons of grist per mash. The pipes are cleared of draff by sending footballs down them under pressure. Outside, at the draff hopper, the footballs are diverted and collected in a device rather like an outsized snooker table pocket. The six gas-fired stills too are the largest on Speyside, a fact easily appreciated on walking into the stillhouse.

Glenfarclas is one of the eight distilleries on the official tourist Whisky Trail and is particularly well appointed to receive the large number of visitors it gets every year. It is one of the very few distilleries where you can watch, from a special viewing gallery, the new spirit being filled into the casks. After a tour visitors are offered a dram in the hospitality suite, the Ships Room, which is lined with the original oak panelling taken from the ocean liner SS *Empress of Australia*.

Glenfarclas bottles its single malt at ten, fifteen, twenty-one, twenty-five and thirty years old, in addition to export versions at twelve and seventeeen years old and the occasional limited edition such as the 40-year-old bottled for the millennium. The 30-year-old was the outright winner of all the whisky categories in the 1996 International Spirits Challenge. The distillery also features in the *Guinness Book of Records* for the strongest malt whisky available in a distiller's 'official' bottling, Glenfarclas 105, the number referring to its proof rating of 105°, or 60% vol! The older vintages come completely from sherry wood, the younger ones from the more usual vatting of bourbon and sherry casks. It is a malt which prompted one blender, obviously a religious man, to remark, 'It goes down singing hymns!'

CRAGGANMORE

At the entrance to Cragganmore Distillery stands a rock which forms the basis of one of the more fanciful stories to emerge from the whisky industry. Cragganmore's founder, John Smith, was known to have been a giant of a man who not only travelled everywhere by rail but had to travel in the guard's van as he was too big to fit through the door of a passenger carriage! He presumably had little trouble shifting the rock when he ploughed it up in a field on his farm, and found beneath it a hoard of buried treasure which ensured his prosperity from then on.

Smith was said to have been one of the most experienced distillers of his time, having previously worked at at least six distilleries between 1851 and 1869, including such luminaries as Macallan, The Glenlivet and Glenfarclas. With such local knowledge it is not surprising that he should have chosen this site at Ballindalloch, virtually next door to the castle and near to the point where the River Avon meets the Spey. It was the first Speyside distillery to be built to take advantage of the railway and had its own private siding from Ballindalloch station. An old smuggling bothy was incorporated into the distillery buildings and used as the spirit-receiving room.

Cragganmore started production in 1869 and was managed by Smith's son William, who conducted Alfred Barnard over the premises when he visited Speyside in the course of preparing his book. By the time the book was published John Smith had died and Cragganmore was run by trustees, guided by his brother George, who was manager of Parkmore Distillery in Dufftown. Control of the business eventually passed to Smith's youngest son Gordon, who had worked as a distiller in the Transvaal.

Gordon Smith rebuilt Cragganmore, the original buildings seeming to have lasted no more than thirty years or so. The work was overseen by Charles Doig and although various labour-saving devices were installed, working methods and production capacity remained the same. The distillery was largely unaffected by the slump following the Pattison crash and its entire production was taken by Smith's agent, James Watson & Co. of Dundee.

Cragganmore was sold by Gordon Smith's widow to a consortium which included Peter Mackie, whose company was to become White Horse Distillers, and so Cragganmore became a partly owned subsidiary of DCL in 1927. The distillery seemed to catch up with the twentieth century rather slowly, for although electric lighting was installed in 1919 the company was ordering new components for the waterwheel as late as 1950 and the steam engine was still in use. An extra pair of stills was installed in 1964, and the spirit stills have T-shaped lye pipes instead of the more usual swan-necked variety. In 1996 a new lauter mash tun was installed. To give it a traditional appearance it has a copper top and oak-clad sides, and is the first of its type in the industry.

Cragganmore is regarded as being the 'spiritual home' of Old Parr, and this is an

association the company has developed over recent years. Its single malt is now bottled at twelve years old as one of those in UDV's Classic Malts range and is described on its packaging as 'haughty', arguably making it the only whisky to have an attitude.

TORMORE

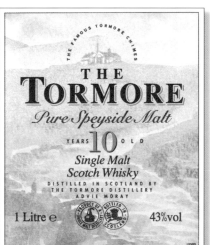

When Glen Elgin Distillery first began to take shape on the drawing board of its architect, Charles Doig, in 1898, he predicted to an associate that it would be the last distillery to be erected on Speyside for fifty years. In January 1899 the liquidators moved into the Leith blending company Pattison's, effectively ending the whisky boom. Doig's prediction was proved to be uncannily accurate, as it was not until the late 1950s that the next completely new Speyside malt distilleries began production.

Tormore was built as part of an expansion programme undertaken by Long John after that company's acquisition in 1956 by the American company Schenley Industries. It was designed by Sir Albert Richardson, a past president of the Royal Academy, as a showpiece distillery, and the unique design is proof that Richardson fulfilled his brief perfectly. The white-painted granite buildings sit amidst landscaped gardens at the foot of the Cromdale Hills. The huge stillhouse is adjoined by the cooperage, atop which is a clock that marks the passage of every hour by chiming the tune of

'Highland Laddie'. Included in the design are an imitation water mill, a curling pond and the housing for the workforce. On the day of the official opening a time capsule was buried in the forecourt. The capsule is in the shape of a pot still and contains a tregnum of Long John whisky, the names of all the employees and of the Scottish clans, samples of the raw materials and a treatise on the history of the industry and the manufacturing process.

I have heard it said that some people find it difficult to believe that such a comparatively new distillery can make so traditional a product. My experience of the new generation of distilleries built since the 1950s is that they are capable of producing often distinctive and individual whiskies that will stand comparison with those of any

distillery built in the previous century. The Tormore (for it is another of those which styles itself with the definite article) is a typical sweet, medium-bodied Speyside malt with a hint of almonds in the nose and a distinctive finish. The distillery's sheltered, north-facing location and the cold water of the Achvochkie Burn contribute to the cleanliness of the spirit.

In its short lifetime Tormore has seen three changes of ownership, the last being in 1990 when, along with Laphroaig, it was sold to Allied Distillers. The rather uninspiring label had by this time given way to a new design featuring a watercolour painting of the distillery commissioned by the previous owner, James Burrough Distillers, which gives the product a nice, 'hand-crafted' feel.

THE GLENLIVET

The history of The Glenlivet Distillery is essentially the history of the transition from illicit to legal distilling on a commercial scale, under the first realistic legislation to govern the industry.

The distillery can trace its origins back to at least 1815, but it is fairly safe to assume that whisky was being produced long before then. The Smith family is known to have settled in this remote part of the Scottish Highlands a hundred years earlier in 1715, at the time of the first Jacobite rising. In 1817 George Smith took a share in the lease of Upper Drumin Farm and no doubt continued to produce illicit whisky to supplement his meagre crofter's income. By this time Glenlivet whisky had established a reputation for being the finest available and was popular amongst the gentry, who did not seem too worried that it was made illegally.

In 1823 the government passed the Excise

Act in an attempt to stamp out illicit distilling. The Act was largely the brainchild of the Duke of Gordon, who was also Smith's landlord, and the duke persuaded Smith to take out the first licence under the new Act in return for assistance in setting up a new distillery at Drumin. The duke was keen to see the new enterprise bring some much-needed and legitimate employment to the glen. Smith's neighbours regarded him as having sold out to the government and made so many threats against him that the Laird of Aberlour gave him a pair of hair-trigger pistols. Smith is said to have carried them everywhere, even taking them to church and sleeping with them under his pillow.

Expansion of both the distillery and its attached farm prompted Smith, now in partnership with his son, to build a second distillery at Delnabo, south-west of Tomintoul.

When it became apparent that both distilleries were unable to satisfy the demand for the Smith's Glenlivet they leased further land from the Duke of Gordon at Minmore, and there built a new distillery with a capacity of 600 gallons per week. The distillery still occupies this site, close to the point where the Livet joins the Avon, and some of the original buildings are still in use. Shortly after, the company appointed Andrew Usher, generally credited as being the first commercial blender, as its agent. Smith's son also brought a test case to try to prevent other distilleries from calling themselves Glenlivets. Although not entirely successful, his action did establish the firm's exclusive right to use the title The Glenlivet.

Today, The Glenlivet is regarded as one of the premier malt whiskies and a classic example of the Speyside style. Deceptively simple at first tasting, its true complexity and depth become apparent with experience. The area seems to produce particularly fine raw materials which, combined with the local climate in the glen, produce beautifully soft, well-balanced whisky. A lightly peated malt is used. Water comes from Josie's Well, which is fed by underground streams, but research has proved that it takes rainwater two years to reach the well and no one has discovered where it goes in the meantime!

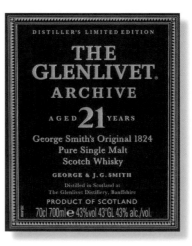

The Glenlivet is bottled at twelve and eighteen years old and occasionally in special vintages, for instance a 25-year-old bottled in 1977 to celebrate the Queen's silver jubilee, and has become the biggest-selling single malt in America. Only the distillery's official bottlings can be called The Glenlivet. It is bottled by the independents but they are restricted by Smith's legal precedent to calling it Glenlivet Whisky, or whisky from The Glenlivet Distillery.

TAMNAVULIN

Of all the distilleries which use the Glenlivet name Tamnavulin's entitlement stands taller than any, as it is the only one which stands literally on the banks of that hallowed water. The village of Tomnavulin, from which its name is corrupted, is situated amidst dramatic scenery on the west bank of the Livet, on the Tomintoul–Dufftown road. Dominated by the Hills of Cromdale to the west and Corryhabbie to the east, the village is surrounded by a knot of smaller hills above which eagles can be seen soaring.

Tamnavulin-Glenlivet is one of the younger generation of twentieth-century distilleries. It was built by Invergordon in 1966 alongside an old wool-carding mill which was converted into a visitor centre. The distillery was mothballed in 1995 and subsequently disappeared from the Tourist Board's Whisky Trail. The name Tamnavulin means 'mill on the hill', and the mill building and its waterwheel help to soften the appearance of the distillery itself, which is basically a collection of rather unprepossessing buildings.

It is a big distillery, its theoretical annual capacity of around 1.5 million proof gallons putting it halfway in size between its Chivas contemporaries Allt a' Bhainne and Braeval. It takes its water from springs rising in the hills to the west, at a place appropriately named Westertown. The water is stored in an underground reservoir and pumped to the distillery through an underground pipeline. Water is only taken from the Livet itself for cooling purposes. As is the fashion amongst new distilleries, Tamnavulin has no maltings of its own and buys in all its malt from outside suppliers who malt to the distillery's specification. Only a light peating is used.

The resultant single malt whisky is bottled after ten years' maturation in plain oak casks, giving it no more than a pale 'white wine' colour. It is an excellent statement of the Glenlivet style: soft, smooth and slightly sweet, and eminently drinkable. This is yet another example of a relatively young distillery whose product can outshine that of many of its much older rivals, and it would provide an encouraging introduction for any newcomer to malt whisky. It has recently been described as the Queen of Malts (the King being Macallan).

An older version of Tamnavulin-Glenlivet is also bottled, labelled as the Stillman's Dram. The first dram was distilled in the first year of production and bottled in 1991, at twenty-five years old. Many distilleries, when they start production, set aside their very first fillings and leave them tucked away at the back of a quiet warehouse where they will be left to mature for far longer than the normal ageing period. Eventually this whisky will be deemed to have matured to its peak, and will be bottled as a limited edition. If left for too long the whisky will pick up an excess of tannin, giving it a woody flavour, but if the casks were chosen carefully enough the results can be extremely satisfying.

BRAEVAL

Formerly the Braes of Glenlivet, a name taken from a horseshoe-shaped glen some 5 miles from Tomintoul, Braeval stands alongside the Crombie Water, a tributary of the Livet, at the foot of the comically named Tom Trumper hill. The road peters out just beyond the distillery, giving the distinct impression that you are in the middle of nowhere. Except for the soft running of the stream the place is eerily quiet, and it is difficult to believe that the nearby hamlet of Chapeltown is only just around the bend in the road. The distillery is the second highest in Scotland, at 1,100ft above sea level a mere 64ft below Dalwhinnie.

In the eighteenth century this was the heart of smuggling country, and the starting point for the journey over the hills to Aberdeen or Perth. It is said that there were 200 illicit stills in Glenlivet at that time, in other words one in every household. The area was raided by the Excise in 1752 and there was a skirmish between the farmers and the soldiers as they attempted to seize the stills.

Braeval was the first distillery to be built in the 1970s, the work commencing on Crown land on 7 July 1972. The first turf was cut by Edgar Bronfman, the son of the president of Seagram Distillers, Sam Bronfman. Construction of the distillery buildings began the following January and it became operational on 29 September 1973. It is a modern-looking distillery, and the company followed the same basic design for Allt a' Bhainne two years later, yet it does not look entirely out of place in the glen, its immaculately landscaped grounds set against a backdrop of heather-covered hills.

Automation allows the distillery to be operated by one man per eight-hour shift. The two large wash stills feed four small spirit stills in an arrangement similar to that at Macallan, but here the spirit stills are not necessarily used in pairs. The amount of low wines dictates the way the stills will be configured on any particular day. Once the distillation is complete, the spirit is reduced with spring water in 10,000-gallon stainless steel vats and tankered daily to Keith for racking into casks. There is no permanent bonded warehousing on site and the distillers do not fill the spirit into the casks themselves. All process water comes from two local springs: the Preenie, and Kate's Well.

Braeval is one of only four distilleries actually in Glenlivet (or the parish of Glenlivet) and undoubtedly its location and original name added a measure of prestige to the group's portfolio in the five years before they actually acquired The Glenlivet Distillers. The company does not bottle the malt itself, although it has recently appeared in Cadenhead's range, and The Master of Malt offers a number of bottlings at cask strength and 43% vol, including miniatures.

TOMINTOUL

I t seems odd that the highest village in Scotland, Wanlockhead, is actually in the Lowlands, and Tomintoul is left with only the runner-up prize for being highest in the Highlands. Tomintoul lies between the River Avon and the Livet and marks the bottom point of the 'Golden Triangle' of Speyside. It is a strange village, built on a grid system like an American city, a legacy of the mid-eighteenth-century fashion for founding planned villages. Its remote location, with the foothills of the Cairngorms visible to the south-east, means it is often snowbound in winter.

Tomintoul grew up around an inn, built to take advantage of traffic passing along the military road from the garrison at Corgarff to Fort George. The inn was selling whisky at 2d (less than 1p) a dram and it is inconceivable that the proprietor was not dealing in produce from Glenlivet's myriad illicit stills. Tomintoul's first legal distillery was opened at Delnabo, probably in the 1830s. The first owner went bankrupt and the premises were taken over and rebuilt by George Smith as an extension to his Glenlivet Distillery. Smith closed the operation at Delnabo when he relocated The Glenlivet to Minmore in 1858.

The present Tomintoul Distillery is about 5 miles from the village itself, on the B9136 Tomintoul–Glenlivet road. Although it stands right on the banks of the Avon it is within Glenlivet parish and used to make a point of this on the bottle label, which gave the distillery's telephone number as Glenlivet 274. It was built as a joint venture between two firms of Glasgow-based whisky brokers, Hay & MacLeod and W. & S. Strong, then owners of Fettercairn Distillery, and was the first of the new twentieth-century malt distilleries to be financed entirely by Scottish capital. A merger in the early 1970s with Whyte & Mackay, the owner of Dalmore, took Fettercairn and Tomintoul into the

W & M fold. Tomintoul is the youngest of this trio of distilleries by some 126 years.

Tomintoul is a functional distillery built to satisfy the need for malt whisky when it was in short supply during the sixties boom and as a result is rather unprepossessing, although the design was approved by the Royal Fine Art Commission. The builders started work in

November 1964 and had to keep at least two weeks' supply of materials on hand in case the site was cut off by snow. Special equipment was used which enabled them to lay concrete blocks in 10 degrees of frost. The plant was commissioned in July 1965 and enlarged after the Whyte & Mackay take-over.

Tomintoul is a big distillery, the casks stacked seven high in the warehouses. Its malt was first bottled in 1975, to celebrate the distillery's tenth birthday. It conforms well to the Glenlivet style, although it is probably the lightest in palate of those malts entitled to use the name. The distillery was acquired on 1 August 2000 by Angus Dundee Distillers.

BALMENACH

To the west of The Glenlivet Distillery, Strathavon and Strathspey are divided by the Haughs (hills) of Cromdale. In a hollow amongst these hills, a mile from the hamlet of Cromdale, is the Balmenach Distillery.

Balmenach was established by James McGregor on the site of one of the largest smuggling bothies in the Glenlivet district. Not far away was a huge cavern in the hillside, the hideout of a notorious smuggling gang who shot an Excise officer during one raid. McGregor came from Tomintoul to farm at Balmenach and was already distilling by the time he took out a licence in 1824. The distillery quickly achieved a good reputation and McGregor's clients included the Earl of Selkirk and the Duke of Bedford. He also supplied his whisky to the Gairloch Hotel at Lochmaree for Queen Victoria's visit.

After McGregor's death the family ran into problems. The constant availability of whisky at home had led to his sons drinking heavily and meeting an early death. Word was sent to the surviving son, who had emigrated to New Zealand to farm, and he returned to set the family and the distillery back onto the straight and narrow. A year later Balmenach almost fell foul of the storm which caused the Tay Bridge disaster. The chimney stack collapsed through the stillhouse roof, damaging the stills and spilling hot liquor into the furnaces. If it had not been for the stillman's presence of mind in running the spirit away through the discharge cocks the entire place could have been destroyed.

McGregor junior was responsible for many improvements at Balmenach. Alfred Barnard commented that it was one of the most primitive distilleries he had seen, all the equipment being of antiquated design and all motive power coming from the waterwheel. Improvements included an extra pair of stills, an oil engine for power and a private siding laid to Cromdale station. More modernisation followed the distillery's acquisition by DCL. The national grid came to Balmenach in 1937, earlier than it did to many of the surrounding distilleries, although the mill was still being steam powered in the 1950s. New building work took place in the 1960s and 1970s, when a Saladin maltings and dark grains plant were installed. DCL also bought a new steam locomotive after the take-over and this was presented, in immaculate condition, to the Strathspey Railway Museum after the Speyside branch line closed.

Part of McGregor's original residence was converted into a reception centre and Balmenach welcomed visitors until it was mothballed in 1993 as part of United Distillers' programme of rationalisation. The distillery has since been acquired by Inver House Distillers, and is now back in production.

(Inver House Distillers Ltd)

CONVALMORE

Convalmore is the first distillery one comes to on arriving at Dufftown from Craigellachie and was the fourth distillery to be established in the town. It takes its name from the Conval Hills, which it faces to the west and which were the source of its water.

The Convalmore-Glenlivet Distillery Co. was formed in June 1893 and all 1,200 shares were taken up by merchants and brokers, mostly based in Glasgow. The managing director was Peter Dawson, a whisky merchant who originally hailed from Dufftown, and so a ready market existed for Convalmore's product when the distillery went into production in February 1894. A decade later the company went into voluntary liquidation to enable its sale to W. P. Lowrie & Co., which was to hold the licence for over eighty years.

Lowrie was a former manager of Port Ellen Distillery on Islay and started his own business as a broker in 1869. His company claimed to be the first with Excise permission to bottle in bond, and also claimed to have originated the practice of blending malt and grain whiskies (Andrew Usher started doing this on a commercial scale around 1852 and may have wanted to argue this point). The company operated as blenders and bottlers for merchants who had no production facilities of their own and probably their best-known customer was James Buchanan, who drew his entire stock from them. When Lowrie's ran into financial difficulties in 1906 Buchanan followed his best course of action to avert the loss of his sole supplier, which was to buy out the company. Lowrie retired, leaving Buchanan to expand the company's premises in Glasgow to meet the demand for his blend Black & White.

Convalmore was virtually destroyed by fire on the night of 29 October 1909. The heat prevented the fire brigade from reaching the hose connections and the fire had to be fought with buckets of water. Many of the locals turned out to help, despite the snowstorm which began just after midnight. The stillhouse was saved, but the malt barn, kiln, mill, mash house and tun room were lost, with the damage estimated at up to £8,000. The distillery was immediately rebuilt and was back in production the following year. In addition to the pot stills, a continuous still was installed with a capacity to distil 500 gallons of wash per hour, but it was distilling the same wash as were the pot stills. It was an interesting and unusual experiment for a Highland malt distillery, and one which later had to be abandoned when it was found that it affected the maturation of the spirit.

Convalmore was transferred to the DCL subsidiary Scottish Malt Distillers Ltd in 1930. Much modernisation took place in the decade from 1962 to 1972, including the provision of a dark grains plant which also served Craigellachie, Glendullan and Mortlach distilleries. Convalmore has never been bottled as a single malt by the distillers themselves, although it is available from the independents. The distillery was mothballed in 1985 and has not worked since. It was sold in 1992 to Wm Grant, owner of its immediate neighbours Glenfiddich, Balvenie and Kininvic, which will be using its warehousing. There are no plans to reopen it for distilling.

GLENFIDDICH

It may seem ridiculous that, as recently as the 1960s, many malt distillers regarded their whiskies as being too distinctive for the 'Sassenachs' south of the border, and Grant's decision to send its single malt to England was greeted with derision by its competitors. It is Grant's which has had the last laugh, however, having spotted a gap in the market that everyone else is now desperately trying to fill. The company sets great store by tradition, and actively involves itself in events which will promote Scotland's heritage, yet it is innovative and extremely skilful at marketing, and if other distillers had had the same foresight then Glenfiddich might not now be the biggest selling single malt in the world.

William Grant was born in 1839. His father was a survivor of Waterloo, boasting that at 4ft 11in all the bullets had gone over his head! Grant worked at Mortlach Distillery, where he eventually became manager. Seeing his future as a distiller he persuaded his family to save every available penny towards the foundation of their own distillery. Two pieces of luck helped him on his way. Legend says that a priest showed him the secret location of the Robbie Dubh spring in the Conval Hills (the company now owns the whole hillside in order to protect its water supply), and the following year he was able to buy second-hand plant from Cardhu for the bargain price of £119 19s.

Grant and his nine children built Glenfiddich literally by their own sweat and toil, hiring only a single mason and carpenter for skilled labour. Grant's children helped to run the distillery, some whilst still at school. The whisky was sold as being suitable for medicinal purposes, every stage in the process being supervised by a qualified doctor! What this really meant was that William Grant's fourth son, Alex, was not only medically qualified but was also the head stillman. His younger brother George was maltman, and Charles was the brewer. All the hard work came to fruition on Christmas Day 1887 when Glenfiddich first ran from the stills.

Grant's big break came when a fire at The Glenlivet Distillery enabled the company to fill an order that The Glenlivet's owner was suddenly unable to meet and, by 1892, William Grant was building a second distillery next door, at Balvenie.

The Pattison crash in 1898 affected many distillers and Grant's answer was to diversify into blending, dealing directly with the retailers themselves. Charles Grant and his brother-in-law, Charles Gordon, were dispatched to England where they set up a sales office in Blackburn. It was perhaps this choice of base which led to their initial lack of success: after 503 sales calls they had sold only one case of whisky! Within ten years, however, they had established agencies in thirty countries. Again bucking the trend, Grant's actually stepped up production during Prohibition in readiness for the reopening of the US market.

Along with Springbank, Glenfiddich and its sisters Balvenie and Kininvie are the only Scottish malt distilleries still controlled by the descendants of their founders and Glenfiddich is now one of the biggest distilleries in Scotland, with twenty-eight stills split between its two stillhouses. They are all replicas of the originals that William Grant bought from Cardhu, as they always have been, one concession to new technology being the electric motors which drive the rummagers. Glenfiddich is the only Highland malt whisky to be bottled on site, and for many years carried no age statement. It is now bottled as a 12-year-old and is consequently a vatting of around 200 casks, of which 8–12 per cent will be first-fill sherry butts. Most of the spirit matures in plain oak. A 15-year-old cask-strength version is available, together with the 18-year-old Glenfiddich Excellence, which comes primarily from first-fill and refill sherry casks.

Glenfiddich was the first distillery to open to the public (in 1969) and now receives 125,000 visitors a year. It welcomed its one millionth visitor, an American tourist from New York, in 1987. Around a thousand visitors each year come from Japan and in 1990 the company was the first to hire a Japanese guide, Tatsuo Suzuki. The sight of him in his clan tartan kilt will be a memory that many people will take home with them.

BALVENIE

On a small hill overlooking Glenfiddich stands the ruin of Balvenie Castle, the residence of Margaret Douglas, 'the Fair Maid of Galloway'. After murdering her first husband and routing the second in battle, King James II took pity on her and reinstated her in Balvenie at an annual rent of a single red rose. When this castle fell into ruin another was built about half a mile away, a mansion designed in the Adam brothers style. This place was supposedly haunted by the laird's wife, whose lover had given her a rabid hound. The dog infected her, and the villagers proclaimed that the only cure was 'suffocation between two feather beds', a cure that was quickly administered.

William Grant was obviously not a superstitious man. Shortly after starting production at Glenfiddich he sold a batch of whisky to a William Williams of Aberdeen, who was so impressed with it that he offered to buy the entire distillery. Grant not only refused the offer, but expanded business at Glenfiddich to the point where he was able to establish a new distillery a mere five years later. That distillery is Balvenie, and was built around the Adam mansion. The original stills were purchased second-hand from Lagavulin and the now-defunct Glen Albyn.

Even today, Balvenie is an old-fashioned and very traditional distillery which could be run by four men. It is one of the few distilleries which still maintains its own floor maltings. Local peat is hand cut for kilning and some of its barley is supplied by Grant's own farm on the flanks of the Conval Hills. The distillery was expanded in 1955 and now has four pairs of stills. Its water comes from the same closely guarded source that supplies Glenfiddich: the Robbie Dubh spring.

Balvenie makes three versions of its single malt. It differs greatly from Glenfiddich, being softer, sweeter and more lingering, with far more sherry

character, and illustrates perfectly how two distilleries next door to each other can produce very different whiskies. About 18 per cent of production is matured in sherry wood, as opposed to 8–12 per cent at Glenfiddich, although like its next-door neighbour it ages the majority in plain oak. The Balvenie Founder's Reserve is a vatting of casks which have matured for a minimum of ten years, and carries a ten-year age statement. The Balvenie Doublewood carries a twelve-year age statement and matures for this period in plain casks, after which the malt is transferred into first-fill sweet oloroso casks where it matures for a further year before being bottled. The Balvenie Single Barrel is bottled at cask strength from 15-year-old casks selected by the company's 'noser', one cask yielding up to 300 bottles which are individually numbered.

Like many distilleries Balvenie sends much of its output for blending, but to prevent it from being sold by independents as a single malt it is vatted with a small proportion of Glenfiddich. Similarly, Glenfiddich sold for blending will be vatted with a small proportion of Balvenie. The mixtures are called Burnside and Wardhead, after areas of the Grant farm, and it is these mixtures which are sent to the blenders. A limited edition of 50-year-old Balvenie recently sold out, the last bottle being sold in the duty-free shop at Hong Kong for £520.

KININVIE

There is a saying in this part of Speyside:

Rome was built on seven hills.
Dufftown stands on seven stills.

This has held true for a long time, the original seven being (in chronological order) Mortlach, Glenfiddich, Balvenie, Convalmore, Parkmore, Dufftown, and Glendullan. When Parkmore Distillery, just downriver from Glendullan, closed down in 1931 its place was taken (although some time later) by Pittyvaich. Convalmore was then mothballed, then Kininvie opened to restore the status quo. Dufftown is without doubt the most densely populated distilling centre in Scotland, all its active distilleries being within a mile radius of the clock tower in the town square.

Driving around Dufftown does not take long and the distilleries are easy to spot; all of them are at the roadside and most have similar stone buildings. Kininvie however is an unexpectedly modern structure, shoehorned in amongst the buildings of Balvenie Distillery, and like its neighbour it belongs to Wm Grant. Named after the Kininvie estate which borders the grounds of Balvenie, it was officially opened in July 1990 by Mrs Janet Roberts, William Grant's granddaughter.

Despite its outwardly modern appearance Kininvie is traditional in its working methods, as are all Grant's malt distilleries. Grant's is a firm believer in the theory that the brewing stage has a significant effect on the outcome of the final spirit and Kininvie uses nine Oregon pine washbacks, all housed in an extension at Balvenie. The distillery has already been expanded in the short time since its inauguration and the stillhouse now contains nine stills – three wash stills and six spirit stills. The spirit stills resemble one of the two that William Grant originally bought from Cardhu, designs still in use at Glenfiddich, with a 'spare tyre' around their waists.

The company describes Kininvie spirit as being heavier, sweeter and fruitier than Balvenie, so it should mature into a very characterful malt. Its flavour is likely to be far removed from that of its elder sister Glenfiddich, which is light and fresh and often described as an ideal introduction to malt whisky. Glenfiddich and Balvenie spirit is sold to blenders as a vatting and Kininvie spirit is sold in the same way, the vatting in this case called Aldunie. Grant's was prompted to build Kininvie in order to supply a third high-quality malt for use in their own blend Grant's Family Reserve (originally named Standfast after the clan battle-cry 'Stand fast Craigellachie!'). If it matures into a whisky of the same quality as its sisters it will receive a warm welcome in the malt whisky marketplace, but with regard to a bottling Grant's is keeping everyone guessing.

MORTLACH

The ancient village of Mortlach dates back to the foundation of its church in AD 566, but it has been completely eclipsed ever since its famous neighbour Dufftown was grafted onto it in the early nineteenth century. The name is so ancient that neither historians nor authors can agree on its origins, but in Gaelic *morthlach* means 'great mound', and *mohrtullich* means 'great hills'. Readers may take their pick! King Malcolm's army fought the Danes at Mortlach in 1010, a time when the Vikings ruled Orkney and the Western Isles. The gravestone of a Viking general killed in the battle became known as the Aqua Vitae Stone, after it was discovered being used as a bar-counter for dispensing whisky to the builders of Balvenie Castle.

The distillery started life as a smuggling bothy and was situated to take advantage of a fast-flowing spring known as Highland John's (Jock's) Well. It went legal following the Act of 1823 and was Dufftown's first distillery. It was over sixty years later that the second, Glenfiddich, was founded by William Grant, who had at that time just become Mortlach's manager. Mortlach's early history was fraught with closures and changes of ownership, and the first licensee, James Findlater, sold it in 1831 for only £270. After a closure in 1837 it was bought by John and James Grant, then still working at Aberlour, and they stripped out the plant, presumably for use in their planned new venture, Glen Grant.

Mortlach spent the next few years unoccupied, save for the granary which was used as a Free church until one was built in Dufftown. The next owner reopened the premises as a brewery but, after enlarging and modernising the place, turned it back to distilling, employing eight men. By-products of the production process were used for animal feed and the owner kept twenty-four cattle and 150 pigs in adjoining byres. In a very efficient arrangement, pot ale was piped directly to the feed troughs, which could be filled by simply turning a stopcock. By the time it was acquired by Johnnie Walker in 1923 Mortlach was the largest of Dufftown's distilleries, its buildings straddling the road alongside Dullan Water. It had two barley lofts, four malt floors, two stillhouses and the biggest mash tun in the district. The machinery was powered by a substantial 50hp steam engine.

Mortlach is a highly regarded

whisky, smoky and malty, and with its peat flavour coming more from the water than from the malt. UDV bottles it as a 16-year-old single malt as part of its Flora & Fauna range, but by far the most interesting variants come from Gordon & MacPhail. Mortlach was one of the few distilleries which managed to stay open for most of World War II, and MacPhail's have a rare distillation from Christmas 1942, bottled at fifty years old. The same company also bottles 50-year-old Mortlach distilled in 1936 and 1939. None of these are cheap of course, the 1936 retailing at £1,000, and 5cl miniatures selling for £50!

DUFFTOWN

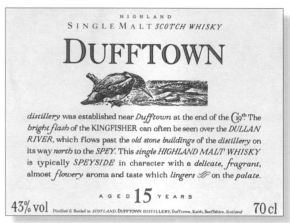

Dufftown marks the point where the Dullan Water meets the River Fiddich and was founded and named by James Duff, the fourth Earl of Fife, in 1817. The four main streets defined by Duff, Balvenie Street, Fife Street, Conval Street and Church Street, still exist today and are laid out in the form of a cross, at the centre of which is the clock tower. Originally the town jail, it once housed an illicit still, despite the fact that the town's Excise officer crossed the square six days a week on his way to and from work. The clock itself came from Banff, where it was known as 'the clock that hanged McPherson'. McPherson was a sort of

Scots Robin Hood who was condemned to death in 1700. He was given a pardon, but the Sheriff advanced the clock by an hour so that he would hang before the reprieve could be delivered.

It is said that the ideal quality of the water is the reason for Dufftown's population of distilleries. Traces of illicit stills are evident even now on river banks in the area, and as we have seen the town has seven distilleries (excluding Convalmore and Parkmore, now closed) crowded within its boundaries. Dufftown was the sixth to be built and was founded by two Liverpudlians, which is not as strange as it sounds as Liverpool itself had two distilleries at the end of the nineteenth century. It was converted from a sawmill and meal mill owned by a local farmer, who also owned Pittyvaich Farm at the top of the hill. Together with a solicitor, the four of them went into partnership as the Dufftown-Glenlivet Distillery Co.

The new distillery commenced mashing on 10 November 1896, using barley from Pittyvaich Farm. The first casks were filled six days later, the first distillation filling nine hogsheads and the

owners pronouncing the new make to be of excellent quality (I have yet to find a record of a distiller who was dissatisfied with his first attempts!). However, Dufftown's early years were blighted by a long-running argument over the distillery's rights to its water source. The local landowner was George Cowie, who also owned Mortlach Distillery and used Highland John's Well in the Conval Hills, which Dufftown was also using. The result was the diversion and re-diversion of water courses in the middle of the night, and the exchange of much acrimonious correspondence before an agreement was reached.

In 1933 the distillery passed to Bell's, which subsequently became part of United Distillers. Bell's output increased threefold between 1970 and 1980, prompting the company to open another malt distillery next door to Dufftown to help meet the demand. The new distillery took its name from Pittyvaich Farm and also appropriated the Glenlivet suffix, more from a sense of tradition than justification. Its four stills were exact replicas of those at Dufftown but its water supply came from two sources, the Balliemore and Convalleys springs. Pittyvaich eventually appeared in UDV's Flora & Fauna range, shortly before the distillery was mothballed as part of a rationalisation programme. It has since been demolished. Dufftown continues in production, supplying Bell's blending operations and bottling its single malt at fifteen years old.

GLENDULLAN

Glendullan was the last of the seven original distilleries built in Dufftown in the nineteenth century and stands on the bank of the River Fiddich on the eastern edge of the town. In its present form it is actually two distilleries sharing a common site, the new plant having been installed in the early 1970s to meet demand for malt whisky from various DCL subsidiary companies.

The original distillery was built in 1897, and various measures were taken to save on running costs. It shared with Mortlach a private railway siding which did away with the need for horse-and-cart transport to Dufftown station, and all its machinery was powered by a huge waterwheel driven by the Fiddich, thereby avoiding the expense of having to run a steam engine. The waterwheel was still being used when Glendullan reopened after World War II. The first consignment of barley was delivered on 28 January 1898, and the first distillation took place on 25 April. The whisky was a main constituent of Strathdon and Three Star, then well-known blends produced by Glendullan's owner, William Williams. In 1902 Glendullan was supplied to King Edward VII, and was granted royal appointment on 2 December that year.

The company merged with Greenlees Brothers to first become Macdonald, Greenlees & Williams Ltd, and finally Macdonald Greenlees Ltd, before being taken over by DCL in 1926. The Greenlees brothers set up as blenders in 1871 and were best known for the deluxe blend Old Parr, named after Thomas Parr who was reputed to have lived for 152 years and is buried in Westminster Abbey. The name is now used by UDV on a range of brands, including the super-deluxe (and super-expensive) blend Old Parr Elizabethan.

The new Glendullan distillery was built in 1971–2 and the stillhouse, which contains six stills, follows the style defined at Craigellachie. It is separated from the old distillery by a distance described by the company as 'short when the weather's good and long when it isn't'. The 11-acre site even has room for its own football pitch! The two distilleries worked in tandem, each having its own mash tun and washbacks, and their spirit was vatted together as Glendullan malt until the old distillery was closed in 1985.

Following the formation of United Distillers a stock-take at Glendullan turned up a small quantity of 60-year-old malt which the company used to make a blended whisky, much more robust than the usual blends of today, and which was intended to recreate the type of whisky popular in the nineteenth century. Unfortunately, due to the limited stock of the 60-year-old Glendullan, supplies are now exhausted.

The distillery's more prosaic 12-year-old is the only single malt I have seen recommended as being suitable for carrying in a hip flask. It is an assertive malt and presumably has a big-enough character to resist the spoiling effects of body heat and contact with a metal container.

143

ALLT A' BHAINNE

The establishment of Glen Keith and Braeval served to indicate the magnitude of Seagram's blending operation in the 1970s. Both these distilleries are capable of producing 1.4 million proof gallons of spirit per annum, and the rate of the company's expansion at that time can be gauged from the fact that Allt a' Bhainne was founded in 1975, just two years after Braeval. The new distillery cost Seagram £2.7 million and was the last to be built in Scotland until Wm Grant established Kininvie in 1990.

The distillery stands alongside the B9009 road, 5 miles from Dufftown, on the windswept south-east flank of Ben Rinnes. The name was chosen by Edgar Bronfman, chief executive of Seagram, and refers to the Milk Burn which runs alongside the distillery and which at one time was used by farmers for washing out their utensils after milking. In many respects the distillery resembles Braeval, both in outward appearance and in its equipment and working practices. The most obvious difference is the lack of a pagoda; neither of the two distilleries does its own malting and at Allt a' Bhainne even the pretence has been dropped.

A high degree of automation enables the distillery to be run by one man per shift, and the process plant is designed for efficient operation. The washbacks and mash tun are all stainless steel, and the mash tun lid is separated from its base by a 15in gap to allow for faster cooling after each mash.

The eight washbacks have conical bottoms for quick emptying. Two hundred and fifty tons of malt are mashed each week. There are two pairs of stills, and the spirit stills are unique in having tall, straight-sided necks. This makes it difficult for the heavier alcohols to reach the lyne arm and contributes to a clean spirit. The distillery takes process water from a total of thirteen springs rising from the red granite on Ben Rinnes, yet still suffered a water shortage during the hot, dry summer of 1995 when a further spring had to be found!

Allt a' Bhainne has no permanent bonded warehousing on site and, after reducing the raw spirit with water, sends it by road tanker to Keith where it is racked into casks. Keith Bond is one of the most extensive bonded warehouse facilities in Scotland and was converted from property purchased by Chivas from the Ministry of Aviation in 1957. A second site, established at Malcolmburn Farm, Mulben, in 1971 now exceeds it in size. The 500 or so casks that Allt a' Bhainne fills each week will be matured at one of these two locations.

The distillers have never bottled Allt a' Bhainne as a single malt and it has been left to the independents to make it available, albeit at a price, to the public. Bottlings have been made by The Whisky Castle of Tomintoul and James MacArthur, and The Master of Malt bottles 10- and 19-year-old versions, together with a 1980 distillation miniature.

THE CASTLE COLLECTION

Distilled 10/79
Bottled 2/93

Number 1

Cask No. 026329

ALLT-Á-BHAINNE
Aged 13 Years

Bottled In Scotland For
The Whisky Castle
Tomintoul

5cl.   43% vol.

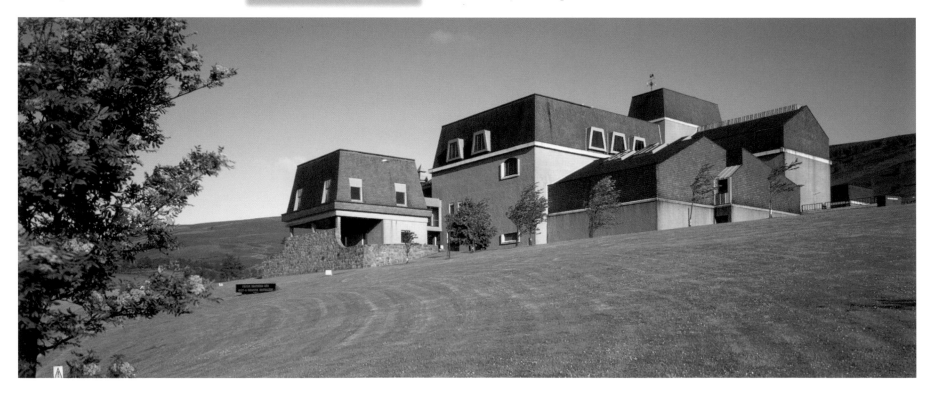

AUCHROISK

Auchroisk commenced distilling in January 1974. It is a spacious distillery, perhaps built a little larger than absolutely necessary, but then this allows for future expansion and provides for a relaxed working environment. It is also extremely clean, a fact which prompted one visitor to comment to the effect that you could eat a meal off the stillhouse floor. Ever since, large visiting groups have been entertained there with a buffet laid out in the open area between the two banks of stills! All four of J & B's distilleries use stills of similar design and Auchroisk's four pairs are larger-sized replicas of those at Glen Spey. Other than the stills themselves, all the process equipment is stainless steel. The lauter tun produces a wort which generates less lather in fermentation so the washbacks need no switchers. The distillery consumes 230 tons of lightly peated malt every week.

Auchroisk's prime claim to fame is The Singleton. The name comes from an expression used by whisky brokers in the early 1900s. If a broker had only one cask of a special malt whisky in stock, he would describe it as being 'a singleton'. It also has the advantage of being easier to say than the name of the distillery, which is one of those Gaelic-derived words whose appearance bears little resemblance to its pronunciation. Introduced in 1987, The Singleton had won eight major awards by 1992, the year in which it also became the Malt Whisky Association's number one seller. A substantial part of the malt spends its final year or so prior to bottling in sherry butts, a method which gives the spirit body and completeness without letting the sherry dominate. The distillers make much of the whisky's smoothness, and well they might. Through the smoke, fruit and hint of mint, comes the unmistakable feel of Dorie's silky water.

A s is the case with most of the new twentieth-century distilleries Auchroisk was built to satisfy a need for malt whisky for blending, and in particular the needs of the International Distillers & Vintners Group (IDV), and it is an important cog in the machinery which produces J & B Rare. However, many of the new distilleries bottle single malts which are more than a match for those from some of their much longer-established competitors, and Auchroisk is the best example of this phenomenon.

The distillery is striking in appearance and its hill-top site is visible from Rothes. It was built in 1973 to a design by Westminster Design Associates, and from the air looks like a very elaborate model. The key to its location is Dorie's Well, a source of pure spring water previously untapped by distillers due to its position halfway down a deep gully. Today, the well is protected inside a small stone building and it is surprising how such a tiny spring can supply enough water for a distillery with an annual production of over 1.5 million proof gallons.

GLENTAUCHERS

Along with Dewar's and Johnnie Walker, one of the original 'big three' whisky companies was that of James Buchanan. Buchanan's start in the industry was as London agent for the blending company Mackinlay's, but after less than five years with them he left to set up his own business. He had little experience and only a small amount of capital borrowed from a friend, but he was a gifted salesman and confessed later that his success was almost entirely due to his sheer self-confidence. He was one of the first merchants to see the potential of bottled whisky and is credited with the first branded blend on the market, Black & White. The company logo of the black and white terriers was also his own idea. Buchanan had a good relationship with W. P. Lowrie, a Glasgow whisky broker from whom he obtained the bulk of his supplies, and it seemed natural that at some point the two companies should embark on a joint venture.

On 29 May 1897, the newly formed Glentauchers Distillery Co. laid the foundation stone of its new distillery in a field on the Tauchers Farm at Mulben, some 3 miles from Keith. It was tucked between the road and the Aberdeen–Inverness railway, from which a siding was laid into the site. The buildings were laid out in the form of a square, an arrangement adopted by a number of distilleries, and interconnected by double iron doors to resist the spread of any fire. The water supply was ample enough to be used not only for distilling but also for powering all the distillery's machinery, thereby obviating the need to buy a steam engine. The water to be used for this purpose was stored in a large dam which covered 3 acres.

It was almost a year to the day after the foundation stone was laid that Glentauchers began malting, and mashing commenced the following month. From starting with Mackinlay's in 1879, Buchanan had by 1919 built up a company which owned five malt distilleries: Glentauchers itself, Dalwhinnie, Convalmore, Bankier in the Lowlands, and Lochruan at Campbeltown. Of these, Bankier and Lochruan have been closed for many years and Convalmore has been sold to Wm Grant, which has no plans to reopen it for distilling. In 1989 Glentauchers was sold to Allied Distillers, leaving only Dalwhinnie still licensed to James Buchanan.

By 1925 Glentauchers was generating its own electricity and was finally connected to the national grid in 1958. Other improvements had been made in the meantime, and the mash house, tun room and stillhouse were completely rebuilt in 1965–6, and the number of stills trebled to six. Prior to the take-over by Allied Distillers Glentauchers had never been bottled as a single malt by the distillers themselves, though it is now bottled under licence by Gordon & MacPhail.

AULTMORE

A ultmore began life as a typical Victorian distillery built, like many others in this area, in the closing years of the nineteenth century, yet its significance lies in the 1950s when experiments were carried out there to develop a process for making animal feedstuffs from distillery by-products. The name Aultmore is derived from the Gaelic *allt mhor*, meaning 'big burn'. One of Dewar's distilleries, it stands on the B9016 Portgordon road, a couple of miles north-west of Keith. Before the Excise Act was passed this area was rife with smugglers, all attracted by the ample supplies of water and peat from the delightfully named Foggie Moss close by, and the ready market for their illicit produce amongst the innkeepers of Keith, Portgordon and Fochabers.

CASK No 2900

ADELPHI DISTILLERY LIMITED

FROM AULTMORE, 14 YEARS OLD

60.1% vol   70cl

Aultmore was built by Alexander Edward in 1896 and entered production the following year. Edward had already inherited Benrinnes from his father David, and co-founded Craigellachie in partnership with Peter Mackie. Aultmore's business took off immediately and by July 1898 production stood at about 100,000 gallons a year, and further malt barns, tun room space and warehousing had to be built. That same year, Alexander Edward bought Oban Distillery and formed the Oban and Aultmore Distilleries Ltd. The company's board of directors included whisky broker F. W. Brickmann, who was also closely associated with the blending company Pattison's, and hence Pattison's became a major client for Aultmore's product. The Pattison crash affected many distilleries and the whisky industry suffered a slump from which it did not revive until 1903–4. Brickmann's own business was a casualty of the crash.

Government restrictions on distilling during World War I, together with the subsequent recession in Britain and Prohibition in the USA, prompted Edward's company to put Oban and Aultmore up for sale in 1923. Oban was bought by a syndicate, and Aultmore was sold to Dewar's

for £20,000. Thus Aultmore was absorbed into DCL when Dewar's amalgamated in 1925, and was transferred to its subsidiary Scottish Malt Distillers in 1930.

DCL modernised many of its distilleries in the 1960s and early 1970s, and Aultmore saw a number of changes in that period. The maltings closed, the waterwheel was demolished and the steam engine, an Abernethy 10hp model, was retired, although it is preserved at the distillery. The stills were converted to steam heating and an extra pair of stills was installed. The refurbishment concluded in 1972 with the building of a dark grains plant, which makes

animal feed from a combin- ation of draff and pot ale. Process water comes from the Burn of Auchinderran and is held in a dam on the distillery's attached farm, Milltown of Tarrycroys. The Burn of Ryeriggs, on the opposite side of the road, provides additional cooling water.

After the Guinness-Grand Met merger in 1997 the distillery was one of four which were acquired by Bacardi, along with the Dewar company itself.

STRATHISLA

Strathisla is literally named after the district in which it lies: the strath, or valley, of the River Isla. The town of Keith, which grew up here, is an ancient town whose history is littered with both saints and brigands, and brewing and distilling have been carried out here since the thirteenth century.

The first reference is from 1208, when it was recorded that the vicar and his churchmen began to make 'heather ale'. The next mention is in 1545, when George Ogilvy received a grant of land from the Bishop of Moray, which included the town of Keith and its brewery. It is the site of that sixteenth-century brewery on which Strathisla Distillery now stands. The original owner, George Taylor, obtained a charter in 1785 from the Earl of Findlater and Seafield for a distillery on the site, the distillery said to have been founded the following year. However, during reconstruction work in a warehouse undertaken in August 1986 workmen uncovered a stone inscribed with the date 1783. The stone was incorporated into the new building work.

Strathisla is now the oldest working distillery in the Highlands, although not the oldest in Scotland (it is predated by Glenturret and Bowmore). By the time it was visited by Alfred Barnard in the late nineteenth century it was known as the Milton (or Milltown) Distillery, a name still used by some of the older local residents. It had also been considerably enlarged and modernised, and stood favourable comparison with the newest Speyside distilleries of the time. It had a single pair of stills: a 5,000-gallon wash still and a 2,000-gallon spirit still, respectable capacities even today. It was said that the spring water fed through the condensers was cold enough to allow distilling to continue even on the hottest summer day. The distiller admitted to Barnard that the spring water was mixed with a small quantity of Isla river water prior to mashing, a custom dating from the distillery's foundation which it was claimed had beneficial results on the spirit! In 1880 the distillery became the first in the north of Scotland to be incorporated as a limited company.

Until 1950, Milton Distillery remained a private company. Its then owner was Jay Pomeroy, who also owned the Cambridge Theatre in London. Pomeroy was a financier who speculated in a number of whisky companies and whose business practices, as described in the Court of Sessions, led to his conviction for tax evasion, owing over £110,000. He caused uproar amongst the distillery's customers by introducing pro-forma invoicing, the customers not being used to paying for their whisky before receiving it! The distillery was sold at auction on 15 April 1950 for £71,000, apparently to a church organist from Aberdeen! He turned out to be a friend of James Barclay, the managing director of Chivas Bros Ltd, who had been sent to the auction on Barclay's behalf in order to conceal the true identity of the purchaser, and his instructions were to buy the distillery whatever the cost. Chivas had itself become a subsidiary of the Canadian Seagram Co. Ltd the year before and had until that point been a blending company, but the purchase of Milton enabled it to move directly into distilling. It was the first step of an ambitious expansion programme which was to establish Seagram firmly in Scotland. The company's first act was to change the name of the distillery back to Strathisla.

The river now provides only cooling water but process water still comes from Broomhill spring (the Fons Bulliens) which rises in the hill above the distillery. Originally a holy well used by the monks, it is reputedly guarded by kelpies (fairies) and their magic circle is faithfully preserved. The water is slightly hard, with very little peat taint, and the malt is also only lightly peated. The stillhouse contains two pairs of stills, all heated by steam coils. The washbacks are wood, the distillers firmly believing that the fermentation stage is vital to the character of the spirit. In fact, Strathisla still functions very much as it would have done 200 years ago, and some of its original buildings are still in use.

The resulting single malt is soft and sherryish, with some maltiness. It appears in Chivas's Heritage Selection at twelve years old, but Gordon & MacPhail bottles it in a range of ages up to thirty-five years old. The bulk of production goes into Chivas's blends and it is known as the heart of Chivas Regal. At the start of 2001 the future of Chivas is yet to be decided as Seagram's wine and spirits business is in the process of being acquired by Diageo and Pernod-Ricard.

GLEN KEITH

converted yet again, this time to steam coils. With the distillery barely celebrating its silver jubilee, Seagram pulled out all the plant and replaced it with new computerised equipment.

Today, Glen Keith is an intriguing mixture of traditional methods and modern technology. It uses similar 12,000-gallon wooden washbacks to those at Strathisla, and mashes 8 tons of grist in each mash using water from Newmill spring. However, it fills 500 casks per week, almost twice the capacity of Strathisla, and thanks to the computer it manages this with only a small workforce.

Chivas now includes Glen Keith in its Heritage Selection, at ten years old and bottled at 43% vol. It has also been available from Wm Cadenhead, and a 1967 distillation appears in Gordon & MacPhail's Connoisseurs Choice range. The bulk of production is used for blending, primarily at present in Seagram's own blends. Should the acquisition of Seagram's wine and spirits business be successfully concluded it looks likely that the distillery will pass to Pernod.

A t the bottom of the hill from Strathisla and on the opposite side of the river, its pagoda visible through the trees, stands its sister and near neighbour Glen Keith. Built to satisfy a demand for single malts for blending purposes during the boom years of the late 1950s, it was one of the first of the twentieth-century malt distilleries to be built.

The site was formerly occupied by the old Keith Mills, a long-established flour and oatmeal milling operation belonging to the Angus Milling Co. Ltd. Seagram acquired the site in 1957 and promptly demolished most of the old mill. Only the most northerly of the original buildings remains and the new distillery was substantially built in local Keith stone. Production began in

December of the following year under the name Glen Keith-Glenlivet. The suffix was later dropped when Seagram acquired The Glenlivet Distillers Ltd in 1978.

Glen Keith was to undergo several changes during its first twenty-five years of existence, both to its equipment and to its operating methods. Initially it used triple distillation, using a single wash still and two spirit stills to concentrate the low wines. The method was more traditionally used in the Lowlands, and although not unheard of further north, it had fallen from favour with Highland distillers by the 1920s. Glen Keith abandoned triple distillation in 1970 and the following year became the first distillery in Scotland to use gas-fired stills. The experiment lasted only three years before the stills were

149

STRATHMILL

The third of Keith's town-centre distilleries is tucked away from public view down a little road off Regent Street, sandwiched between Fife Keith golf course and the River Isla, and not far from the Auld Brig, a picturesque packhorse bridge dating back to 1609 and one of the oldest bridges in Scotland.

Strathmill started life in 1823 as Strathisla Mills, an oatmeal mill. The first distillery to use the Strathisla name, founded by John Keith in 1825 and surviving for a brief four years, was also reputed to stand on this site. The mill was rebuilt as a distillery in 1891, when it was named Glenisla-Glenlivet, and became Strathmill after being purchased by W. & A. Gilbey in 1895 for £9,500. Gilbey's was in the process of expanding into the whisky trade, having started with the acquisition of Glen Spey in 1887 and continuing with that of Knockando in 1904. The company was also later to acquire, through various mergers, that of Justerini & Brooks. J & B, to which Glen Spey, Strathmill and Knockando were licensed, can trace its history back to 1749, when Giacomo Justerini came to London from Bologna and set up as a wine merchant in partnership with George Johnson. Their first advertisement for whisky was placed in the *Morning Post* on 17 June 1779. The company was purchased by Alfred Brooks in 1831, when it became J & B. It in turn merged with Twiss, Browning & Hallowes in 1952 to form United Wine Traders Ltd, which merged with Gilbey's in 1962 to create International Distillers & Vintners (IDV). Subsequent take-overs took it into Grand Metropolitan, which merged with Guinness to become United Distillers & Vintners. UDV thus acquired the J & B brand, together with its four associated distilleries (now including Auchroisk), at the expense of divesting four of its own existing distilleries, and the Dewar company, to Bacardi.

CONNOISSEURS CHOICE

SPEYSIDE
Single Malt Scotch Whisky

DISTILLED AT
STRATHMILL
DISTILLERY
Proprietors: Justerini & Brooks Ltd

DISTILLED
1991

Specially selected, produced and bottled by
Gordon & MacPhail
Elgin . Scotland
Product of Scotland

70cl   40% vol

Strathmill continued to operate virtually unchanged until the late 1960s, when Gilbey's began a major reconstruction of all its distilleries. The maltings was converted into a warehouse, and the double kilns into a malt storage area. An additional pair of stills was installed and the old worm tubs were replaced by condensers. The stills are heated with steam coils and kettles, and the spirit stills have purifiers fitted into the lyne arms. The River Isla provides cooling water, but process water comes from the distillery's own spring, which rises behind one of the warehouses. Strathmill's warehouse capacity is limited, and most of the spirit is tankered to Auchroisk for maturation.

Strathmill is scarcely found as a single malt, even in independent bottlings, and virtually all of its production is destined for blending, in particular as a component of J & B Rare.

KNOCKDHU

In a dip between the A95 and the B9022 a few miles east of Keith lies the tiny, blink-and-you-miss-it, hamlet of Knock. Overshadowed by the 1,412ft Knock Hill, a local landmark, Knockdhu Distillery stands in a tranquil setting amidst stands of trees. Historically, Knockdhu is significant in that it was the first malt distillery to be built by DCL. It was specifically built to supply whisky to Haig's, which was under contract to buy all its blending whisky from DCL, and for its part DCL was keen to prevent Haig's from building its own malt distillery.

In 1892 the Knock estate was purchased from the Duke of Fife by John Morrison. Morrison subsequently discovered a spring on Knock Hill and, so the story goes, was so impressed with the quality of the water that he sent samples to a firm of analysts for their opinion. The company also happened to work for DCL, and shortly afterwards the Distillers Company approached Morrison with a view to buying land on his estate on which to build a new distillery. A deal was struck and work on Knockdhu commenced in

(Inver House Distillers Ltd)

May 1893, the distillery being built of local grey granite and served by a siding and station built for it by the Great North of Scotland Railway. Production began in October 1894 with a projected output of 2,500 gallons per week. By the winter of 1898–9 more warehouses had been built and the distillery's workforce had grown to nineteen. The *Banffshire Journal* confidently, but erroneously, predicted that Knock would become a thriving village.

In 1924 DCL formed a new subsidiary company, The Distillers Agency Ltd, to handle the business of its export branch. The Distillers Agency acquired the licence for Knockdhu and ran the distillery until 1930, when it was transferred to Scottish Malt Distillers, the subsidiary formed to take over the running of all DCL's malt distilleries. Knockdhu later passed to James Munro & Son Ltd, which was part of Macdonald Greenlees, and had also operated Dalwhinnie on behalf of Cook & Bernheimer.

In 1928 the distillery saw the first of a number of improvements. to its equipment, a new explosion-proof Boby malt mill. The manager must have been glad to see the back of the old one as it had caused him considerable alarm on a number of occasions, the worst being when an explosion partly demolished the stillhouse wall, took off the roof and set fire to the rafters. The distillery closed briefly during the Depression and again during World War II, when a unit of the Indian Army was billeted in the malt barns. The horsemen used to train on the slopes of Knock Hill.

After the war the distillery was gradually rebuilt and refitted, a new chimney being constructed as recently as 1980. Three years later DCL closed a number of its distilleries and Knockdhu was one of the casualties. It remained closed until 1988, when it was acquired by Inver House and put back into production. Its malt is now sold as An Cnoc, to avoid confusion with Knockando.

GLENDRONACH

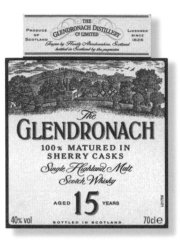

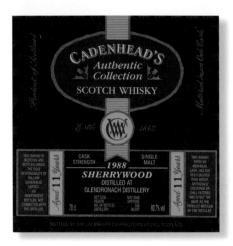

The Glendronach takes its name from the Dronac Burn, whose banks it straddles, and stands in tranquil countryside on the very eastern edge of Speyside's 'Golden Triangle'. It is one of half a dozen distilleries recorded in the area around Huntly and Insch, of which only one other, Benachie, ever enjoyed any degree of success. It was first licensed in 1826 to James Allardes, and has had a succession of illustrious owners. Allardes himself found favour with the fifth Duke of Gordon after introducing him to his product, and all went well until 1837 when a serious fire occurred. This must surely have been before The Glendronach acquired its colony of rooks, whose presence is meant to confer good luck! The next owner, Walter Scott, was an experienced distiller, having learned his trade at Teaninich on the Cromarty Firth. Scott went on to become a shipping magnate and a pioneer in breeding Aberdeen Shorthorn cattle, and the home he built at The Glendronach housed an impressive collection of trophies and awards for prize animals. After a further change of ownership The Glendronach was sold in 1920 to Captain Charles Grant, the fifth son of William Grant of Glenfiddich.

The Glendronach remained under the Grant family's control until 1960, when it was acquired by Wm Teacher & Sons. In 1976 Teacher's itself was absorbed by Allied Brewers, the distilling branch of which company was in 1988 to become Allied Distillers. Although capacity was increased at The Glendronach, the company was at pains to preserve the old working methods as much as possible in the belief that the old ways contribute greatly to the character and quality of the final spirit. The distillery still has its floor maltings, Oregon pine washbacks and coal-fired stills, and uses locally grown barley. The old steam-powered wagon is preserved in concourse condition and still makes appearances at local events.

For a number of years The Glendronach was unique in offering two different versions of its 12-year-old single malt, one vatted from a combination of plain oak and sherry casks and the other from sherry casks alone. For the enthusiast it was the only commercially available way of testing the effect that total sherry ageing has on malt whisky. Sadly, the company abandoned this idea in favour of The Glendronach Traditional, which as the name suggests was a more traditional vatting from bourbon and sherry wood, although it came extensively from first-fill sherry casks. This too has now gone, the distillers having taken the opposite tack and introduced a 15-year-old which comes entirely from sherry wood. Aficionados wishing to compare the effects of bourbon and sherry ageing side by side may still do so, thanks to Springbank's current bottlings of Longrow.

ARDMORE

Ardmore was founded in 1898 at the village of Kennethmont in Aberdeenshire and, along with its sister The Glendronach a few miles to the north-east, marks the eastern edge of Speyside. The distillery is about a mile from Leith Hall, a Scottish baronial manor dating from 1650, and between here and Aberdeen itself is an area rich in antiquities, castles and National Trust properties.

Ardmore stands alongside the B9002 and was built by William Teacher's son Adam, although he died before it was completed. Until it became part of Allied Breweries in 1976 Teacher's was the largest independent Scotch whisky company still controlled by its founder's descendants. William Teacher was a Glasgow merchant with a chain of successful shops. His activities in whisky blending, making up batches of whisky to his customers' specifications, led him to build up a portfolio of blend recipes, and it was inevitable that he would eventually develop from these his own house blend. This was to become Teacher's Highland Cream, and the brand name was registered in 1884. Although there were other blends marketed by the company, it is Highland Cream which has stood the test of time. The company rationed supplies to its clients during World War I, and so during the war built up a good stock of whisky. This attracted the attention of DCL, which tried unsuccessfully in 1921 to gain an interest in the company. Thus Teacher's remained independent until 1976 when it became part of Allied Breweries, and subsequently Allied Distillers.

Ardmore was the first malt distillery to be built by Teacher's, and is now one of Allied's largest. It was extended from two to four stills in 1955, and a further four were added in 1974. The wash and spirit stills are the same size, with a capacity of 3,300 gallons, and six are coal fired. Malt is supplied by Allied's central maltings, Robert Kilgour & Co. at Kirkcaldy, and is well peated in comparison to the usual Speyside standards. Twelve tons of grist are mashed at a time. The wort is fermented in fourteen washbacks, the largest of which hold over 13,000 gallons. Process water comes from springs on Knockandy Hill. The company also has research laboratories situated at Ardmore. Some 35,000 casks rest maturing in the warehouses, the oldest one a relatively recent 1974 distillation. The malt is one of those bottled under licence for the company by Gordon & MacPhail and, like Imperial's, has a 'vintage' rather than an age.

153

The Eastern & Southern Highlands

Glen Garioch •

Royal Lochnagar •

Fettercairn •

Glencadam • • Glenesk

Blair Athol • • Edradour

Aberfeldy •

• Glenturret

• Tullibardine

• Deanston

• Glengoyne

• Loch Lomond

GLEN GARIOCH

With the exception of Campbeltown, Morrison Bowmore Distillers has a portfolio representing each of Scotland's whisky-producing regions, and of these the Highland representative is Glen Garioch. It is one of the few remaining eastern Highland distilleries and re-entered production in November 1997 after a two-year closure.

Glen Garioch is situated in the village of Oldmeldrum, about 18 miles from Aberdeen.

Following the closures of Glenugie at Peterhead and Glenury at Stonehaven it is now Scotland's most easterly distillery. Oldmeldrum's other claim to fame is that it was the birthplace of Sir Patrick Marson, a nineteenth-century researcher in tropical medicine, perhaps a strange choice of job for someone from a village further north than Moscow!

The distillery is said to have been founded in 1797 and the village appears to have grown up around it: it stands on Distillery Street. It has had a number of owners including William Sanderson, the blender of Vat 69, who took it into DCL in 1937. The Distillers Company was not satisfied with its water supply and, after suffering shortages, closed it down in 1968. Two years later it was sold to Stanley P. Morrison, which sank a well in a nearby field and tapped a new and more reliable water source. With distilling under way again Morrison's made various improvements, including the purchase of a new wash still, and trebled production in three years. For DCL it must have been like giving away a winning lottery ticket.

Until its closure in 1995 Glen Garioch shared two particular features with its sister Bowmore: its own floor maltings, and its innovative use of heat recovery. The malt was lightly peated, using peat taken from New Pitsligo Moss, the peat moistened before being burnt to reduce the amount consumed, but the increase in distilling capacity meant that the maltings was only capable of providing about 30 per cent of the distillery's malt. The waste energy scheme began in 1976 and was the only scheme of its kind in the whisky industry. Glen Garioch was the first malt distillery to convert to using North Sea gas, and boiler flue gases were used to generate steam for firing the stills. Hot water was drawn off the condensers and used to heat some surprisingly large greenhouses built behind the distillery which yielded around 180 tons of tomatoes a year. Carbon dioxide recovered from the washbacks was used to enhance the growth of the crop.

Glen Garioch single malt is bottled at eight, fifteen and twenty-one years old, and with the eldest two at 'export' strength, or 43% vol. The current range also includes a 29-year-old single cask bottling and a 'selected cask vatting', an 18-year-old produced from a marriage of selected casks from a single year's distillations. Like its sisters Bowmore and Auchentoshan the distillery holds the ISO 9002 accreditation, awarded in 1997.

ROYAL LOCHNAGAR

lost no time in writing to her private secretary and inviting her to view the distillery. He was rewarded with a private royal visit the next day and presented a dram to Victoria, Albert and their three eldest children. They were obviously impressed: it is said that Victoria began to lace her claret with Lochnagar, and Begg received a royal warrant a few days after the visit.

By the time of his death Begg had expanded the distillery and established company offices and warehousing at Aberdeen, and he played a major role in the blending trade. In 1906 his son transferred the operation to Glasgow and rebuilt and re-equipped the distillery, but he lacked his father's gift for the business and the family sold out. Lochnagar was acquired by Dewar's in 1916 and passed to DCL in 1925.

The distillery was rebuilt for the second time in the late 1960s and the stills converted to steam heating. Waterwheels were still being used to drive machinery as recently as 1963, and lighting was by paraffin lamps until 1949. The company also holds the lease on the surrounding farm, as if to emphasise the link between farming and distilling. The farm buildings and the distillery are all made from the red granite of Lochnagar itself.

UDV has equipped the distillery with an excellent visitor centre and reinstated the 'Royal' prefix, which for a time seemed to have fallen from favour. After the demise of Glenury, Lochnagar is now one of only two distilleries to use a regal title. Its single malt is normally bottled at twelve years old, but a special edition was introduced in 1988 called Selected Reserve. Bottled, as the name suggests, from specially selected casks, and with a greater proportion of sherry-aged spirit, it has a price tag that even the Royal family would probably look twice at!

The area of Deeside around Lochnagar has long been associated with the royal family, thanks to Balmoral Castle, built on an estate whose lease was acquired by Prince Albert in 1852 for £31,000. Lochnagar itself is actually a twin-peaked mountain lying at the head of a small range separated from the Cairngorms by the Dee valley, and has given its name to the only distillery on Deeside.

The first of the illicit distillers on Deeside to take out a licence under the 1823 Act was James Robertson. This noble gesture was rewarded with the burning of his distillery in Glen Feardan by his former compatriots. Undeterred, he built a new distillery called Lochnagar, for which he was recorded as licence-holder in 1826, and which also burned to the ground in mysterious circumstances. It would appear that at this point Robertson gave up and his distillery was rebuilt by Farquharson & Reid in 1842, surviving for another eighteen years. In 1845 a second distillery, referred to as 'New Lochnagar', was built to the south of the Dee by John Begg and partners. The partnership was dissolved in 1851 and Begg was left to run the business alone.

Begg coined one of the first advertising slogans to be used in the whisky trade: 'Take a peg of John Begg'. He also had an eye for the main chance, and when Queen Victoria first visited Balmoral he

FETTERCAIRN

After The Glenlivet, Fettercairn is reckoned to be the second distillery to be licensed under the 1823 Act, although it was operating previous to this on a site 2 miles higher up the slopes of Cairn o' Mount, one of the Grampian hills over which passes the road to Deeside. The old still was abandoned when a new and larger distillery was built at the edge of Fettercairn village in 1824.

Fettercairn itself is a small village on the edge of the moorland plain known as the Howe O' the Mearns, an area of rich farmland where barley growing has fuelled the whisky industry for generations. Victoria and Albert visited the place in 1861, calling it a 'small, quiet town', and Fettercairn commemorated the visit by building an archway just off the village square. Just to the north-east was Kincardine Castle, said to be the place where Macbeth's head was brought as a trophy after his final defeat.

The distillery was originally a grain mill which, in addition to its legitimate endeavours, probably also supplied grist to the area's illicit stills. When the 1823 Act was passed, the mill was converted into a legally licensed distillery by Sir Alexander Ramsay and leased to its first tenant, James Stewart, for an annual rent of £21. It passed through a succession of anonymous private owners until 1887 when the Fettercairn Distillery Co. was formed with Sir John Gladstone as chairman. It can be no coincidence that when Gladstone's son became prime minister he was responsible for the legislation relating to the angel's share, an allowance against duty to account for spirit lost through evaporation during the maturation period. He became one of the few friends the industry has ever had in government. After a lengthy closure between the two world wars, Fettercairn was acquired for Train & McIntyre, which also managed Bruichladdich Distillery on Islay. Eventually, through subsidiary companies, the distillery passed to Whyte & Mackay.

Fettercairn was rebuilt around the end of the nineteenth century and extended in the 1960s. Gone now are the cooperage and the condenser pipes laid in the bed of the stream. An additional pair of stills was installed, together with modern vertical condensers, and an extra three washbacks, taking the total to eight. Fettercairn's single malt is bottled at ten years old after maturing in a combination of sherry butts and refill bourbon casks. Refill casks are used to avoid the bourbon's vanilla flavour becoming too prominent.

Late in 1989 Fettercairn opened its own dedicated visitor centre. It is set to become an important attraction in Aberdeen's hinterland and is already catering for around 10,000 visitors a year.

GLENESK

L ike many distilleries Glenesk has had a parade of owners, many of whom have sought to impress their own identity on it, and as a result it has changed its name more times than any other distillery. When it closed in 1985 it was licensed to Wm Sanderson & Sons Ltd, and used to sport a giant Vat 69 bottle painted on the building lest any visitor should not realise this!

The distillery stands on the edge of the valley of the River North Esk, just outside Montrose. Montrose itself is a historically important fishing port, with parts of the town unchanged in two centuries. The 300-year-old Curfew Bell in the church is still rung every night at 10pm. Being coastal the area was rife with smugglers at the beginning of the nineteenth century, and was associated with one of Scotland's most famous Excise men: Malcolm Gillespie. Gillespie used a bull terrier on his campaigns against the smugglers (which was shot dead in one action) and cheated death himself on several occasions before meeting a rather ignominious end, being executed for forgery in Aberdeen.

Glenesk Distillery was founded in 1898 on the site of a flax mill. It was a good site, close to Hillside station, with plenty of water available from the river, and it was surrounded by barley fields. Its first owner was the unforgettably named Septimus Parsonage & Co., which christened it Highland Esk Distillery. It subsequently became North Esk, Montrose and Hillside before finally adopting the name Glenesk in 1980. Along with six other distilleries, including nearby Fettercairn and the now-defunct Glenury just up the coast at Stonehaven, it was a member of the Associated Scottish Distilleries, a company formed with the National Distillers of America to supply whisky to the Americans following the repeal of Prohibition.

Associated Scottish Distilleries converted the buildings for grain distilling but it became a malt distillery once again after being taken over by DCL, as the small scale of the operation was uneconomical beside their existing grain distilleries. In 1968, DCL built a huge drum maltings alongside the distillery which is capable of germinating over 740 tons of barley at any one time.

The story of Vat 69, often jokingly referred to as the Pope's telephone number, is an interesting one. William Sanderson was a merchant with a wide repertoire of recipes for blends. He decided to adopt one in particular as his house blend and in order to make the selection invited a group of friends to a tasting. If the story is to be believed, the choice was unanimous that the blend in cask, or vat, number 69 was the best, and the name stuck. Glenesk's single malt formed a component of Vat 69 as well as being bottled in limited quantities at twelve years old. However, all maturing stocks have been removed, and both the distillery and the maltings have recently been acquired by Paul's Malt.

GLENCADAM

T he city of Brechin, for city it is, is one of Scotland's oldest, and stands on the River South Esk on the edge of the foothills of the eastern Grampians. It boasts a twelfth-century cathedral and the tenth-century Round Tower, an 87ft high former watchtower which is one of only two in Scotland. Nearby at Arbroath Abbey, Scotland's noblemen swore their independence from England in 1320.

Four distilleries are recorded in or around Brechin. Two of these flourished only very briefly in the middle years of the nineteenth century. North Port, named after the north gate in the long-vanished city walls, survived from 1820 until it became a casualty of the DCL distillery closures of 1983. It was demolished in 1994 and its site is now marked by a supermarket and, rather ironically, a funeral director's premises. Only a plaque marks its passing. One taster described its malt as having the aroma of a pickle, which probably set the seal on its fate!

That leaves only Glencadam. It was said to have been founded in 1825, but first appears registered to a David Scott two years later. It passed through the hands of a number of owners until it was acquired in 1891 by Gilmour, Thomson & Co. Ltd of Glasgow, which traded as the Glencadam Distillery Co. Gilmour, Thomson operated Glencadam until 1954, when the distillery was sold to Hiram Walker, which was busily setting about expanding its portfolio at that time. Walker's had taken over Ballantine's in 1936 and already owned three distilleries. Along with Glencadam it also acquired Scapa Distillery from Bloch Bros the same year, and Pulteney Distillery from Robert Cumming the following year. Walker's licensed Glencadam to Ballantine's and brought it up to date. Ballantine's parent company, Allied Distillers, sold the distillery in May 2003 to the owner of Tomintoul Distillery, Angus Dundee Distillers.

Glencadam is not a large-scale operation. It has but a single pair of stills, steam heated, both wash and spirit stills having the same 3,080 gallon capacity, and having slightly upward-pointing lyne arms. The mash tun mashes 4½ tons of grist per mash, and there are six steel washbacks which each hold just over 6,000 gallons of wort. (Allied being ambivalent about the argument which rages in some quarters concerning the flavour contribution of wooden washbacks). The distillery's water supply comes from springs at Unthank. Its product is rare as a bottled single malt, being bottled only by the independents, but tasters seem to agree that it is worth seeking out.

CONNOISSEURS CHOICE

HIGHLAND
Single Malt Scotch Whisky

DISTILLED AT
GLENCADAM
DISTILLERY
Trade Mark of Proprietors: The Glencadam Distillery Co. Ltd.

DISTILLED
1987

Specially selected, produced and bottled by
and under the responsibility of registered bottler

Gordon & MacPhail
Elgin   Scotland
Product of Scotland

70cl   40% vol

BLAIR ATHOL

On the slopes of the Grampian Mountains stands Pitlochry, a pretty Victorian town which has been a holiday resort since the mid-nineteenth century. The Victorians came here to escape the London smog and breathe the clean Highland air and Pitlochry established a reputation as a health spa. The main street is part of a road built by General Wade which crosses the Grampians *en route* to the northern Highlands and is lined with stone-built Victorian houses and mansions, many now converted into hotels and guest-houses. At the southern end of this street stands Blair Athol Distillery.

Whisky was being made in this area during the Jacobite rebellion of 1745, and near the distillery stands an oak tree in which the local laird, Robertson of Faskally, hid from the redcoats of 'Butcher' Cumberland's army after the defeat of Bonnie Prince Charlie. A distillery was founded on this site in 1798 by John Stewart and Robert Robertson and named Aldour, after the burn which flows through the grounds – the Allt Dour, or 'burn of the otter'. It subsequently closed and was refounded in 1826, when it was renamed Blair Athol. By 1882 it had passed to P. Mackenzie & Co., which increased its capacity. That company reconstituted itself in 1897 as P. Mackenzie & Co. Distillers Ltd, when it acquired Dufftown-Glenlivet Distillery. It in turn was taken over in 1933 by Arthur Bell & Sons, now part of United Distillers & Vintners.

After a period of closure Bell's rebuilt Blair Athol in 1949, and have since steadily improved the distillery both technically and environmentally. Production capacity was increased in 1973 by the addition of a second pair of stills, and a visitor centre was opened in 1987 which now attracts 100,000 visitors a year. It has a function suite for wedding receptions and a shop which provides an outlet for local craftsmen to sell their goods. The distillery's stone buildings are beautifully maintained and the grounds landscaped with rhododendron and rose gardens. In 1991, working in conjunction with the Freshwater Fisheries Laboratory, a small fish ladder was built to aid research into trout breeding.

Blair Athol is Bell's showpiece and proudly proclaims itself 'the home of Bell's whisky'. Its single malt is now bottled in UDV's Flora & Fauna range and gives much of its character to Bell's 8-Year-Old, the most popular blended whisky in Britain, as well as being a significant component of Bell's 12-Year-Old.

EDRADOUR

Edradour likes to call itself the 'last hand-crafted single malt whisky' and to see the distillery is to understand why. It is the smallest distillery in Scotland and operates very much as it would have done when it was first founded in 1825, and on a similar scale. The mash tun, washbacks and stills are all about a tenth of the size of those in an average distillery and the entire process takes place in one building. The workforce of three men, one of whom is the manager, is outnumbered by the tour guides, and in the space of a year Edradour produces the same volume of whisky that an average modern distillery would make in a week.

Everything really is done by hand; there is no automation. A local farmer takes the draff for cattle feed and this involves physically shovelling it out of the mash tun through an open window and into his waiting trailer. In some places the original equipment is still in use, such as the worm pipes which can be seen in sunken tanks behind the stillhouse, and the Morton wort refrigerator, now the oldest working model in the world.

In 1922 Edradour was acquired by William Whiteley, known in the industry as the 'dean of distillers'. He used The Edradour to perfect a top-quality blend which he named King's Ransom. In an attempt to ensure the perfect marrying of the component whiskies Whiteley dispatched fifty sherry casks of the blend on a round-the-world sea voyage, during which the sea air and constant rocking of the ship gave a unique quality to the whisky that normal

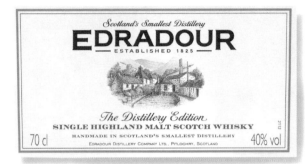

warehousing on dry land never could. Whiteley went on to create the blend House of Lords, and ran into trouble with the real House of Lords, which barred him from using the name in the UK. This did not stop Whiteley from selling the blend in ninety-four other countries, and the problem was neatly circumvented when Britain entered the EU. A name registered in any EU country is valid throughout the Union and House of Lords was registered in Italy.

Edradour enjoyed a boom during Prohibition. King's Ransom was very popular in America and bootleggers used every method at their disposal to ensure its delivery. It was even fired onto Long Island beaches by torpedo. The most resourceful bootlegger was the so-called 'prime minister of the underworld', Frank Costello, who backed up his whisky boats with a seaplane and a U-boat! It is said that Costello secretly funded the American company which took over Whiteley's business after his death.

In July 2002 Edradour was acquired from its owner Pernod-Ricard by Signatory, at a cost of £5.4 million, making them the third independent bottling company in recent times (along with Gordon & MacPhail and Murray McDavid) to move into distilling. The company has no plans to change the operation at Edradour, other than the introduction of further expressions of its malt. To read some people's tasting notes you could be forgiven for thinking more of wedding cake than of whisky; fruity, nutty, marzipan and almonds being some of the descriptions, but to visit this distillery and taste its whisky is to understand what malt whisky must have been like 150 years ago.

ABERFELDY

contacts in his pocket. He must have been somewhat dismayed to find that one of these was bankrupt and the other dead, but undeterred he exhibited at the Brewer's Show and employed pipers to draw attention to his whisky. The stunt was outrageous but effective, and by 1893 Dewar's was exporting around the world and was awarded Queen Victoria's royal warrant. In order to ensure adequate supplies of whisky for their blending operations, the brothers decided to set up their own distillery and chose to site it near to their father's birthplace at Aberfeldy.

The distillery opened in 1898 and some of its original buildings are still in use. A new stillhouse was built in 1972 and houses two pairs of stills. In the interests of efficiency, the company built its own railway siding at its Perth headquarters and a rail link direct to the

distillery was in use until the 1960s. The water supply comes from the Pitilie Burn, a tributary of the Tay.

Much of Aberfeldy's production goes for blending, particularly into Dewar's White Label, one of the biggest-selling Scotch whiskies in the USA. United Distillers also bottled Aberfeldy's single malt at fifteen years old as part of its Flora & Fauna range, reflecting its involvement with the Countryside Commission in building a nature trail at the distillery to create a habitat for red squirrels. However the distillery, and Dewar's itself, were divested to Bacardi in 1998 following the merger of Guinness and Grand Metropolitan.

Aberfeldy is a small town on the south bank of the River Tay some 15 miles by road from Pitlochry, in an area rich in history and folklore. It stands on another of General Wade's roads and boasts the finest example of his bridges, this one designed by William Adam in 1733. Robert Burns came here from Crieff in 1787 and wrote the song 'Birks of Aberfeldy'. The nearby village of Fortingall was the site of a Roman camp which legend says was the birthplace, believe it or not, of Pontius Pilate (doubtful, as Pilate was born some decades before the Romans first arrived in Scotland) and in the local churchyard stands a

yew tree reputed to be 3,000 years old. Glen Lyon, which extends westward from here, was the home of Captain Robert Campbell, who was responsible for the massacre of Glencoe.

If Blair Athol can be said to be the home of Bell's whisky, then Aberfeldy is the home of Dewar's. John Dewar set up his own business blending and bottling whisky in Perth in 1846. The firm was amongst the first to sell whisky in branded bottles and Dewar began to look for sales further afield. His two sons, Tommy and John Alexander, joined the family firm and Tommy was despatched to London on a sales drive with the names of two

GLENTURRET

Depression took hold, the Mitchells sold off the plant. Five years later the premises were sold to the owners of the adjacent land, the Murrays of Ochtertyre, who used it for warehousing.

Glenturret's renaissance came in 1957 when it was sold to James Fairlie. Fairlie, like Peter Mackie, was an enthusiast who believed in the old traditional methods and had a wealth of 'hands-on' experience in the trade. Under his management, Glenturret was producing again by June 1960. More warehouses were added, built in a style matching the existing buildings, some of which date from the distillery's foundation. His son Peter joined him in the business, which passed first to Cointreau in 1981, then later to the Highland Distilleries Co. in 1990. It was on Peter Fairlie's initiative that the distillery was first opened to the public in 1980.

Glenturret is not a large-scale operation. There is only a single pair of stills, producing around 100,000 proof gallons annually, but the distillery is notable for its extensive range of bottlings. It makes a malt whisky liqueur as part of its standard product range and its single malt has won a number of awards, including the gold award at the 1991 International Wine & Spirit Competition.

Glenturret also rates a mention in the *Guinness Book of Records* thanks to the distillery cat, Towser. Born in the stillhouse in April 1963, she is named as World Champion Mouser having caught 28,899 mice during her lifetime, according to the stillmen, who apparently kept count! Her successor, Amber, has a tough act to follow.

T here are a number of distilleries which claim to be the oldest in Scotland, and Glenturret is one of them. The Lowland distillery Littlemill, which started life as a brewery, was also reckoned to be the oldest in Scotland, having changed over to distilling in 1772, this being the year in which accommodation for a resident Excise officer was first erected on site. Glenturret proudly claims a foundation date of 1775, with illicit antecedents going back to 1717 when there were reputedly five smuggling bothies on the present site. Littlemill's records from this period are unclear but Glenturret is certainly the oldest distillery in the Highlands.

The distillery lies between two high hills at the point where the Shaggie Burn enters the River Turret, about a mile from Crieff. It was originally owned by smugglers, who selected the site not only for its water supply, but also for the concealment offered by the hills and the vantage points from which a look-out could be kept for any approaching Excise men. Glenturret changed hands a number of times throughout the nineteenth century, the most prominent owner being Thomas Stewart, a Crieff landowner.

The distillery was closed for the duration of World War I, after which it was bought by the Mitchell brothers. They operated it for only two years before closing it down to be used for storage purposes. In 1923, as the

TULLIBARDINE

B elow Glenturret the A9 skirts the northern fringes of the Ochil Hills as it passes from Perth to Stirling. The most notable modern landmark here is the famous Gleneagles hotel and golf course, but the area is rich in antiquities, particularly those dating from the Roman occupation. To the north of Gleneagles, just off the A823, stands the red sandstone Tullibardine chapel, founded as a collegiate church in 1445 by Sir David Murray and used as a burial vault for the Drummond Earls of Perth.

Most of the distilleries recorded in this area have been in or around the conservation village of Muthill. Of eight distilleries licensed here the last survivor was Overhill, which failed in 1838 after a life of twenty-four years. The first distillery to use the name Tullibardine was founded in 1798. Its location near Blackford has been lost in the mists of time, but it was run by its founders, the Bannerman family, until 1837. The name Blackford is said to be derived from a ford on the Allan Water, a little further to the west of the village, where Queen Helen of Scotland was drowned.

The existing Tullibardine Distillery was converted from a brewery and stands on a site which has been used for brewing since the seventeenth century. Brewers were attracted to the site originally by the quality of the water, and today Blackford village is the home of the Highland Spring mineral water company. Their water is essentially the same as that used by the distillery, except that theirs is drawn from an artesian well whilst the distillery takes its supply from springs which feed the Danny Burn, which rises on the 2,073ft Blairdenon Hill, 3 miles to the south. The brewery was converted in 1949 (the year in which George Orwell published *1984*) by Delmé Evans, creator of Glenallachie and Jura, and C. I. Barrett. In 1953 it was acquired by Brodie Hepburn, a member of the consortium which later built Macduff Distillery, and then in 1971 by Invergordon which rebuilt and expanded it a couple of years later.

Invergordon itself was taken over in November 1993 by Whyte & Mackay which had fought a protracted battle for its ownership, attracted by the prospect of acquiring the Invergordon grain distillery on the Cromarty Firth, the most northerly grain distillery in Scotland. Once it had taken over the company it found itself with more than double its original portfolio of distilleries, and in the economic climate of the 1990s sacrifices had to be made. Tullibardine was mothballed in 1995, along with Bruichladdich and Tamnavulin. The closures were keenly felt in their respective communities.

However, the outlook improved for the distillery in 2003 when it was acquired by a consortium from Whyte & Mackay's parent company, Kyndal, for a reported £1.1 million and the new owners announced plans to reopen the distillery and build a retail outlet and visitor centre.

The distillery's sweet and malty 10-year-old has been unfairly damned with faint praise by some tasters, but 27-year-old and 30-year-old versions are also available, bottled as part of the distillers' Stillman's Dram range.

DEANSTON

The mill eventually came into the ownership of the textile company James Finlay & Co. Ltd, which by the early 1960s had closed it and moved elsewhere. Finlay's was approached by Brodie Hepburn, which had interests in Macduff and Tullibardine distilleries, with a plan to convert the building into a distillery. It was well sited for the purpose, with the river right outside and the mill's water turbine and generator still installed and in working order. The Deanston Distillery Co. Ltd was established, with Brodie Hepburn holding a third share and Finlay's the majority, and work began on the conversion, which included the removal of four internal floors. The distillery's hydroelectric power station generates so much power that excess production is sold to the national grid. Warehouse No. 2 occupies a vaulted weaving shed which dates from 1836, and is now Grade 1 listed.

In 1972 Deanston passed to Invergordon, which operated it for ten years before closing it down. Burn Stewart Distillers acquired it in 1990 and set about renovating the plant, discovering the now highly polished copper piping hidden for years under layers of paint. The four stills each have a reflux bulge at the base of their necks and the lyne arms point slightly upwards, all contributing to a lighter spirit. The company owns a 1½-mile stretch of the river by the distillery, the fishing rights being used to the full by both the workforce and the colony of herons which live there.

Deanston makes its whisky from unpeated malt, a feature it shares with its sister distillery Tobermory (which Burn Stewart acquired in 1993), and has recently been licensed by the Organic Food Federation to make organic whisky, using organically grown barley. The company's standard bottling of Deanston malt is as a 12-year-old, although 17- and 25-year-old versions are bottled from spirit distilled during the time of Invergordon's tenure. In 1996 the distillery diversified by installing a gin still, which runs on neutral spirit bought-in for the purpose.

The royal burgh of Stirling occupies a prominent place in Scottish history. It was near there on 24 June 1314 that Robert the Bruce, outnumbered by three to one, defeated the English forces at Bannockburn for possession of Stirling Castle, a victory which established Bruce on the Scottish throne. At the nearby village of Doune is Deanston, whose label tells the story of the battle. Doune caters quite well for visitors, having as it does a safari park and a fourteenth-century castle, at which the Monty Python team shot some of their 1975 film *The Holy Grail*.

Deanston is a relatively young distillery, commencing distilling in September 1966, but it occupies an unusual and historic building, a former cotton mill which stands on the bank of the River Teith. The mill dates from 1785 and was equipped with Sir Richard Arkwright's new spinning frames, a successor to, and improvement upon, Hargreaves's spinning jenny. Deanston village was built alongside the mill as a self-contained 'model' village for the mill workers.

165

GLENGOYNE

One of the prettiest distilleries in Scotland, Glengoyne is a mere 10 miles from the northern fringe of Glasgow and its accessibility has made it a popular attraction for visitors to the area. It classes itself as a Highland malt, although it sits right on the Highland Line, which supposedly runs right through the distillery's grounds, putting the process buildings on the Highland side and the warehouses in the Lowlands!

Glengoyne stands at the foot of Dumgoyne Hill, on the A81 just south of Killearn. With the Campsie Fells on one side and the Kilpatrick Hills on the other it is difficult to believe that the bustle of Scotland's largest city is so close. The area is famous as Rob Roy MacGregor's stamping ground, and within yards of the distillery is an old oak tree said to have been one of his hiding places. Strathblane was then home to thirteen illicit stills. Glenguin, as it then was, straddled two parishes and as neither minister would admit to having a distillery in his parish its existence was not recorded in the Excise returns.

Glenguin was the only one of those thirteen illicit stills to be licensed under the 1823 Act, and that was not until 1833 when it was licensed to Archibald McLellan. Its name had changed to Burnfoot by the time Lang Bros Ltd bought the distillery in 1876 and they changed it back to Glenguin. The resident Excise officer was Arthur Tedder, who was later Chief Inspector of Excise and was knighted in 1909 for his part in the Royal Commission set up in the wake of the famous 'what is whisky' case. His son, born in Glengoyne's customs house, became Marshal of the RAF.

The distillery was modernised in 1965 when Lang Bros was taken over by Robertson & Baxter, and some interesting features have been tried before giving way to tradition. Like Macallan, Glengoyne derives a particular character from the use of small low wines stills, used in conjunction with a single wash still. Until 1990 the two low wines stills were of an unusual straight-sided design, but these have now been replaced by standard-shaped stills with no detrimental change to the spirit. At one time the distillery's mash tun had a glass-fibre dome, but the material failed to hold its shape and had to be abandoned in favour of something stronger. The new tun is stainless steel with a traditional domed copper top. Water comes from springs on the Campsie Fells and falls down a 50ft cascade into the distillery's dam.

Glengoyne uses completely unpeated malt and this, together with the influences of its location, gives it a character more akin to a Lowland than to a Highland malt whisky. It is bottled as a single malt at ten and seventeen years old, together with various limited editions. A cask-strength millennium edition was released, presented in a grandfather clock! t also forms an important component of Lang's Supreme. The company used to have bonded warehouses in Glasgow's Argyll Free church, Lang's occupying the basement whilst church services were conducted on the floor above!

LOCH LOMOND

Loch Lomond is the largest inland loch in Scotland and its beauty and accessibility have made it one of the most popular tourist destinations. Part-way along its western shore it is almost met by the tip of Loch Long, where the first distillery to use the Loch Lomond name flourished briefly at Arrochar from 1814–17. The new Loch Lomond Distillery is hidden away from public view on an estate at Alexandria, and on the company's own admission is not one of Scotland's prettiest distilleries. It is, however, one of the more interesting ones.

Loch Lomond was built on the site of an old printing and bleach works in 1965 by the American owner of Littlemill, Barton Brands, and was acquired in 1985 by Glen Catrine Bonded Warehouse Co. Ltd, a company which evolved from the retail chain A. Bulloch & Co. Following the upheavals of the late 1980s Loch Lomond has emerged as the current owner of Littlemill and its sister Glen Scotia. The Loch Lomond brand received an unexpected bit of publicity when it featured in Hergé's *Tintin and the Black Isle*, when Tintin's dog Snowy inadvertently got drunk on Loch Lomond whisky!

Loch Lomond's stills are highly unusual. Two of its three pairs have thick, straight necks, topped with reflux condensers which can be adjusted by varying the supply of cooling water to alter the character of the distillate. At any one time the two pairs could be making completely different spirits. A pair of conventional, fat, onion-shaped pot stills was installed in August 1999, in order to make a further type of spirit which was outside the capabilities of the rectifying stills. Altogether, these stills are used to make seven different malts. Inchmurrin, named from an island in Loch Lomond, and Rhosdhu, named after the home of the area's principal landowners, the Colquhoun

family, have been sold for some time as bottled single malts, and these have been joined by the new Loch Lomond brand. The others are sent for blending, although it is possible that one of those, Croftengea, which is more heavily peated than Lagavulin, may well find its way into bottle at some point in the future.

Restrictions in the supply of grain spirit led the company in 1994 to build its own on-site grain distillery at a cost of £8.5 million. It is Scotland's smallest grain plant, and is operated by two men. The yeast is pitched manually into the twelve huge washbacks, but everything else is computerised. It has a stainless steel analyser, an all-copper rectifier,

and extra columns for making neutral spirit. The grain spirit is filled into first-fill bourbon casks. Some of the malt is finished in sherry wood. The casks are stored on pallets in the warehouses, stacked up to nine pallets high. The distillery is one of only a tiny number which still maintains its own cooperage, and employs five coopers and an apprentice.

Loch Lomond is now the only distillery in Scotland making both malt and grain whiskies, and as a result the company is virtually self-sufficient. The plan is to use the Loch Lomond brand as a single malt, a single grain and a 'single blend', a blended whisky made entirely from Loch Lomond's own malt and grain whisky production.

The Lowlands

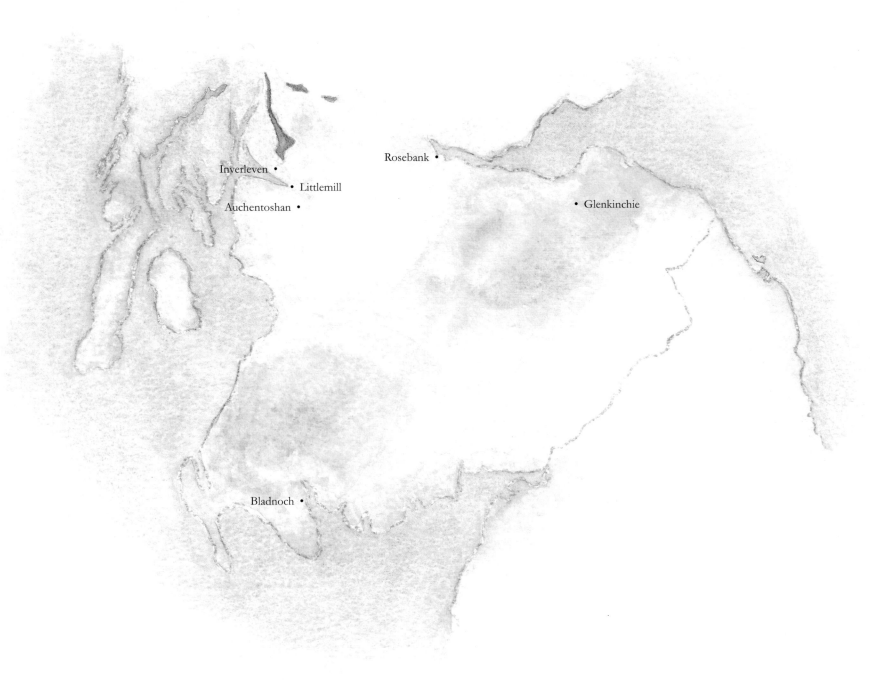

Inverleven •
• Rosebank
• Littlemill
Auchentoshan •
• Glenkinchie
Bladnoch •

INVERLEVEN

In 1930 the Canadian company Hiram Walker, in preparation for the repeal of Prohibition, took its first step in expanding into Scotland by taking a share in James & George Stodart Ltd. Six years later it took full control of Stodart's and acquired the Glasgow blending company Ballantine's. The company consolidated its position as a 'Scottish' distiller by making for its headquarters a new grain distillery, the largest in Scotland at the time, on the site of the old McMillan shipyard on the River Leven at Dumbarton. It was actually a complex comprising Dumbarton Grain Distillery and the Inverleven Malt Distillery, the latter producing two distinct Lowland malts, Inverleven and Lomond.

Inverleven, which is behind the trees on the left of the picture, came on stream shortly after Dumbarton began production in 1938 and made its different malts by using two spirit stills of different designs (compare this with Springbank, which makes two distinct malts but in the same stills), and was reputed to be the first malt distillery to use steam heating in both its wash and its spirit stills. The mash tun, washbacks and wash still were common to both spirit stills. When the original pine washbacks were due for replacement in 1970 they were replaced, for the sake of efficiency, with Colclad – mild steel with a stainless steel lining (Allied is not convinced that the washback's construction has a bearing on the final spirit). Process water came from Loch Lomond and the tiny Loch Humphrey in the Kilpatrick Hills. It was spirit from the conventionally designed pot still which became Inverleven malt.

Lomond malt, not to be confused with Loch Lomond Distillery at nearby Alexandria, was made in a variant of the pot still known as a Lomond still. This still shared the same spirit receiver (but not at the same time!) and low wines charger as the Inverleven pot still but was cylindrical in design, and carried a water jacket on top of it which could control the degree of reflux. Lomond-type stills were installed at a number of other Hiram Walker distilleries, notably Glenburgie and Miltonduff, and their heavy, oily spirit matured into a malt which was usually different enough from that which came from the distillery's pot stills to be regarded as a distinctly separate product. Some of these malts can still be found in independent bottlings, even though the plant has long since been decommissioned.

Of the Dumbarton complex itself, only the grain distillery is still working. Inverleven's pot still was mothballed in 1991, although its single malt is still available in a Gordon & MacPhail bottling, and is also sold in miniatures. It was never bottled by the distillers themselves. The Lomond still has not been removed but ceased production in 1973, and its product was never officially bottled.

LITTLEMILL

Driving a few miles along the A82 from Dumbarton towards Glasgow the old Dumbarton road passes through the village of Bowling. On this road, beside the railway station, stands Littlemill. Until it closed it was one of the strongest contenders for the title of oldest distillery in Scotland, its buildings straddling the road against the backdrop of the Clyde. The distillery marks the western end of the Antonine Wall, a defence built by the Romans to keep the Picts at bay.

It is possible that the site was originally that of a brewery, and the changeover to distilling is said to have been made in 1772. It is noted that accommodation for an Excise officer was present

on the site at that time, but whether the officer was overseeing a brewery or a distillery is not clear. There is little record from the first forty-five years of its existence but after a closure resulting from a ban on distilling following legislation in 1813–14, it is registered as being licensed to Matthew Clark & Co. in 1817. This was a tough time for the distilling industry. Whisky production fell significantly and many companies faced bankruptcy. The Lowlands were particularly hard hit. Clark's tenure was short, as was that of a number of Littlemill's many owners.

Clark's successor built up production to 20,000 gallons a year and himself gave way to a list of licensees an arm's length. The American company Barton Brands took a share in Littlemill in 1959 and, when it reached its maximum production capacity six years later, built it a sister on the site of an old printing and bleach works at nearby Alexandria. The new distillery was called Loch Lomond and its single malt named Inchmurrin, the name of the largest island in the loch. After a

further wave of take-overs and buy-outs which culminated in the failure of Gibson International in 1994, Loch Lomond Distillery has emerged as Littlemill's latest owner.

Although a Lowland distillery Littlemill took its water from the Kilpatrick Hills, and also used Highland peat until the closure of its Saladin maltings. Its stills were unique in Lowland malt distill-eries, having pot-shaped bases and straight necks; and instead of a normal lye pipe were fitted with reflux condensers known as

dephlegmators (dephlegmate means 'to free from water'), in which the spirit vapour could be controlled by varying the temperature of the cooling water. Similar stills are used at Loch Lomond itself.

Despite its recent acquisition by Loch Lomond Littlemill's future looks bleak, although it is up for sale and a change of ownership could give it a new lease of life. It has been partly demolished, but the old part is a listed building and may eventually be reopened as a visitor centre. The distillery's 8-year-old single malt was increasing in popularity and is still available, thanks to stocks in bond, but the closure leaves a paltry three malt distilleries now operating in the Lowlands.

AUCHENTOSHAN

distillation, but at a higher strength – about 80% vol. It is one of only three working malt distilleries remaining in the Lowlands, although its water comes from a loch north of the Highland Line. The use of unpeated malt and the triple distillation combine to produce a whisky which is light and fragrant.

The distillery was badly damaged in an air raid on the night of 13 March 1940, and fifty-three butts of maturing whisky were lost. Despite rebuilding after the war, production was relatively small-scale by today's standards, until Eadie Cairns re-equipped the place shortly after taking over. In 1984 the distillery was acquired by Stanley P. Morrison, now Morrison Bowmore, the owner of Bowmore and Glen Garioch distilleries. Under its management Auchentoshan has become the first malt distillery to gain BS 5750 accreditation, a quality control standard which applies not only to a company's product but also to its staff and the procedures they operate. The company was awarded the certificate on 23 April 1993, narrowly ahead of Bushmills in Northern Ireland.

As with its sister Glen Garioch, Auchentoshan includes in its range a single cask bottling, in this case a 31-year-old, and a 21-year-old 'selected cask vatting'. There is also the Auchentoshan Three Wood, which is not simply 'finished' in a different type of cask but matured in three different woods in sequence, being first filled into American bourbon casks, then transferred into oloroso sherry butts, and then completed in Pedro-Ximénez barrels.

No more than a mile or so beyond Littlemill the traveller comes to the Clydebank suburb of Duntocher. Here, the view is dominated by the vast concrete construction of the Erskine Bridge and one could be forgiven for failing to notice the immaculate white warehouses which screen Auchentoshan Distillery from the road.

The first reference to the name Auchentoshan occurs in a print dated 1649, which shows the present site occupied by a monastery. Since the distilling of aqua vitae was carried out throughout Scotland's religious establishments it is fair to assume that whisky was being made on this site at least three, if not four, centuries ago. The present distillery was founded at the turn of the nineteenth century, and licensed following the 1823 Act. It has had many owners, some of whose interests were in brewing rather than distilling. It was owned by Tennents and Bass Charrington before being sold by the latter to Eadie Cairns in 1970. This company was formed in the nineteenth century when Cairns, a Glasgow publican, teamed up with John Eadie, a member of a prominent brewing family. It was through their retail interests that Auchentoshan became one of the first Lowland malt whiskies to be sold as a bottled single malt.

Auchentoshan is now the only distillery in Scotland still using traditional Lowland triple distillation in its original form. In this method an intermediate still is used to separate strong alcohol and strong feints from the low wines prior to the final distillation. The spirit still yields less spirit than in conventional double

ROSEBANK

The industrial revolution transformed Falkirk from a cattle drover's meeting place into an important industrial manufacturing town. Cheap fuel from the coalfield on which it stands provided the catalyst for this change and the Forth and Clyde canal gave easy access to the ports for movement of products and supplies. Collieries and ironworks began to spring up, and cannons for Nelson's fleet were made here. Distilling was in progress almost two centuries ago, when statistical records show the presence of the Stark Bros Camelon Distillery.

Rosebank Distillery, which occupies more or less the same site, was founded in 1840 by James Rankine and was originally based on Camelon's maltings, which Rankine bought and enlarged. Unfortunately, the work got him into financial difficulties and it was left to his son to complete the modernisation in 1864. The following year Camelon's main buildings on the opposite side of the canal were demolished and a new maltings built. The two complexes were connected by a swing bridge over the canal. The new maltings, downhill from the main distillery, was cleverly built to allow farmers' wagons direct access from the roadway into the top-floor barley loft. Shortly after, the distillery acquired probably the most unfortunately named Excise officer in Scotland, William Bastard.

Rankine's whisky was very well received. In the 1890s, when the whisky boom was at its peak, Rosebank's annual production stood at 123,000 gallons. Demand was such that customers were often allocated less than their full order and Rankine was the only malt distiller at that time able to charge his customers warehouse rent. The company went public in 1894, with Rankine holding half the shares.

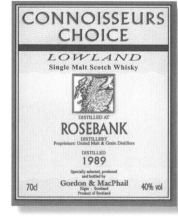

The Pattison crash affected Rosebank as it did many other distilleries, and it struggled to survive for some years until DCL came along. DCL was expanding rapidly and the Pattison fiasco enabled it to buy distilleries at knock-down prices.

Rosebank was one of five distilleries which were amalgamated to form Scottish Malt Distillers in 1914, the other four being Glenkinchie, St Magdalene, Grange and Clydesdale.

In 1993 Rosebank was mothballed, along with three other malt distilleries, as part of United Distillers' rationalisation programme, and has since closed permanently. Much of the area has changed – the canal is closed to navigation and the maltings has gone to make way for a new road. However, the distillery was at the time maturing stocks in bond so it is likely that its 12-year-old triple-distilled single malt will be available for some time to come. After all, it is still possible to find St Magdalene, if you know where to look.

GLENKINCHIE

Glenkinchie Distillery stands in wide open farmland at the foot of the gently rolling Lammermuir Hills, in an area sometimes referred to as 'the back garden of Edinburgh'. Some of the best barley for distilling is grown in this region of Scotland. The village of Ormiston, some 4 miles away, was the home of John Cockburn, the founder of the Society of Improvers of Knowledge of Agriculture, a group of experts which revolutionised Scottish farming. The distillery still has an 85-acre farm attached to it which in the 1940s and 1950s was farmed by the distillery manager himself and whose Aberdeen Angus herd, fed on the by-products of the distillery's malting and mashing processes, won many of the fatstock prizes at the Birmingham, Edinburgh and Smithfield shows. Buchanan's Clydesdale drayhorses, which pulled carts of whisky through the streets of Glasgow, were brought to Glenkinchie's stables for their 'summer holidays'.

The distillery was founded in 1825 by two local farmers, John and George Rate. It was originally called the Milton Distillery (as was Strathisla), and it could well have been confusion over the name which led to it being changed in 1837 to Glenkinchie. The name comes from the glen of the Kinchie Burn which flows through the village. The Rates, being farmers, were quite self-sufficient and distilled from barley grown on their own farms. The operation was quite successful until production stopped in 1853 and the premises were bought by another farmer named Christie. Christie was not interested in distilling and used Glenkinchie partly for sawmilling and partly as a cowshed. When the market for blended whisky began to expand in the 1880s, Glenkinchie was acquired by a syndicate of companies from Edinburgh, which formed itself into the Glenkinchie Distillery Co. Ltd. In 1914 Glenkinchie joined forces with the now-defunct Rosebank, St Magdalene, Grange and Clydesdale Distilleries to become Scottish Malt Distillers Ltd, which subsequently became a wholly owned subsidiary of the fledgling Distillers Company Ltd.

Glenkinchie is distilled conventionally in a single pair of stills, as opposed to being triple-distilled in the traditional Lowland manner. The distillery is licensed to John Haig and not so long ago its entire output went for blending, but it is now bottled as a 10-year-old single malt and Glenkinchie is the Lowland malt representative in UDV's Classic Malts range. The distillery's water supply comes from reservoirs in the hills which are fed from the same springs that feed the Kinchie Burn. The burn itself has not been used since 1954 in view of the possibility of its contamination by farming chemicals.

Glenkinchie is apparently the only distillery which provides a bowling green for the use of its employees, and it also caters well for visitors. A new visitor centre has been built which incorporates the Museum of Malt Whisky Production, originally opened in 1968 on the initiative of the distillery manager. The museum houses a collection of the various implements and instruments used in a distillery. The most impressive exhibit is a model of a malt distillery used at the British Empire Exhibition of 1924–5, which was formerly displayed at the Science Museum.

BLADNOCH

Dumfriesshire has never been a particularly busy distilling area, no doubt on account of its isolation from the mainstream distilling centres, but since records began some nine distilleries have existed here, strung out from Langholm, by the English border, to Stranraer. Some of those nine lasted a good length of time, and some were owned by major companies: Glentarras, at Langholm, was owned for a time by Seager Evans; and Annandale, at Annan, spent its last twenty-five years licensed to Johnnie Walker.

Bladnoch Distillery is situated near Wigtown, on the Machars peninsular, and is the second most southerly distillery ever recorded in Scotland. The area is associated with St Ninian who, according to tradition, established Scotland's first Christian church in AD 397. The settlement was at Whithorn, a few miles south of Wigtown, where the most southerly recorded distillery, the short-lived Smallhills Distillery, met its end at the close of the eighteenth century.

Bladnoch was built between 1814 and 1817 by Thomas McClelland, and remained in his family for nearly a century. From 1911 to 1937 the company, whilst still trading as T. & A. McClelland, was a subsidiary of the Irish company Dunville & Co. Ltd, the proprietor of the Royal Irish Distillery at Belfast. Dunville's was wound up in 1937 and the plant was sold off during and after the war. In 1953 the three stills (Bladnoch was then triple-distilled) were sold to a Swedish company which made Skeppit (meaning 'ship') whisky. The make was not a success and two of the stills were sold to Absolut, where they are reportedly still in use. The third found its way into the Wine and Spirit Museum at Stockholm.

In 1956 the distillery was revived by the Bladnoch Distillery Ltd, and was subsequently acquired by Ian Fisher, chairman of the now-defunct Glasgow blending company McGown & Cameron. Fisher operated the distillery until 1973, when it was sold to Inver House Distillers. Ten years later it passed to Bell's, and subsequently to United Distillers, which closed it down, along with three other distilleries, in 1993. On the wall in the stillhouse is a framed UD memo dated

1 April 1992, placing Bladnoch first and Rosebank second in their efficiency league table. Cardhu was third. Obviously efficiency is no guarantee of survival. Both Bladnoch and Rosebank were in need of investment, although being situated out on a limb, or merely in an unfashionable location, cannot have helped. Neither could the workman, if the story is true, who turned the wrong tap and ran off a batch of whisky into the River Bladnoch!

When Alfred Barnard visited Bladnoch he found a distillery with a single, huge, 13,000-gallon wash still, at odds with the tiny pair of 400-gallon spirit stills; and the wort cooled in the underback, which was sunk into the watercourse which drove the waterwheel. When it closed the distillery had a wash still of 3,000 gallons and a spirit still of 2,200 gallons. The lauter tun mashed 5.3 tons of grist, there were six washbacks, and the spirit safe was unusual in being stainless steel. United Distillers bottled Bladnoch's malt at ten years old in its Flora & Fauna range. The distillery is once again in Irish hands, having being sold to a property developer from the Emerald Isle, who began operating it as a museum. He has since succeeded in buying back the plant from UDV and restarted distilling on a small scale in December 2000.

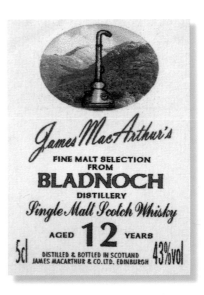

Lost Distilleries

Brora •

Ben Wyvis •

Banff •

Glenugie •

•
Glen Albyn
Glen Mhor
Millburn

Glenury-Royal •

• Glenlochy

North Port • • Lochside

• Strathmore

• St Magdalene

• Glen Flagler
• Kinclaith

• Ladyburn

There have been over seven hundred legally licensed malt distilleries recorded in Scotland since the mid-eighteenth century. There are now around eighty-five. So what happened to all the others? There are many reasons why businesses fail. The industry as a whole has moved away from being a collection of small, family-run concerns, each perhaps operating only a single distillery, towards ever-larger multinational companies all vying for the title of 'biggest drinks company in the world'.

Distilleries have come and gone because of many different factors. In the industry's early days many distilleries were tied to farms, little more than an illicit still run by the farmer as a sideline. His whisky would be sold locally, within weeks of being made, to his neighbours and to nearby inns. Eventually the still would be licensed as a commercial venture. Some of these would prosper and others would fail, as different forces came into play – the additional time and labour on top of that needed to run the farm, transport, and the fact that many of his neighbours were all trying to supply the same markets. Many 'distilleries', which the farmers had taken the trouble to license, disappeared from the Excise records, often after only one year. As distilleries grew from being little more than a still and an improvised worm tub installed in a bothy on the farm to being larger-scale purpose-built establishments so different factors came to play a role in their survival. The introduction of commercial blending saw a vast new market open to the distillers, and with it more competition. They were each forced to compete with their rivals in terms of both economics and product quality. Economically the small firms were at a disadvantage and the larger firms, which grew in the wake of the industrial revolution, made the most of it. Distilleries were bought out and closed down as some companies sought to displace the competition.

The whisky industry has always operated on a cyclical basis, sometimes, but not always, of its own making. Bust regularly follows boom. The Pattison crisis pricked the balloon of the blending boom, closing almost thirty distilleries in its aftermath. The two world wars and Prohibition also took their toll. The economy emerged from the doldrums of World War II and companies began to expand, only to have to shrink again as recession took hold in the 1980s. Conditions were ripe for a wave of take-overs by predatory companies, especially by those from overseas.

Overproduction has been a particular enemy of the whisky industry, and steps have been taken to control the situation since the amalgamation of Lowland grain distillers which led to the formation of DCL. Distilleries may be mothballed – closed temporarily – in order to regulate stock levels, but temporary closures have a habit of becoming permanent. Some companies have found a solution in sporadic production, where a distillery will work maybe one week each month. In this way its whisky is still available to its markets without saturating them. Mistakes have been made, and distilleries with good reputations have been closed and offered for sale, then acquired by rival companies which have gone on to make them successful again. Some distilleries have been irretrievably closed, and one has to ask why. They may be in an 'unfashionable' area, one which does not carry the cachet of some of its more illustrious neighbours; they may need more work to bring them up to present-day standards, particularly with regard to environmental issues, than it is economical to carry out; they may be surplus to requirements following a take-over; or it may be that their product is simply not good enough in today's marketplace. Once a whisky receives a thumbs-down from the blenders then its death knell has been sounded.

The distilleries described here are recently departed. With few exceptions there is nothing left to see – they have been demolished, their sites redeveloped, their plant ripped out for use in other distilleries or sold for scrap. All the malt distilleries built within the grain plants are long silent, as are Allied Distillers' Lomond stills. Other 'lost' distilleries were described in the previous chapter, their buildings still standing and in some cases still equipped. A change in the economic climate, or an enthusiastic and well-heeled businessman with grand ideas, may be all that is needed for them to fire up their stills anew. Their spirit lives on – both literally and figuratively – only in the finite stocks preserved by their former parent companies and the independent bottlers. It is up to the consumer to weigh the possibilities and decide if a bottle is worth the asking price. As stocks dwindle so the price rises accordingly. You must ask yourself if you would pay the price for a whisky for its rarity value alone. Was it that good in the first place, or would your money be better spent on one of the finer, and more readily available, malts?

Banff

Banff Distillery was one of the casualties of DCL's 1980s cut-backs and was one of a dozen or so closed in 1983. Two incarnations of the distillery existed, the first founded in 1824 by James McKilligan & Co. and acquired on the founder's death by James Simpson. Simpson's company ran the distillery from 1852 to 1863, when it was closed by his son and moved to a site at Inverboyndie, a hamlet to the west of Banff. It was known to the locals by that  name, despite being officially registered as Banff. In 1877 it was rebuilt after a fire, at which point the company, in a classic case of shutting the stable door after the horse has bolted, purchased its own fire engine! In 1932 the company was liquidated and Simpson sold out to Scottish Malt Distillers for £50,000.

The spectre of fire raised its head at Banff on two further occasions. The distillery was one of those to suffer damage during World War II, being bombed by a single German JU-88 on 16 August 1941. Some 16,000 proof gallons of spirit were lost, some of which contaminated nearby fields and streams, intoxicating farm animals there. One fireman who filled his helmet with spirit liberated from the damaged casks was prosecuted! In October 1959 a coppersmith managed to cause an explosion whilst carrying out repairs on the spirit still. Fortunately the man was not injured, although the still was a write-off. Scottish Malt Distillers was fined £15 for contravening safety regulations in a court case the following January.

Despite the fact that two planning applications were submitted and approved for a new distillery at Banff, one from SMD itself, the distillery was closed in 1983 and demolished shortly afterwards.

Brora

Although Brora no longer survives its torch is still carried by its sister Clynelish, which was built on the same site in 1967 and which was christened with the original name of the old distillery.

The first Clynelish Distillery was founded in 1819 by the Marquis of Stafford, later the first Duke of Sutherland, who is still reviled in the Highlands for his part in the clearances. Demand for wool in the late eighteenth century led to landowners turning over entire estates to sheep farming. Such farms, tended by a single shepherd, were highly profitable. Tenants were either allotted smallholdings on the coastal strip, or moved out *en masse* with transport ships laid on. Although many people moved to the newly growing Lowland industrial centres others emigrated to Canada, America or the Antipodes. The duke and duchess between them evicted some 10,000 of their tenants altogether. Those moved to the coast were forced to eke out their existence on pitiful crofts and inevitably turned to distilling to supplement their income. Realising that he was in effect promoting an illicit industry the marquis decided that a licensed distillery would afford his tenants a legitimate market for their grain.

Clynelish was first licensed to James Harper, who was succeeded by Andrew Ross, and then by George Lawson. At the time of Barnard's visit Clynelish was so successful that Lawson was only accepting private orders, rather than those from the trade. The distillery was then acquired by the Glasgow blending company James Ainslie & Co., and passed after its bankruptcy to a company jointly owned by DCL and John Risk, the former owner of Bankier Distillery in Stirlingshire. Johnnie Walker took a share in the company in 1916, and by 1930 Risk's share had been bought out and the distillery absorbed into DCL.

In 1967 a new distillery was built alongside the existing one and designated Clynelish A. The old distillery became Clynelish B. Customs and Excise, however, insisted that the two distilleries be treated as separate entities and so the old Clynelish reopened after rebuilding as Brora Distillery in April 1975. Recession forced its closure in 1983, and its buildings are now used by the new distillery for warehousing and for a visitor centre.

Glen Albyn

Inverness had a thriving distilling industry in the early nineteenth century, with around a dozen distilleries recorded in or around the town. Of those, only three survived into the twentieth century – Glen Albyn, Glen Mhor and Millburn.

Glen Albyn was founded on the site of the abandoned Muirtown Brewery alongside the Caledonian Canal by Provost James Sutherland, who was its licensee from 1847 to 1852. It then fell into disuse for a while, after which it was turned into a flour mill. It was rebuilt and refounded as a distillery by Grigor & Co. in 1884. One unusual feature was that the worm pipes were D-shaped, rather than cylindrical as was usual, which was supposed to cool the spirit more quickly. The distillery closed during World War I and, like Dalmore, was used as a base for making mines for the US Navy. It was purchased in 1920 by Mackinlay & Birnie Ltd, the owner of its immediate neighbour Glen Mhor.

In 1972 Mackinlay & Birnie Ltd was acquired

by DCL and the distillery licence transferred to Scottish Malt Distillers. The distillery ceased its own malting in 1980 (it was one of the first distilleries in Scotland to be equipped with Saladin maltings) and closed for good in 1983. Five years later it was demolished and a supermarket built on the site.

Glen Mhor

Although the younger of the two by almost fifty years, Glen Mhor was to become partner to its near neighbour Glen Albyn, which it faced across the Great North Road at Inverness.

Glen Mhor was built in 1892 by James Mackinlay, of the Leith blending company Charles Mackinlay & Co., and John Birnie, Provost of Inverness, who was the distillery's first manager. The company was incorporated as Mackinlay & Birnie Ltd in 1906 with Charles Mackinlay as chief shareholder. It acquired Glen Albyn in 1920 and operated the two distilleries until it was taken over by DCL in 1972. Mackinlay & Birnie Ltd disappeared as a distinct company shortly after the DCL take-over. The distillery closed in 1983 and was demolished to make way for a shopping complex.

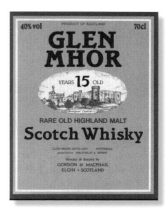

Glen Mhor was bottled by Mackinlay's as a single malt from its early days and seems to have maintained its reputation even to the present. It is still available in bottlings at various ages and strengths from Gordon & MacPhail. The name Glen Mhor means 'Great Glen', and refers to the geological fault marked by lochs Ness, Lochy and Linnhe which virtually split the Scottish mainland in two. In his early years, writer Neil Gunn was an Excise man at Glen Mhor.

Glenlochy

Glenlochy is one of three distilleries to be established at Fort William and was built in 1898

by the Glenlochy-Fort William Distillery Co. Ltd, founded by David McAndie of Nairn. The distillery was in direct competition with Long John's Ben Nevis Distillery and also (until 1908) its partner Nevis, which Long John built nearby in 1878. McAndie was doubtless hoping to ride the crest of the whisky boom, but instead built his new distillery just in time to catch the Pattison crash. Glenlochy worked until 1919 then fell silent, apart from a short period around 1925, until 1937.

Towards the end of this period the distillery was purchased by a local motor hirer, Thomas Rankin. He sold it in 1937 to Train & McIntyre, which transferred it the following year to its subsidiary Associated Scottish Distilleries Ltd, which also acquired at around the same time Bruichladdich, Benromach, Fettercairn, Glenesk, Glenury-Royal and Strathdee distilleries. ASD was run by Joseph Hobbs on behalf of its parent, the National Distillers of America. Hobbs finally sold the company for £38,000 and settled in Fort William, where he bought Inverlochy Castle and established the Great Glen cattle ranch. Train & McIntyre was acquired by DCL in 1953 and the National Distillers of America withdrew from the Scottish industry. Along with Glenlochy, DCL acquired Benromach, Glenesk and Glenury-Royal as part of the deal, with Fettercairn and Bruichladdich finding other buyers and Strathdee not reopened after World War II.

DCL operated Glenlochy until 1983, when it became a victim of its rationalisation programme. The site was sold in 1992 to West Coast Inns Ltd after DCL's application to demolish the distillery was rejected by the District Council, probably due to the fact that the maltings and kilns are listed buildings.

Glenugie

With the exception of a distillery named Kirktown, which was built on the opposite side of Peterhead Bay in 1825, Glenugie is the eastern-most distillery to be licensed in Scotland. Kirktown was a mere ½ mile further east, any further and it would have been in the sea, but operated for only five years. Glenugie, on the other hand, survived for some 150 years before it succumbed to cut-backs in 1983.

Glenugie was founded in 1831 by Donald, McLeod & Co. and was originally known as Invernettie. It was built on the site of an old windmill, and the main distillery building was constructed around a cast-iron frame. It passed in 1837 to the Glenugie Distillery Co. which, strange as it may seem, converted it into a brewery. It was later rebuilt as a distillery by the Scottish Highland Distillers Co. Ltd, but the company languished and was eventually wound up. The distillery was sold in 1879 to George Whyte & Co., which seemed to be no more successful and sold it around 1884 to Simon Forbes, who operated it until 1915. The distillery was silent for a number of years after World War I until it was taken over by a new company, also calling itself the Glenugie Distillery Co., which was owned by Seager Evans & Co. of London. In 1956 Seager Evans became a subsidiary of Schenley Industries and its Scottish distilleries were transferred to Strathclyde & Long John Distilleries, which became Long John Distillers Ltd. As a preliminary to the Schenley take-over the company was briefly controlled by Hugh Fraser, later Lord Fraser of Allander. Seager Evans was reconstituted as Long John International in 1970 and was sold by Schenley to Whitbread in 1975 for a reported £18 million.

The following year the distillery suffered a catastrophe when an

oil tank overflowed and oil contaminated the watercourse and the beach nearby, and Long John was given the bill for the clean-up operation. As the industry sank into recession in the early 1980s Glenugie became surplus to requirements and Long John closed it down. Some of the plant was taken out and transferred to the company's recently acquired Ben Nevis distillery at Fort William, and the site was eventually redeveloped for use by engineering companies working in the North Sea oil industry.

Glenury-Royal

Glenury is another of those distilleries built on the east coast of the Grampian region and one of the many to be founded shortly after the introduction of the Excise Act. It was built on the north bank of the River Cowie at Stonehaven in 1825 by Barclay, McDonald & Co., the Barclay of which was Captain Robert Barclay, the MP for Kincardine. He controlled the distillery until 1852 and obtained its 'Royal' title apparently through his friendship with a lady he referred to as 'Mrs Windsor', and her influence on King William IV!

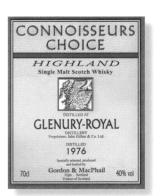

The distillery was then said to have been acquired by a William Ritchie of Glasgow. The company was incorporated as William Ritchie & Co. in 1890 and continued at Glenury until 1938, when the distillery was sold to Joseph Hobbs's Associated Scottish Distilleries, which was then newly incorporated into Train & McIntyre, a subsidiary of the National Distillers of America. When Train & McIntyre was acquired by DCL in 1953 Glenury passed to Scottish Malt Distillers, which licensed it to John Gillon.

Gillon's was established by Sir John Gillon of Linlithgow in 1817 and became a subsidiary of DCL through a complicated series of take-overs and mergers. The company amalgamated in 1913 with Ainslie's and two other companies to become Ainslie, Baillie & Co., which in turn was acquired after World War I by Sir James Calder, whose company Macdonald, Greenlees & Williams owned Glendullan and Benromach distilleries. Calder had already taken over David Heilbron & Son and merged the two with Campbeltown distillers Colville Greenlees & Co. to form Ainslie & Heilbron, which became a subsidiary of Macdonald, Greenlees & Williams. That company was acquired by DCL in 1926.

Glenury was rebuilt in 1965 and extended from two to four stills, and Gillon's bottled its malt at twelve years old. It closed in 1985 and its licence was revoked in 1992. The following year planning permission was granted to turn the site into a housing development.

Lochside

Lochside was a distillery of striking appearance, standing at a crossroads on the main road into Montrose. It took its name from the filled-in loch by which it stood, and on whose reclaimed land its warehouses were built. The site was that of an eighteenth-century brewery, and the distillery was converted from a later brewery building dating from the 1890s and built in the German 'brauhaus' style. That brewery was owned by Deuchar's, which became part of Scottish & Newcastle Breweries Ltd. It was the only location outside Newcastle itself to brew Newcastle Brown Ale, which was then shipped by sea down the coast to its 'home' town.

The brewery was rebuilt by Macnab Distilleries Ltd, which was a company set up by Joseph Hobbs after he had sold Associated Scottish Distilleries Ltd in 1953. The name came from John Macnab, the proprietor of Glenmavis Distillery at Bathgate to the west of Edinburgh, whose brand names Hobbs had acquired. Between 1855 and its closure in 1910 Glenmavis unusually used, or rather underused, a Coffey still to make malt whisky,

and this peculiarity seems to have piqued Hobbs's interest. He had moved to Fort William and bought Ben Nevis Distillery, in which he installed a Coffey still with the intention of making both malt and grain whisky, and he repeated the exercise at Lochside.

Joseph Hobbs died in 1964 leaving Lochside to his son. The Coffey still was mothballed in 1970, but left *in situ*, and the distillery sold in 1973 to the Spanish company Destilerias y Crianza. DYC operated the distillery for nearly twenty years, producing Lochside malt and a blend called Sandy Macnab, which was bottled on site. The company was acquired by Domecq, which itself passed to Hiram Walker and subsequently to Allied Distillers. Production stopped at Lochside in April 1992 and the warehouses were gradually cleared out. A local campaign was set up in an attempt to preserve the brewery tower, which it was discovered was not even a listed building.

Millburn

Unusually for one of the distilleries described in this chapter, there is still something of Millburn left to see. The distillery was converted after its closure into a Beefeater restaurant, and its chimney is still a landmark.

Of the dozen or so distilleries recorded in Inverness only three survived into the twentieth century, Millburn, Glen Albyn and Glen Mhor, and of those Millburn was the oldest by a considerable margin. The distillery was built at the foot of a hill on the outskirts of Inverness, by the Mill Burn, on a tightly hemmed-in site. It is said to have been founded in 1807 by a Mr Welsh, who leased the land for a rent of £16 a year, but the earliest positive reference is in 1825 when it was licensed to Rose & Macdonald. It changed hands three times in less than thirty years before being acquired by corn merchant David Rose, who may have used it as a mill. It was rebuilt in 1876 and operated from 1881 by Rose's son George, who sold it in 1892 to the Haig family. Haig's in turn sold it in 1921 to Booth's, the gin distillers, which saw its new acquisition burn down the following year. In 1943 Millburn was acquired by Scottish Malt Distillers and licensed to

Macleay Duff Ltd, a blending company established in 1863 and taken over by DCL in 1933.

Millburn closed in 1985. It was small and old-fashioned and offered little scope for expansion. Its process water was by that time being piped eight miles from Loch Duntelchaig, in the hills above Loch Ness to the south-west. Its whisky apparently had a good reputation, and for the time being is still available from the independents.

North Port

North Port took its name from the north gate in the old city walls of Brechin, and is said to have been founded in 1820 by David, John and Alexander Guthrie. The distillery was originally known as Townhead but changed its name after three years to Brechin Distillery, just prior to the company being reconstituted as Guthrie, Martin & Co. The distillery was still called Brechin at the time of Barnard's visit. Guthrie's survived, in one form or another, until 1922, when the distillery was purchased by DCL and W. H. Holt & Co. Ltd and transferred to Scottish Malt Distillers.

North Port was then licensed to Mitchell Bros Ltd (not to be confused with J. & A. Mitchell of Springbank Distillery). The company was a subsidiary of the Distillers Finance Corporation, which itself was owned by a syndicate of Irish distillers and blenders, and which was also taken over by DCL in 1922. North Port remained within SMD until it was closed in 1983. The cooling water dam was filled in and a funeral parlour built on the reclaimed land. A supermarket marks the site of the old warehouses, and all that now remains of North Port is a commemorative plaque.

St Magdalene

The royal burgh of Linlithgow was the birthplace of Mary, Queen of Scots, and once held an annual fair on the site of St Magdalene's hospital, a twelfth-century leper colony established by the Knights Templar. St Magdalene Distillery was one of five recorded in Linlithgow. The others worked

for twenty or thirty years, one for only a single year, yet St Magdalene lasted for 185 years, proving to be one of the longest surviving of all the Lowland malt distilleries. Only nine out of nearly seventy malt distilleries licensed in the Lowlands before 1800 survived into the twentieth century, and most of those had gone before the end of World War I.

St Magdalene is believed to have been founded by Sebastian Henderson in 1798 and stood next door to Bonnytown Distillery, which was built three years previously. Its proprietors, the Dawson family, quickly took over St Magdalene and eventually Bonnytown was absorbed into St Magdalene's site as it expanded. Barnard found St Magdalene to be a thriving distillery, with an annual output of over 200,000 proof gallons from its five stills. It had forty staff and a chief Excise man with the improbable name of Allice Robertson. The distillery was operated by Adam Dawson and his successors until 1912, when the company was liquidated. Two years later it was bought by DCL and it became one of the founding members of Scottish Malt Distillers, along with Glenkinchie, Rosebank, Grange and Clydesdale.

St Magdalene was later licensed to William Greer & Co., a subsidiary of Mitchell Bros Ltd which was to become licensee of North Port Distillery at Brechin. Greer came to Glasgow in 1893 from Belfast, where his family was involved in distilling through Kirker, Greer & Co. Mitchell's parent company, the Distillers Finance Corporation, was acquired by DCL in 1922. In November 1979 DCL transferred the business of William Greer to its subsidiary John Hopkins & Co. Ltd, the licensee of Oban Distillery. St Magdalene closed in 1983, after a working life of almost two centuries, and some of the distillery buildings have been converted into flats.

Malt-within-grain distilleries

With the notable exception of DCL a number of major blending companies have decided at some time that it might be a good idea to have a malt distillery virtually within arm's reach, and so have built one within their grain distilling complexes. With the exception of Inverleven, built within Ballantine's Dumbarton complex in 1938, they were all built from the late 1950s to the mid 1960s, and were closed down in the mid 1970s. Long John built Kinclaith within Strathclyde grain distillery, Inver House built Glen Flagler within its Garnheath plant and Wm Grant built Ladyburn at Girvan. George Christie's Strathmore Distillery was not strictly a malt plant within a grain distillery, but rather a malt distillery which was converted to a grain plant after an unsuccessful start. All these distilleries were Lowland-based with the exception of Ben Wyvis, built within the Invergordon grain distillery on the Cromarty Firth.

Somehow the experiment never seemed to pay off. It may have appeared convenient for the grain distillers to have a malt distillery so close to hand, yet such small plants never stood much chance of long-term survival, built as they were on the doorstep of a huge grain distillery, whose operations inevitably took precedence. Inverleven is the exception to the rule, having worked for fifty-three years when it was closed in 1991. It actually made two malts, one of those in a

Lomond-type still, and Inverleven malt is still available in a distillers' bottling. Inver House bottled Glen Flagler at one time, but it has been left largely to the independents to bring these malts to the market. Even then they are rare. A bottling of Ben Wyvis has been made from three recently discovered casks, but no Strathmore malt is known to survive at all.

Ben Wyvis

Ben Wyvis is a 3,428ft peak to the west of Alness, which has lent its name to two distilleries in the region. The original Ben Wyvis Distillery was situated at Dingwall, at the head of the Cromarty Firth. It was built in 1879 and passed through the hands of a number of licensees including the Irish distillers Kirker, Greer & Co., which changed its name to Ferintosh, an evocative name harking back to the days of Duncan Forbes, who was granted the right to distil duty free as a reward for his loyalty to William of Orange in the face of the Jacobites. When the privilege was withdrawn Forbes's descendants closed down their distilleries and Robbie Burns himself mourned the passing of their whisky. Kirker, Greer's parent company was acquired by DCL and the Ferintosh company liquidated. At the time the distillery was taking its water from Loch Ussie, into whose depths the Brahan Seer supposedly threw his 'stone of vision' after being condemned to death.

The name Ben Wyvis was appropriated again in 1965 when Invergordon built a malt distillery within its recently constructed grain plant, the most northerly grain distillery in Scotland. It was one of the smaller malt-within-grain plants, with only a single pair of stills, and lasted until 1976 when it was closed down to make way for expansion of the grain distillery. A fourth continuous still, with extra columns for neutral spirit production, was commissioned in 1978. It has previously been reported that Ben Wyvis's malt has apparently never been bottled as such, even by the independents, but whilst the company was stock-taking in the labyrinthine warehouses at Invergordon it discovered three casks of a 1972 distillation of Ben Wyvis malt which had lain there forgotten for twenty-seven years! A check of the original stock books, by then in archive storage, confirmed the identity of the find. The malt was bottled on 26 October 2000, the three casks yielding seventy-eight cases of whisky.

Glen Flagler

In 1965 Inver House Distillers Ltd, whilst a subsidiary of the American company Publicker Industries, built itself a grain-distilling complex, converted from the old Moffat Mills paper mill 3 miles east of Airdrie. The distillery, and the grain spirit produced by it, was called Garnheath. Inver House also built a large-scale commercial maltings and a malt distillery as part of the complex. Glen Flagler was the largest of the malt-within-grain distilleries with six stills, and made in total four different malts.

Glen Flagler was distilled conventionally until 1969, when the production method changed and the wash was run through a continuous 'beer still' in the bourbon fashion. Until 1970 three other malts were also distilled – Killyloch, the more heavily peated Islebrae, and Glen Moffat. The distillery took its water from Lilly Loch and that was intended to be the name of the malt until, so the story goes, the cask stencil was delivered with a spelling mistake. Rather than delay production the company decided to use the name on the stencil – Killyloch! Inver House have sold Glen Flagler bottled at five and eight years old, and Killyloch, though intended for blending, has appeared in independent bottlings. Islebrae and Glen Moffat were only used for blending.

Overproduction problems in the industry in the late 1970s and early 1980s led Inver House to take drastic action at Garnheath. Killyloch,

Islebrae and Glen Moffat were dropped, and the maltings was sold off in 1978 to Associated British Maltsters. Glen Flagler continued until July 1985. Garnheath itself closed in July 1986, and was demolished following the management buy-out of 1988.

Kinclaith

Strathclyde grain distillery was built in 1927 by the Scottish Grain Distilling Co. Ltd, a subsidiary of Seager Evans, and shoehorned into a tiny site in the Gorbals region of Glasgow where St Andrew's suspension bridge crosses the Clyde at the southern end of the park known as Glasgow Green. Seager Evans had acquired the Long John brand name when it purchased the London wine and spirit merchant W. H. Chaplin & Co. in 1936, and created Long John Distillers Ltd as a subsidiary company. It was taken over in 1956 by Schenley Industries of Cincinnati, which was expanding its Scotch whisky interests. Shortly after the take-over Schenley built itself two new malt distilleries, Tormore on Speyside, and Kinclaith, within Strathclyde itself.

Kinclaith was built primarily for a convenient supply of malt whisky for the Long John blend. Of the three dozen or so malt distilleries recorded in Glasgow, the oldest of which were licensed in 1770, it was the last to be built by a margin of over a hundred years. It survived until 1975, a time when most of the malt-within-grain distilleries were being discarded. Long John was sold to Whitbread in that year and the company began to refurbish Strathclyde and gear up for gin and vodka production. Kinclaith had to go.

Ladyburn

Little has been written about Ladyburn, which was built by Wm Grant in 1966 within its Girvan grain distillery on the Ayrshire coast. Girvan, which is on the fringe of the town of the same name, looks out to sea towards the island of Ailsa Craig and was built three years previously at a cost of £1.25 million, a phenomenal sum at that time. The distillery was built in record time, a mere nine months, and when complete was the largest and

most sophisticated grain distillery in Europe. Charles Grant Gordon, William Grant's great-grandson, lived on the site in a caravan during the construction, in order to spur on the builders, and some of the workmen were offered jobs at the plant once it was complete. Ladyburn was built with four stills, making it the second-most ambitious malt-within-grain distillery after Glen Flagler. It was closed in 1976.

Ladyburn's malt has been bottled by some of the independents, which is unusual in itself as Wm Grant generally takes precautions to prevent other companies bottling its products as single malts. Glenfiddich and Balvenie are supplied to blenders each vatted with a tiny proportion of the other for this very reason. However, Gordon & MacPhail list an 'Ayrshire malt' distilled in 1970, and of the eight licensed malt distilleries recorded in Ayrshire only one was in production in that particular year!

Strathmore

Strathmore, also known as the North of Scotland Distillery, was built in 1957 by George Christie's North of Scotland Distilling Co. Ltd and started its life making malt whisky in a patent still, as had Glenmavis some years before. The distillery was converted from Knox's Forth Brewery at Cambus, close to Cambus Distillery itself. For its first two years it made Strathmore malt whisky, but the patent-still technique was not successful and the plant was converted for grain distilling. Three new column stills were installed, but they were too tall for the stillhouse and, as planning regulations forbade raising the roof, the only solution was to sink them into pits in the floor! Knox's was reputedly haunted by the ghost of a former brewer, and one has to wonder if this was not his idea of mischief!

George Christie sold out in around 1980 to DCL, which annexed the plant to Cambus. Christie was by that time working on his new malt distillery near Kingussie, having bought the site in 1956. He has since retired, but not before seeing the new Speyside Distillery come into production in 1990.

The increasing number of distilleries throwing open their doors to the public is testament to malt whisky's growing popularity, and more and more distillers are recognising the advantages of welcoming visitors. Attendances vary widely, from maybe 600 per year for a small, out-of-the-way distillery, to the huge attendances recorded at some of the popular Whisky Trail distilleries. Glenfiddich, for instance, the first distillery to open to visitors back in 1969, now caters for some 125,000 per year. Facilities are becoming increasingly sophisticated, with exhibitions, audiovisual presentations, multilingual commentaries to cater for the high number of overseas visitors, and even gardens and picnic areas.

The Whisky Trail itself is a tourist attraction unique to Scotland and comprises a cooperage and eight Speyside distilleries: The Glenlivet, Glenfiddich, Glenfarclas, Glen Grant, Cardhu, Strathisla, Benromach, Dallas Dhu and the Speyside Cooperage at Craigellachie. The trail is signposted throughout the area and all nine attractions would be accessible within a two-day period, although having a designated driver would be a good idea! If any criticism could be levelled at the Whisky Trail it would be that the distilleries mostly represent the traditionally accepted character of Speyside malts – lightish, fragrant and flowery – and that some opportunities to demonstrate Speyside's variety are missed.

The following list shows which distilleries are open to visitors, and on what basis. Those with visitor centres have regular organised tours, and unless yours is a large party pre-booking is usually not necessary. At the end of the tour a 'wee dram' will see you on your way. The current fashion, especially amongst those distilleries which have recently invested large sums in refurbishing their visitor facilities, is to levy a small admission charge, some or all of which may be credited against the purchase of a bottle of whisky from the gift shop. I have even been charged for the tour myself when visiting one of the distilleries listed here in the course of researching this book! Distilleries which accept visitors by appointment only will have no fancy facilities, and will probably not even be licensed to sell you a bottle of their malt. A phone call in advance is necessary so that a member of staff can be made available to show you around. The advantage of visiting these distilleries is that you may have the manager or brewer as your personal guide, and if you are seriously interested in the subject they will be in a much better position to answer your questions than a tour guide conducting a party of a dozen people.

Bowmore tun room

Distillery	Reception Centre	Whisky Trail	Visit By Appt	Telephone
ABERFELDY	Y			01887 822010
ARDBEG			Y	01496 302244
ARRAN	Y			01770 830264
BALBLAIR			Y	01862 821273
BEN NEVIS	Y			01397 700200
BENRIACH			Y	01542 783042
BENRINNES			Y	01340 871215
BENROMACH	Y	Y		01309 675968
BLADNOCH	Y			01988 402605
BLAIR ATHOL	Y			01796 482003
BOWMORE	Y			01496 810671
BUNNAHABHAIN			Y	01496 840646
CAOL ILA			Y	01496 302760
CARDHU	Y	Y		01340 872555
CLYNELISH	Y			01408 623000
DALLAS DHU	Y	Y		01309 676548
Historic Scotland				0131 668 8600
DALMORE			Y	01349 882362
DALWHINNIE	Y			01540 672219
EDRADOUR	Y			01349 882362
FETTERCAIRN	Y			01561 340244
GLENDRONACH			Y	01466 730202
GLENDULLAN			Y	
Heritage Dept				0131 5192000
GLENFARCLAS	Y	Y		01807 500257
GLENFIDDICH	Y	Y		01340 820373
GLENGOYNE	Y			01360 550254
GLEN GRANT	Y	Y		01542 783318
GLENKINCHIE	Y			01875 342004
THE GLENLIVET	Y	Y		01542 783220
GLENMORANGIE	Y			01862 892477
GLEN MORAY			Y	01343 542577
GLEN ORD	Y			01463 872004
GLEN SPEY			Y	01340 810215
GLENTURRET	Y			01764 656565
HIGHLAND PARK	Y			01856 874619
JURA			Y	01496 820240
KNOCKDHU			Y	01466 771223
LAGAVULIN			Y	01496 302400
LAPHROAIG			Y	01496 302418
LONGMORN			Y	01542 783042
MACALLAN			Y	01340 872214
MACDUFF			Y	01261 812612

Distillery	Reception Centre	Whisky Trail	Visit By Appt	Telephone
OBAN	Y			01631 572004
PULTENEY	Y			01955 602371
ROYAL LOCHNAGAR	Y			01339 742700
SPEYBURN			Y	01340 831213
SPEYSIDE COOPERAGE	Y	Y		01340 871108
SPRINGBANK			Y	01586 552085
STRATHISLA	Y	Y		01542 783044
STRATHMILL			Y	01542 882295
TALISKER	Y			01478 614308
TOBERMORY	Y			01688 302647
TOMATIN	Y			01808 511444
TOMINTOUL			Y	01807 590274

Distilleries not listed here do not generally accept visits from the public.

If you cannot wait to travel to Scotland and see the distilleries at first hand, then the internet has made it possible to undertake 'virtual visits'. Many distillers, and even some individual distilleries, have a presence on the web. Feeding various combinations of the words 'malt', 'whisky' and 'distillery' into your web browser and checking out the results will take up an entertaining evening or two, and the number of search matches may surprise you. There are also sites devoted to the subject which have been established entirely independently of the distilling companies by individuals or groups of enthusiasts in a number of countries and further sites, both official and otherwise, are in development.

Many of the larger companies have their own corporate websites which offer a good basic starting point, some of which are listed below. Some are better than others for finding information on individual distilleries.

UDV	www.diageo.com
Classic Malts	http://scotch.com/
Allied Distillers	www.allieddomecqplc.com
Morrison Bowmore	www.Morrisonbowmore.co.uk
Inver House Distillers	www.inverhouse.com
Invergordon	www.invergordon.com
Pernod-Ricard	www.pernod-ricard.com/
Seagram	www.seagram.com

The following distilleries can be found either on their own websites, or on those of their parent companies as shown. It is possible to make a 'virtual' visit to some distilleries which are closed to visits by the public.

Distillery	Website
ABERFELDY	www.dewars.com/worldofwhisky
ABERLOUR	www.aberlour.com
ARDBEG	www.ardbeg.com
ARRAN	www.arranwhisky.com
AUCHENTOSHAN	www.Morrisonbowmore.co.uk
BALBLAIR	www.inverhouse.com
BALMENACH	www.inverhouse.com
BEN NEVIS	www.fort-william.net/bennevis-distillery/
BENROMACH	www.benromach.com
BLADNOCH	www.bladnoch.co.uk
BOWMORE	www.Morrisonbowmore.co.uk
BRUICHLADDICH	www.murray-mcdavid.com
DALMORE	www.invergordon.com
EDRADOUR	www.edradour.com
FETTERCAIRN	www.invergordon.com
GLENFARCLAS	www.glenfarclas.co.uk
GLENFIDDICH	www.glenfiddich.com
GLEN GARIOCH	www.Morrisonbowmore.co.uk
GLENGOYNE	www.glengoynedistillery.co.uk
GLENLIVET	www.glenlivet.com
GLENMORANGIE	www.glenmorangie.com
GLEN MORAY	www.glenmoray.com
GLEN ORD	www.glenord.com
GLENTURRET	www.glenturret.com
HIGHLAND PARK	www.highlandpark.co.uk
JURA	www.isleofjura.com
KNOCKDHU	www.inverhouse.com
LAPHROAIG	www.laphroaig.com
MACALLAN	www.themacallan.com
PULTENEY	www.inverhouse.com
SPEYBURN	www.inverhouse.com
SPEYSIDE	www.speysidedistillery.co.uk
TAMNAVULIN	www.invergordon.com
TOBERMORY	www.tobermory.mull.com/distillery
TOMINTOUL	www.angusdundee.co.uk

There are many other sites of interest, as a search will reveal. The Scotch Whisky Association and the Scotch Malt Whisky Society both have comprehensive sites from which many other destinations can be reached:

Scotch Whisky Association   www.scotch-whisky.org.uk
Scotch Malt Whisky Society   www.smws.com

The Speyside Whisky Trail is well represented on the web, the 'official' site being: www.ifb.net/webit/whisky.htm
Other sites, which also have links to accommodation in the area, include: www.net-trak.com/~ecs/culture/cult03.htm
www.maltwhiskytrail.com

There is also The Edinburgh Malt Whisky Tour at: www.dcs.ed.ac.uk/home/jhb/whisky

For readers wishing to know more about Islay the island has its own site, which includes details of the distilleries, accommodation, etc. and links to their sites: www.isle of islay.com

The following two independently run sites were created by groups of enthusiasts in Denmark and contain many links to further sites. With the caveat that the material is not for commercial use The Alternative Whisky Academy shamelessly reproduces articles from whisky books which have caught their interest, including, I should be flattered to say, my own!

Alternative Whisky Academy   www.awa.dk
UISGE   www.uisge.dk

The Online Distilling Network – www.distill.com – is a more commercially oriented site aimed at the industry itself. It has links to the home pages of distilleries and related organisations around the world, including distillery auctions and used equipment dealers. Readers toying with any ideas of founding their own distilleries should start here!

Historic Scotland, which is the curator of Dallas Dhu, has its own website: www.historic-scotland.gov.uk

Readers wishing to join the debate on the origins of the distillery names should visit The Scottish Place Names Society: www.gaclic.nct/cli/links.htm

AGE: As stated on a label applies to the youngest *whisky* in the bottle. By law, whisky must be at least three years old.

ALCOHOL: Hydrocarbon compound resulting from *fermentation* of saccharine solutions. Forms the intoxicating component of fermented and distilled liquors.

ANGEL'S SHARE: Quantity of *spirit* lost from *casks* during the *maturation* period due to evaporation – approx. 2 per cent per year. Also known as *ullage*.

BARLEY: *Cereal* which is *germinated* to produce *malt*, the raw material from which *malt whisky* is made.

BARNARD, ALFRED: Victorian journalist and author of a major survey of distilleries published in 1887: *The Whisky Distilleries of the United Kingdom*.

BARREL: A small *cask* containing about 40 gallons.

BLEND: A *whisky* which is a mixture of *grain* and *malt* whiskies, for instance Famous Grouse, Bell's etc. The better the blend, the more malt whisky it will contain. Devised to produce whiskies which would appeal to a wider range of tastes, in particular those of the English.

BLENDING: The art of combining *malt* and *grain* whiskies in various proportions.

BODEGA: A particular kind of Spanish wine cellar which specialises in the production of certain wines only, for instance sherry.

BOILING POINT: The principle on which distilling works. If a mixture of liquids such as *alcohol* and *water* is boiled, the liquid with the lower boiling point will be vaporised and driven off first and so the components of the mixture will be separated.

BOND: A warehouse in which new *whisky* may be stored without payment of *duty* until such time as it leaves that warehouse at the end of the *maturation* period.

BREWER: Middle manager responsible for the day-to-day running of the *distillery*.

BROKER: An individual or company which acts as an intermediary between the distillers and the blenders and bottlers. A broker will hold a portfolio of whiskies from which he supplies his clients.

BURNT ALE: See *POT ALE*.

BUSHEL: A dry measure of 8 gallons, which for grain equates to 56lb, or half a hundredweight.

BUTT: Largest sized *cask* usually used in a *distillery*. Contains 108 gallons. See also *PUNCHEON*.

CARAMEL: Dark brown substance made from sugar which is used as a colouring agent in some whiskies. Most likely to be found in *blends*, where it is used to ensure continuity of colour from one batch to the next. Malt whiskies achieve their colour from the judicious use of bourbon, new *oak* and sherry *casks* in predetermined ratios.

CARBON DIOXIDE: A by-product of the *fermentation* process. It is heavier than air, and the danger of suffocation is the reason why the lower *tun* room is kept locked whilst the *washbacks* are in use.

CASK: Storage vessel made of wooden staves bound with metal hoops, used to store *whisky* during *maturation*. In a malt distillery they are always *oak* and have usually been used previously to store sherry or bourbon. See also *BARREL, BUTT, HOGSHEAD, OCTAVE, QUARTER*.

CASK STRENGTH: New *whisky* is filled into *casks* at about 63.5 per cent *alcohol* by volume. Also refers to whisky which has been bottled straight from the cask with no further dilution.

CEREAL: A grass-type crop yielding starchy seeds suitable for food. Rich in carbohydrates.

CHARGER: A tank usually used to store a liquid prior to passing it on to the next stage of the process. See also *LOW WINES CHARGER, WASH CHARGER*.

CHARRING: The insides of new *oak* bourbon *casks* are briefly set alight thus charring them. Adds colour to the *spirit*. Also used to rejuvenate previously used casks, cracking the surface to expose 'new' wood to the spirit.

CHILL-FILTRATION: Filtration of the *spirit* at low temperature to remove the clouding which occurs if *whisky* is allowed to get too cold. Some would argue that it also filters out some of the character.

CLEARIC: New make *spirit*.

CLING: The oily trails which a *malt whisky* leaves on the inside of a glass. Caused by *fusel oil* in the *spirit*.

COFFEY STILL: See *PATENT STILL*.

COLOUR CODE: The pipework in a *distillery* is colour-coded to show what liquid is inside – red for *wash*, blue for *low wines* (including *foreshots* and *feints*), black for *spirit*, white for *water*. Required by law.

CONDENSER: A system of tubes cooled by running *water* and attached to the neck of the *still*, used to reduce the *alcohol* vapour coming off the still to liquid form.

CONGENERS: The constituents of the *spirit*, in particular impurities such as *fusel oil*, which contribute to its character.

COOPER: *Distillery* worker responsible for the assembly and maintenance of the *casks*. In the nineteenth century, probably the highest-paid man in the distillery.

COOPERAGE: A workshop where the *casks* are made and maintained. Also used as a general term for the casks themselves.

CROWN LOCK: Lock bearing Customs and *Excise* seals to prevent unauthorised access to any liquor in the *distillery* which has an alcoholic content (all *alcohol* being liable to *duty*).

CULM: Dried rootlets still attached to the *malt* grains after kilning.

CUSTOMS AND EXCISE: See *EXCISE*.

CUTTING: Dilution of the *spirit* with *water* to reduce it to a specific alcoholic content. Done when filling the *whisky* into *casks* for *maturation* and usually again at the bottling stage. Demineralised water is usually used as it contains no calcium which could throw a precipitate later.

DARK GRAINS: A cattle feed, usually in pellet form, made from *distillery* by-products *draff* and *pot ale*.

DCL: The Distillers Company Ltd. Originally formed out of a 'trade arrangement' made between six Lowland grain distillers in 1857. After a slight 'reshuffle, the companies merged in 1877. Taken over by Guinness in 1987.

DEPHLEGMATOR: A pre-condenser mounted on top of a *still* to control the degree of *reflux*. Sometimes called a purifier. Dephlegmate means 'to free from water'.

DIASTASE: *Enzyme* complex secreted during *germination* of *barley* which converts *starch* to soluble starch and *sugars*.

DISTILLATION: Separation of alcoholic liquor from a mixture of *alcohol* and *water* by evaporation and condensation. The resulting liquor is known as the distillate.

DISTILLERY: A place where *alcohol*, and especially alcoholic beverages, are produced by a process of *distillation*.

DOIG, CHARLES: Architect responsible for design or alteration work on many Speyside distilleries around the end of the nineteenth century.

DRAFF: Waste material left in the *mash tun* after draining off the *extraction waters*. Basically *malt* husks and usually used for cattle feed. See *DARK GRAINS*.

DRAM: Originally a late-eighteenth century measure of whisky of about a third of a pint (which in that era would have been at 60 *per cent volume*), or in today's terms about eight normal pub measures! Modern usage implies a much smaller, though imprecise, measure.

DRESSING: The removal of dust, rootlets and any foreign contaminants from the *malt* before it passes to the *mill* for grinding into *grist*.

DRUM: A type of *maltings* in which the *barley* is *germinated* in large revolving drums through which air is drawn. A drum will usually have a capacity of 20–50 tons of barley.

DUNNAGE: Method of warehousing in which *casks* are stacked on each other, separated by wooden rails. The floor is often bare earth.

DUTY: A tax on certain commodities administered by Customs and *Excise*.

ELUTION: Spraying hot *water* on to the *grist* in a *lauter* tun to wash the *sugars* away from the grist solids.

ENZYME: Biochemical catalyst, naturally occurring in living cells, which causes a particular chemical reaction to take place, for instance conversion of *sugar* to *alcohol* and *carbon dioxide* during *fermentation*.

EXCISE: HM Customs and Excise. The branch of the Civil Service responsible for the collection of *duty*.

EXTRACTION WATERS: The three or four batches of liquid drawn off from the *mash tun* and passed to the *underback*. The bulk liquid is then known as *wort*.

FEINTS: The heavier alcohols present in the *low wines*, and therefore the last to be driven off during the second *distillation*.

FEINTS RECEIVER: A tank in which *foreshots* and *feints* are stored prior to being fed back for redistillation with the next batch of *low wines*. Foreshots and feints are sometimes diverted straight to the *low wines charger*.

FERMENTATION: A slow decomposition of organic substances usually induced by *enzymes*, for instance the conversion of *sugars* to *alcohol* and *carbon dioxide* by *yeast* enzymes. Distillers allow fermentation to progress to completion whereas brewers stop the process part-way through, the final fermentation taking place in the *cask*.

FIRST FILL: Refers to *casks* which are being filled with *whisky* for the first time, even though they may have already been used for bourbon or sherry. See also *REFILL*.

FORESHOTS: The lightest alcohols present in the *low wines*, and therefore the first to be driven off during the second *distillation*. An undesirable element in the distillate as it is not *potable* spirit.

FUSEL OIL: One of the heavier alcohols present in the *feints*, some of which are kept along with the *middle cut* in order to add character to the *spirit*.

GERMINATION: The sprouting of a seed grain at the start of its growth cycle.

GLEN: A deep valley.

GRAIN WHISKY: *Whisky* made mainly from *cereals* other than malted *barley*, usually wheat. Maize may also be used, but as it is more expensive (though the results are arguably superior) most grain distillers go for the cheaper option. In practice, a quantity of *malt* (usually 10 per cent) is added to the mixture as the enzyme *diastase* must be present in the *mash tun* to convert the *starch* into *sugar*, and

UK law prohibits the use of artificial *enzymes*. *Distillation* usually takes place in a *patent still* and is a continuous process, as opposed to the batch process by which *malt whisky* is made.

GREEN MALT: *Barley* which has completed its *germination* phase but which has yet to be dried in the *kiln*.

GRIST: The fine powder which results from milling grain and which is passed to the *mash tun* to be mashed with hot *water*.

HEADS AND TAILS: *Foreshots* and *feints* respectively.

HEART OF THE RUN: See *MIDDLE CUT*.

HEAT RECOVERY: Large quantities of heat are generated in a *distillery* and it is not usually wasted. Mash water can be heated by heat generated by the *wort cooler* and *condensers*, fresh *wash* by the *pot ale*, and *low wines* and *feints* by heat from the *spent lees*. Bowmore also uses waste heat to heat the public swimming pool next door to the distillery.

HIGHLAND LINE: An imaginary dividing line drawn from Dundee in the east to Greenock in the west, and which defines a *distillery* as being Highland or Lowland depending on its situation either north or south of this line respectively.

HOGSHEAD: Common size of *cask* used in a *distillery*. Contains 55 gallons.

HYDROMETER: A floating device which gives an indication of the *specific gravity* of the liquid in which it is placed.

INTERMEDIATE STILL: The second *still* in the process of *triple distillation*. Removes strong *alcohol* and strong *feints* (between strengths of 70 *per cent volume* and 20 per cent volume) from the *low wines*.

IOLM: International Organisation of Legal Metrology. The EU standard of *proof* measurement whereby *spirit* strength is expressed as a percentage of *alcohol* by volume at 68°F (20°C). Thus 70° proof is 39.9 per cent volume. See also *PER CENT VOLUME, PROOF*.

KILN: Essentially a large oven. A chamber, having a perforated floor, in which *malt* is dried by heat from a source underneath the floor. For at least part of the drying cycle, the heat is usually supplied by a *peat* fire. Kilning prevents any further growth in the malt which would use up its stored food reserves.

LADE: A mill stream.

LAUTER: A modern type of *mash tun* which incorporates improved *rake gear* and is self-venting of the *draff*. *Sugars* are washed off the *grist* solids by *elution*.

LOMOND STILL: Peculiar, column-shaped *still* which produces a heavier, oilier *spirit* than would a normal pot still, although it works on the same principle. Found at one time in a number of Hiram Walker (Ballantine's) distilleries.

LOW WINES: The product of the first distillation in the *wash still*. Approx. 25 per cent alcohol by volume.

LOW WINES CHARGER: Storage tank for the liquor produced in the first, or wash distillation until the *low wines stills* are ready to receive it. *Foreshots* and *feints* may also be held here to be recycled with the next batch of *low wines*.

LOW WINES STILL: The second *still* in the conventional *distillation* process.

LPA: Litres of pure alcohol – the EU standard measurement of a distillery's capacity which is replacing the use of *proof gallons*. One proof gallon is 2.59 LPA. See also *PROOF*.

LYNE ARM: The vapour-delivery pipe which connects the top of the *still* neck to the *condenser*. Sometimes called the lye pipe.

MALT: *Barley* which has been allowed to germinate, then dried to prevent further growth.

MALT FLOOR: Stone floor, usually in a warehouse or vault-like building known as the malt barn, where *barley* is spread out after steeping and allowed to germinate in controlled conditions.

MALTINGS: A building which has the facility for germinating *barley* under controlled conditions to make *malt*. Distilleries would originally have made their malt on a *malt floor*, today it will more likely be made in a *drum* or *Saladin box*.

MALTOSE: Crystalline *sugar*, chemical formula $C_{12}H_{22}O_{11}$, formed by the action of the enzyme complex *diastase* on *starch*.

MALT WHISKY: *Whisky* distilled from a fermented solution derived entirely from malted *barley*, with which no other grain has been mixed.

MARRYING: Allowing a number of whiskies, or batches of whisky, to homogenise fully when *blending* or *vatting*.

MASHING: The process of soaking the *grist* in hot *water* in the *mash tun* in order to dissolve all the fermentable *sugars* derived from the *malt*.

MASH TUN: Large circular tank, usually of wood, cast iron, copper or *stainless steel*, in which the *grist* is mashed with hot *water* (in the same way that tea is mashed with hot water) in order to dissolve all fermentable *sugar*. The tun is operated by the mashman.

MATURATION: A period during which *whisky* is stored in order that the harsher *alcohols* may evaporate and the *spirit* be 'mellowed'. The legal minimum is three years before the spirit can be called 'whisky'. Whisky intended for use in standard *blends* is usually used at three years old. *Single malts* are usually matured much longer – ten or twelve years on average.

MEAL: See *GRIST*.

MIDDLE CUT: That part of the spirit *distillation* which will be kept and subsequently matured to become *whisky*. May be as little as 15 per cent of the total runnings of the *still*.

MILL: Device for grinding *malt* into *grist* in preparation for *mashing*. In practice, the grist is milled to differing degrees of coarseness to ensure maximum extraction of *sugars* in the *mash tun*.

MORTON REFRIGERATOR: A particular type of *wort cooler* dating from the nineteenth century and still in use at Edradour.

MOTHBALLED: Temporarily closed. A *distillery* is usually mothballed in order to prevent the build-up of too much *whisky* in stock given the trading conditions at the time. Although such a distillery may not be producing, it could still be maturing stocks in *bond*.

NEUTRAL SPIRIT: Grain *spirit* distilled above a strength of 94.7 *per cent volume*. Also called neutral alcohol, and used to make gin and vodka. Grain spirit which is to become *whisky* must by law be distilled at less than this strength.

NEW SPIRIT: The unadulterated product of the *spirit still*. Sometimes called new make, or *clearic*.

NOSING: A method of sampling *whisky* by sense of smell only. Used by professional tasters and blenders to avoid fatiguing the palate and/or intoxication.

OAK: The traditional timber from which *casks* are made. Bourbon casks are made from American white oak, sherry *butts* from European oak.

OCTAVE: A small *cask* with a capacity of a quarter of a *hogshead*.

ORIGINAL GRAVITY: Refers to the *specific gravity* of the *wort* from which the final *spirit* is derived.

PAGODA: Characteristic style of roof found on a distillery *kiln*.

Roughly pyramidal and surmounted by a square chimney which has its own pyramid-shaped cover. The chimney usually contains a fan which draws the smoke up through the *malt*.

PAJARETE: A colouring agent, similar to *caramel*, used by smearing it on the insides of the *casks*. Made from grape juice and used in Jerez for colouring and sweetening certain sherries.

PATENT STILL: A device for the *distillation* of *whisky* from grain. Two column stills are used, known as the analyser and rectifier, and the process runs continuously. Originally invented by Robert Stein and updated to the twin-column design by Aeneas Coffey, former Inspector-General of Excise in Ireland. See also *GRAIN WHISKY, NEUTRAL SPIRIT*.

PEAT: Organic fuel laid down over thousands of years by accumulation and partial decomposition of plant remains in waterlogged conditions.

PEAT REEK: Smoky flavour imparted to the *malt* during kilning due to *peat* smoke condensate settling on the grain and increasing its phenol content.

PEDRO-XIMÉNEZ: A grape used to make sweet wines which are used in the blending of the sweeter sherries.

PER CENT VOLUME: Easy-to-understand measurement of alcoholic strength, abbreviated '% vol'. Fifty per cent volume would be an equal mixture of pure *alcohol* and *water*. See also *IOLM, PROOF*.

PIECE: A bed of *barley* grain on a *malt floor*.

PITCHING: Introducing *yeast* into the *wort* in a *washback*.

POTABLE: Of drinkable quality.

POT ALE: Residue left in the *wash still* after the first *distillation*. Usually mixed with *draff* and used for cattle feed. Apparently known colloquially on Speyside as 'happy cow juice'! See *DARK GRAINS*.

POT STILL: Large, onion-shaped copper retort used for distilling batches of *malt whisky*.

PROOF: A system of defining alcoholic strength. Proof spirit is that which, at a temperature of 51°F (11.5°C), weighs twelve-thirteenths that of an equal volume of distilled water at the same temperature, and this is said to be 100° proof. Such a mixture would be 57.1 per cent alcohol and 42.9 per cent water. The measurement of 'proof gallons' has now given way to 'litres of pure alcohol', 1 LPA being 0.386 Imperial proof gallons. The new EU standard is a more logical system of expressing alcoholic strength as percentage volume, in other words the volume of alcohol in a mixture expressed as a percentage of the total volume of the mixture. Standard bottlings are now usually made at 40 per cent alcohol by volume, the legal minimum strength for whisky. See also *IOLM, PROOF GALLON*.

PROOF GALLON: One Imperial gallon of *spirit* at proof strength i.e. 57.1 per cent alcohol by volume at 51°F (11.5°C). Now giving way as a method of expressing a distillery's capacity to litres of pure alcohol. See *LPA*.

PUNCHEON: A *cask* of equal capacity to a *butt*, although shorter and fatter.

QUARTER: A small *cask* with a capacity of half a *hogshead*.

RACKING: Transferring *spirit* into *casks* from another container, for instance a damaged cask or a tanker.

RAKE GEAR: Stirring rakes and blades in the *mash tun*.

REFILL: Refers to *casks* which have already been used once for *whisky* and are being pressed into service again.

REFLUX: The condensing of *spirit* vapour on the *still* neck, the condensate then running back down into the still to be distilled again.

RUMMAGER: A device consisting of a number of chains connected to a revolving arm and fitted inside *wash stills* which are fired from below by open flames. The purpose of the chains is to scrape the bottom of the *still* and prevent any particles of unfermented matter or *yeast* from settling and sticking to it and being scorched by the fire underneath. The gear which drives the chains used to be fitted with a bell so that the *stillman* knew it was working correctly. The use of *steam coils* has largely made the rummager redundant.

SACCHARINE: See *SUGAR*. Also 'saccharified' – being converted into sugar. See also *MALTOSE*.

SALADIN BOX: A type of *maltings*. *Barley* is placed in a long metal box and continuously turned by large revolving forks which move along the inside of the box. Came into use in the 1950s, originally at the North British, Tamdhu and Glen Ord distilleries.

SHERRIED: Flavour characteristic arising from the *whisky* being matured in *casks* that have previously been used for maturing sherry. Many distilleries use sherry *butts* to mature some of their stocks, but only Macallan uses them exclusively.

SHIEL: Wooden shovel used to turn *barley* on the *malt floor*.

SILENT SEASON: A period of around four to six weeks when the quality of the water supply drops during the warmer weather and distilleries usually close down. The time is used to carry out essential maintenance, for staff holidays, etc. Traditionally harks back to the time when locals were otherwise occupied on the farms during the harvest.

SINGLE MALT: A *whisky* derived from *malt*, and which is the product of a single *distillery*, i.e. not *blended* or *vatted* with any other whiskies.

SLAINTE MHATH: Basically Gaelic for 'Cheers!' Pronounced 'slarnjer var', it means 'good health'. You will usually hear it, shortened to just 'Slainte', from a distillery guide as they present you with a *dram* at the end of a tour.

SLIT WINDOW: A narrow window in the upper part of the *wash still* which allows the *stillman* to see if the contents are starting to boil up (in much the same way that a milk pan will suddenly boil up).

SPARGING: Pouring hot *water* on to malt *grist* in the *Steel's masher* or *mash tun*.

SPECIFIC GRAVITY: The weight of a substance compared to the weight of an equal volume of *water* under the same conditions. Usually used to measure alcoholic content and measured with a *hydrometer*. See also *PROOF*.

SPENT LEES: Residue left in the *spirit still* after the second, or *low wines* distillation. Mostly deoxygenated water and usually run to waste after treatment.

SPIRIT: A distilled liquor consisting of an aqueous solution of ethyl *alcohol*.

SPIRIT RECEIVER: The first destination of the distillate from the *spirit still* after passing through the *spirit safe*.

SPIRIT SAFE: Brass-bound glass tank, sealed with *Crown locks*, through which the raw *spirit* passes on its way to the *spirit receiver*. The safe contains apparatus for sampling the spirit and testing its quality, and a device for routing the flow from the *still* to the spirit or *feints receivers*.

SPIRIT STILL: The second *still* in conventional malt *distillation*, in which the *low wines* are concentrated from around 25 per cent to around 68 per cent *alcohol*. Also known as the *low wines still*.

STAINLESS STEEL: Material increasingly used in the manufacture of *mash tuns* and *washbacks*. Easy to keep clean and does not harbour bacteria as wood does.

STARCH: Carbohydrate food material stored in plants.

STEAM CANS: Cylindrical attachments to *steam coils* which distribute the heat more evenly through the liquid in the *still*.

STEAM COIL: Coiled copper pipe in the bottom of a *still* through which steam is passed in order to heat the liquid contents of the still. Does not scorch the liquid as an open flame can.

STEEL'S MASHER: Device attached to the bottom of the *grist* hopper which mixes the grist with hot *water* and introduces it into the *mash tun*.

STEEP TANK: Large metal or concrete tank in which *barley* is soaked in *water*, or steeped, prior to being germinated on the *malt floor*.

STILL: See *POT STILL*.

STILLHOUSE: A building, or in some distilleries simply a large room, in which the *stills* and their associated heating gear are situated. Usually the building sprouting the tall chimney.

STILLMAN: *Distillery* worker responsible for operating the *stills*. The quality of the finished product depends on his expertise in judging which part of the *distillation* will be retained as the *middle cut*.

STRATH: A broad, flat-floored valley.

SUGAR: An energy source from which *alcohol* and *carbon dioxide* can be produced by the action of *enzymes*. A member of the carbohydrate family.

SWAN NECK: See *LYNE ARM*.

SWITCHER: Revolving blade in the top of a *washback* which cuts through the head of bubbles on the fermenting liquor and prevents it from overflowing.

TOP MALTS: Those *malt whiskies* used to impart the 'top notes' to the flavour of a *blend*.

TRIPLE DISTILLATION: Traditional Lowland method whereby strong *alcohol* and strong *feints* are produced by an *intermediate still* and then concentrated in the *spirit still*.

TUN ROOM: A double-decker room in which the *washbacks* are situated. The lower, ground floor part is kept locked during the *fermentation* process (see *CARBON DIOXIDE*). The washbacks stand on the ground floor and project up into the first floor area. The fermentation process is controlled by the tun room man.

UISGE BEATHA: Pronounced 'OOSH-kuh BAE-huh'. Gaelic for 'water of life', as good a description of the subject of this book as you'll find, and the origin of the word 'whisky'.

ULLAGE: See *ANGEL'S SHARE*.

UNDERBACK: A deep, usually semi-circular tank alongside the *mash tun* which indicates the level of the *wort* as it drains from the mash tun. Balances the flow between the tun and the *washbacks*, enabling the tun to be drained slowly.

VANILLIN: A fragrant substance used as an aromatic for flavouring and found in the succulent fruit of a West Indian climbing orchid. Also found in the form of vanillic acid in the *oak* from which the *casks* are made, and influential in the flavouring of bourbon.

VATTED MALT: A mixture of two or more *malt whiskies*.

VATTING: The mixing together of whiskies. Vatting is usually taken as meaning that only *malt whiskies* are contained in the mixture. If *grain whiskies* were to be added, the process would be *blending*.

WASH: *Wort*, after being *fermented* in the *washback*. A liquid containing 7–8 per cent *alcohol* which is sent to the *wash still* for the first *distillation*.

WASHBACK: Huge cylindrical vessel, up to 18ft deep, in which *wort* is *fermented*. Traditionally made from larch or pine, now more likely to be *stainless steel*.

WASH CHARGER: Tank into which the *washbacks* discharge the fermented liquor and where it is held until the *wash stills* are ready to receive it.

WASH STILL: The first of the (usually) two stills used in the *distillation* of *malt whisky*. Concentrates the *wash* from 7–8 per cent *alcohol* to around 25 per cent alcohol.

WATER: An essential raw material in the making of *whisky*. A *distillery* usually uses the same supply for steeping and *mashing* so obviously the quality of the end product is directly dependent on the purity of the water. Most distilleries have a soft water supply, a notable exception being Glenmorangie.

WHISKY: 'A spirit obtained by distillation from a mash of cereal grains saccharified by the diastase of malt', according to the Royal Commission of 1908. By law, it cannot be called Scotch whisky unless it has been distilled in Scotland. The legal jargon cuts straight through the romance which usually shrouds the subject, and which would prefer to define it in only two words – *uisge beatha*.

WHISKY TRAIL: A signposted tourist route in Strathspey between Glenlivet and Keith on which lie a number of participating *distilleries* and a *cooperage* which are open to visitors.

WORM: Coiled copper pipe immersed in cold running water in which the vapour given off from the *stills* is condensed back into liquid. See also *CONDENSER*.

WORM TUB: Large tank containing the *worm*, filled with circulating cold water. Usually seen sunk into the ground, or in the form of large wooden vats, behind the *stillhouse*, although this is now an old-fashioned system.

WORT: The liquid which is drawn off from the *mash tun*. A liquid containing the fermentable *sugars* derived from the *malt* in solution.

WORT COOLER: A device for reducing the temperature of the *wort* from the 148°F (64°C) at which it leaves the *mash tun* down to around 67°F (20°C) for *fermentation*. It must be cooled to prevent decomposition of the *maltose* and destruction of the *yeast*. The wort cooler also recovers heat which heats the water for the next mash.

YEAST: A mould, consisting of single living cells, each capable of producing the enzyme *zymase* which *ferments* carbohydrates to *alcohol* and *carbon dioxide*. Added to the *wort* in the *washbacks* the yeast multiplies, feeding on the *sugars* in the solution, and producing alcohol which eventually kills it.

ZYMASE: The *enzyme* found in *yeast* which causes *fermentation*. Zymase is actually a compound of enzymes, each catalysing a small step in the process.

APPENDIX

A Lesson in Gaelic

Distillery	Gaelic & pronunciation	Meaning
Aberfeldy	Obar Pheallaidh O.pur F^y AL.ee	mouth of Peallaidh's water (water sprite)
Aberlour	Obar Lobhair O.pur LA.oo.ir	mouth of the noisy burn
Allt a' Bhainne	Allt a' bhainne A.oolt uh VAN.yuh	milk burn
Ardbeg	an Àird Bheag un ahrsht vek	the small cape/point
Ardmore	an Àird Mhòr un ahrsht voer	the great height
Arran	Arainn	origin unknown
Auchentoshan	Achadh an Oisein ACH.ugh OSH.in	the corner field
(Previously published derivation *achad oisnin* is incorrectly spelled, and syntax and definition do not match either.)		
Auchroisk	Àth an Ruadh-uisge ah un ROO.ugh OOSH.kuh	ford of the red water
Aultmore	an t-Allt Mòr un TA.oolt moer	the big burn
Balblair	Baile a' Bhlàir BAL.uh uh vlar	the field of battle
Balmenach	am Baile Meadhanach um BAL.uh MEE.un.uch	the middle town (speculation)
Balvenie	Baile Bhainidh BAL.uh VEN.ee	St Bean's stead
Ben Nevis	Beinn Nibheis	mount of the Nevis (venomous river)
Benriach	a' Bheinn Riabhach uh vaen REE.uh.vuch	the grizzled/greyish mountain
Benrinnes	Beinn Ruaidhñeis baen ROO.uh.ee.nish	unknown
Bladnoch	Blaidneach BLATCH.nuch	unknown
Blair Athol	Blàr Athall blahr A.hul	the plain of Athol (New Ireland)
Bowmore	Bogh Mòr BOE moer	the great bend
Brackla	a' Bhraclaich uh VRACH.kleech	the warren/den
Bruichladdich	Bruthach a' Chladaich BROO.uch uh CHLAT.eech	hillside of the stony shore

Distillery	Gaelic & pronunciation	Meaning
Bunnahabhain	Bun na h-Aibhne boon nuh HUH.ee.nuh	mouth of the river
Caol Ila	Caol Ìle keul EE.luh	Sound of Islay
Caperdonich (cf. Ben Donich	Caibeal Dòmhnaich KAP.ul DAW.neech Beinn Dòmhnaich	the Lord's chapel (speculation) the Lord's mount)
Cardhu	a' Chathair Dhubh uh CHA.hir ghoo	the black town/fort
Convalmore	Cona Mhcall Mòr KON.uh v^{y}al moer	Great Conval (name of hill)
Cragganmore	an Creagan Mòr ung KREK.an moer	the great rock
Craigellachie	Craig Eileachaidh crek EL.uch.ee	rock of the stony place
Dallas Dhu	Dalais Dhubh DAL.ish ghoo	the dark dale of the homestead
Dalmore	an Dail Mòr un dal moer	the great meadow
Dailuaine	an Dail Uaine un dal OO.an.yuh	the green meadow
Dalwhinnie	Dail Chuinnidh dal CHUN.yee	the dale of the champion (speculation)
(Distillers' 'meeting place' would be based on *dail coinneachaidh* – v. *coinnich*, to meet – which is incorrect. 'Dale of the champion' fits with the clan battle.)		
Edradour	Eadarra Dhobhar ET.uh.ruh Ghoe.ur	between two waters
Fettercairn	Fothair Chàrdainn FO.hir CHARSH.teen	slope of the woods
Glenburgie	Gleann Bhorghaidh GLA.oon VOR.uh.ghee	glen of Burgie
Glendronach	Gleann Droighneach GLA.oon DROYN.yuch	glen of the brambles
Glen Elgin	Gleann Eilginn GLA.oon EL.ik.in	glen of Elgin (Little Ireland)
Glenesk	Gleann Easg GLA.oon esk	glen of the River Esk
Glenfarclas	Gleann an Fheòir Ghlais GLA.oon un YAW.ir ghlash	glen of the green grassland
Glenfiddich	Gleann Fhiodhaich GLA.oon YUGH.eech	glen of the woodsman (contradicts distillers' 'valley of the deer')

Distillery	Gaelic & pronunciation	Meaning
Glen Garioch	Gleann Ghairbhich GLA.oon GHU.ruh.veech	glen of the rough place
Glengoyne	Gleann a' Gheòidh Fhiadhain GLA.oon uh YO.ee EE.ugh.in	glen of the wild goose
Glen Grant	Gleann Ghrainnd GLA.oon ghrantch	Grant's glen
Glen Keith	Gleann Cheith GLA.oon chae	Keith's valley
Glenlivet	Gleann Lìobhait GLA.oon LEE.uh.vitch	glen of the smooth river
Glenlossie	Gleann Losaidh GLA.oon LOS.ee	glen of the water of herbs
Glen Mhor	Gleann Mòr GLA.oon moer (Not 'voer' as often stated.)	great glen
Glenmorangie	Gleann Mhòraistidh GLA.oon VOER.ush.tchee	glen of great tranquillity
Glen Moray	Gleann Mhoireibh GLA.oon VOER.iv	glen of the seaboard settlement
Glen Ord	Gleann an Ùird GLA.oon un oorshtch	glen of the hammer-shaped hill
Glenrothes	Gleann Rathais GLA.oon RA.ish	glen of the lucky dwelling
Glen Spey	Gleann Spè GLA.oon spae	glen of the River Spey (hawthorn burn)
Glenturret	Gleann Turraid GLA.oon TOO.ritch	glen of the dry pass
Inchgower	Innis nan Gobhar IN.ish nung GOE.ir	island of the goat (speculation)
Inverleven	Inbhir Lìobhann IN.yur LEE.vun	mouth of the elm-water
Jura	Diùra	derivation uncertain but correct Gaelic name
Kininvie	Cinn Fhinnmhuighe kin.IN.uh.voo.yuh	head of the white plain
Knockando	an Cnocan Dubh ung KROCH.kan doo	the little black hill
Knockdhu	an Cnoc Dubh ung krochk doo	the black hill
An Cnoc	an Cnoc ung krochk	the hill

Distillery	Gaelic & pronunciation	Meaning
Lagavulin	Lag a' Mhuilinn lak uh VOO.lin	the mill hollow
Laphroaig	Lag Bhrodhaig lak FRO.ik	(best speculation which agrees with distillers' definition – Gaelic-Norse hybrid, hollow of broad bay)
Lochnagar	Loch na Gàire loch nuh GAH.ruh	lake of laughter
Longmorn	Lann Marnoch	the church of St Marnoch

Lann being Gaelic for 'church' & St Marnoch – missionary, died AD 625. (Chivas)

Distillery	Gaelic & pronunciation	Meaning
Macallan	MacAilein machk EL.an	son of Allan
Macduff	MacDhubhaich machk GOO.eech	son of the black-haired one
Miltonduff	Baile a' Mhuilinn Dhuibh BAL.uh uh VOO.lin GHOO.ee	milltown of the Black Burn
Mortlach	Morthlach MOHR.hlukh	great mound (speculation)

(Correct Gaelic spelling based on *mòr thulach*, 'great mound'. Also Gaelic *tolg* meaning 'hollow'. Distillers give 'great hollow' as definition.)

Distillery	Gaelic & pronunciation	Meaning
Oban	an t-Òban un TAW.pan	the little harbour
Speyburn	Allt Spè A.oolt spae	the hawthorn burn
Strathisla	Srath Ìle stra EE.luh	the valley of the River Isla
Strathmill	Srath a' Mhuilinn stra uh VOO.lin	river valley of the mill
Talisker	Talaisgeir TAL.ish.kir	Gaelic spelling, origin Norse
Tamdhu	an Tom Dubh un TA.oom doo	the black knoll
Tamnavulin	Tom Mhuilinn TA.oom uh VOO.lin	the hill of the mill
Teaninich	Taigh an Aonaich TUH.ee un EU.neech	house of the market
Tomintoul	Tom an t-Sabhail TA.oom un TOE.il	the knoll of the barn
Tormore	an Tòrr Mòr un tawr moer	the great rounded hill
Tullibardine	Tulach Bàrdainn TOO.luch BARSH.teen	the hillock of the copse (speculation, possibly hybrid Gaelic-Brythonic)

INDEX